Makin' Stuff Up

secrets of song-craft
& survival in the music-biz

by Rand Bishop

About the Author

Rand Bishop is a Grammy-nominated, BMI Award-winning, Million-play songwriter with well over 200 cuts to his credit by such artists as Tim McGraw, David Ball, Lorrie Morgan, Beach Boys, Heart, Cheap Trick, Indigo Girls, Richie Havens and Vanilla Fudge—among many others. Bishop's *My List*, recorded by Toby Keith (co-written with Tim James) spent five weeks at number one on the Billboard country singles chart in the spring of 2002 and became country radio's most played song for that year. Bishop and James also co-authored the profitable companion book, *My List (24 Reflections on Life's Priorities)*, published by McGraw-Hill in 2003.

In his nearly 40-year career, Bishop has filled just about every role in the creative end of the music business: recording artist, session vocalist, producer, A&R exec and publisher. Other notable credits include Bishop's screenplay, *The Tin Roof* (First Place, The National Screenplay Showdown, 2004), and the stage play, *The Viewing*, which debuted at Nashville's prestigious Darkhorse Theater in 2006.

Bishop continues to pursue a career as a writer, publisher, talent-development consultant and music producer in Nashville, Tennessee, where he lives with his wife, Stacey, and youngest daughter, Glendyn.

Library of Congress Control Number: 2008940372
ISBN-10: 0-61523-165-9
ISBN-13: 978-0-61523-165-5

Edited by Steve Trinward ≈ Design by Laura Hardy

Visit Makinstuffup.net — *Improving your songcraft, one song at a time*

Acknowledgments

I wish I could list every single everyone who has inspired me, encouraged me, invested in me, vouched for me, stood by me, signed me, dropped me, hired me, fired me, listened to me, disregarded me, informed me, argued with me, loved me, despised me, made me laugh, brought me to tears, quickened my heart, or bored me into a state of numbness. There are no bit-parts. But in a life drama as rich as mine has been so far, to recount every one of those absolutely essential role players would take a good part of forever—and certainly fill volumes.

I must, however, specifically acknowledge some of the mentors who, knowingly or not, have helped me immeasurably along this journey: Marc Ellington, Bob Segarini, John T. Frankenheimer, Gary Usher, Spencer Proffer, Seymour Stein, Dr. J. Robert Prete and Dr. Mitch Johnson, to name a few. I'm also indebted to some inexplicably generous patrons: Norm and Jean Bishop, Jac Holzman, André Perry, Charlie Pullman, Kate Cunningham, Naomi Taylor, Donald Seitz and Parker MacDonnell, among others. Thank you all for believing in ... and gambling on ... my promise.

To my friends and family—who have for the most part held their tongues, but have occasionally nailed me to the cross, while I bull-headedly plowed ahead through the decades from one wild-eyed notion to the next—I offer each one of you my undying love and gratitude. (Especially my children, Emily, Dustin, and Glendyn, who never signed up for the uncertainties of my creative career, my unpredictable temperament or my marital misadventures, but despite it all, grew into the two wonderful ladies and one true gentleman they are today.)

A trainload of thanks to Lisa Catherine Cohen for teaching me so very much about authoring a book, and to Steve Trinward for his precise and astute editing.

It's truly an infinitely abundant, forgiving and charitable universe that has granted me permission to learn the craft of writing on the job: to create, stumble, then get back up again and create some more. It's the same loving God-force that allows me the time and imbues me with the vitality and inspiration to share these stories with you, along with some of the most important lessons I've learned along the way.

For Stacey...

Remind me how it is that this very
fortunate man is so blessed to wake
day after day next to this much
love, light, laughter, and beauty.

Contents

Preface

On its surface, this volume may appear to exhibit a split-personality. *Persona number one* is a basic primer on the process and craft of writing a well-composed, solidly structured, contemporary pop song—coming from the unique point of view of a seasoned vet, who harbors no compunctions whatsoever about raising the curtain on a trove of heretofore-secret guidelines, tricks and techniques, learned by trial and error, over a lengthy tenure as a creative professional.

However, a second glance reveals a memoir—some might call it a name-dropping cautionary tale—exposing sometimes provocative, hopefully entertaining glances behind the scenes, at a journey that commenced with those first Oregon garage bands in the '60s, and somehow found its serpentine path ascending to the top of the charts—in a new millennium.

It is this author's hope that these two seemingly divergent literary guises will meld into one cohesive, inspirational lesson in possibility, in a text that spells out some of the do's and don'ts of pop song-craft, while simultaneously unveiling real-life examples of how (and how *not)* to negotiate the tangled, brutally political underbrush of the music-biz, while interacting with the various predators and tender-hearted natives populating its alien netherworld. Honing both of these skills is critical to your ultimate success as a songwriter, and *your* ultimate success is, ultimately, the single focus of this twin-themed tome.

So what gives *this* guy the credibility to offer you (or anyone else) advice in your pursuit of songwriting achievement? Lord knows, I certainly can't come close to competing with the discography of Jimmy Webb, or profess to the academic prestige of Pat Pattison—both of whom have waxed brilliantly on the subject.

However, if longevity and perseverance carry any weight, I can claim those qualities in spades. Meanwhile, when it comes to a wide range of industry experience—and experien*ces*—I'll willingly put my adventures along Bizzaro Boulevard against anyone's. I've survived on PB 'n' J and celebrated with *Duck à l'Orange*, guzzled gallons of jug wine and toasted warmed snifters of Remy Martin *VSOP*. I've brushed against geniuses, eccentrics and the certifiably insane. Living to tell these tales, surviving to collect and share my theories on the creative process, has imbued me with a distinct perspective you would surely never hear from any other journeyman songwriter.

As a recording artist with numerous labels, contributor to myriad feature film soundtracks, platinum producer, studio singer/musician/engineer and music-publishing and A&R exec, I've seen our industry from nearly every possible creative angle. At the end of the day, I know that the song is the spark igniting the motor. Songwriters are responsible for contributing the most vital and indispensable component to a wondrous and inexplicable equation—one that, generation after generation, profoundly affects the hearts and lives of millions of human beings. Time and time again, I've learned that, for me, there's nothing more compelling, mysterious, inspiring, heartbreaking or fulfilling than the process of writing.

Now, there's always the chance that I've made a gross miscalculation, a foolhardy presumption in thinking anybody out there cares at all about what I think, what I've done, where I've been, and what I've learned along the way. Maybe I've tossed away six months of my life putting all this stuff down in black and white.

But, hey, it wouldn't be the first time, and it won't be the last. We songwriters are used to being ignored. It's just that, over the last four decades, I've found out a thing or two about a thing or two. And I've got a powerful hankerin' to share some of the life experience, craft and philosophy I've accumulated—with *whomever* might be willing to listen.

Writing is what I do. A writer is who I am. To have my work read is divine. Thanks a bunch for pickin' up my book. I hope you enjoy it—and that it works for ya.

Introduction

*The only thing I was fit for was to be a writer, and this notion
rested solely on my suspicion that I would never be fit
for real work, and that writing didn't require any.*
                                   - Russell Baker

Y ou wanna know what really cracks me up?

   Okay. Since you've asked, let me paint the scene for you: A pair
of eager, young song scribes emerge presuming victory from a tussle
with those fickle, prickly muses. It's mid-afternoon, and the tag-team has
put in a full four hours of comprehensive brainstorming, jamming away
on a brand-new original song. (BTW, the four-hour figure is arrived at
when that 90 minutes the collaborators took for a filling, rumor-
mongering lunch/schmooze is subtracted from their exhausting 10 a.m. to
3:30 p.m. workday.)

   "Man!" emotes scribe A. "It's a freakin' smash!"

   "Yeah, Dude," agrees his partner in crime. "If this song doesn't get
cut, there's somethin' wrong with this business."

   Ya gotta love these guys' enthusiasm. Besides, if a writer doesn't
believe in his or her work, who will? But, at the risk of being branded as
a cynic, an old fuddy-duddy, a *get-off-my-lawn-you-damned-kids*
curmudgeon, please allow me share this little tidbit of truth:

   *IT TAKES A HECK OF A LOT MORE THAN UNANIMOUS GUSTO
FOR YOUR LATEST COMPOSITION TO ACTUALLY ROCKET TO
THE TOP OF THE CHARTS.*

   I once heard tell of a Nashville songwriter who believed so wholeheartedly in the tune he'd just penned one fine Tennessee day, that he
felt motivated to grab his lyric sheet and scoot on down to the Music

Makin' Stuff Up

Row franchise of SunTrust Bank. There, Mr. Zesty waited in the lobby for an opportunity to receive an audience with the branch president, Brian Williams. At his first availability, Williams (who was, until his tragic, premature, accidental drowning, one of the most creative and compassionate bankers in the history of show-biz) welcomed the writer (now nearly bursting with zeal) into his office.

"What can I do for you today?" inquired Williams.

Mr. Z placed his lyrics on the bank president's desk, patted the sheet of paper and asked smugly, "How much are you gonna give me for this song? It's a surefire smash!"

While Nashville banks commonly extend substantial credit lines on promising single releases by established, major-label artists, SunTrust didn't build its solid financial foundation by speculating on the latest, unrefined, unproven inspirations of Music Row's legion of tunesmithing optimists. (Leave that kind of high-risk gamble to the many music publishing mavens carrying on their risky business in the environs of Music City.)

Williams knew that the stars must align in a multitude of mysterious and serendipitous ways for any song to even get recorded, let alone rise to the top and establish itself in the firmament of Hit Heaven. After Williams no doubt offered some diplomatic and encouraging words, the overly fervent writer exited the bank, his pockets still empty, as they remained unlined with SunTrust cash.

However, let's not despair. As my friend Mark Alan Springer once told me, "Good things happen to good songs." So if a CMA song-of-the-year recipient says it, let's believe it and endeavor to craft us some gems. Good things can happen to your good songs, too. But, first things first—let's make sure they're good.

≈   ≈   ≈

I was, for all intents and purposes, retired from the music business when I received a phone call virtually out of the blue one early-spring Monday morning. After more than 30 years as a music-biz journeyman—starting out as a recording artist who wrote a few songs; drifting into the role of songwriter/producer; adding six years as an A&R "exec;" then returning fulltime to the craft that reflected my true passion: the writing of the tidy, three-minute pop song—I'd finally arrived at a state of genuine gratitude.

Makin' Stuff Up

After all, over those three previous decades, I'd received more creative opportunities than most folks could expect in ten lifetimes: Record deals with Elektra, A&M, MCA and Epic. Playing, singing and touring with an impressive array of luminary talents. Writing with numerous gifted and inspired collaborators. Having my songs recorded by some of the most unique and iconic artists of the '70s, '80s and '90s. I'd also produced gold and platinum records—in the studios of Los Angeles, Nashville, Montreal and London. My songs had been recognized with a Grammy Nomination and BMI Awards. I had certainly been, I finally realized, a very fortunate man.

However, I hadn't always felt so lucky. There had been far more years of struggle than periods of plenty. One day I'd be luxuriating in a limo (on my record company's dime), enjoying a royal chariot ride through the opulent avenues of New York City. The next, I was traversing across L.A. in a rusty, antique Volkswagen bug, with a leaky sunroof and a broken starter. In my envious heart, that guy in the Porsche with his $200 haircut, streaking past me—no doubt on his way home to his multi-million-dollar digs in Malibu—*he* was the lucky one, not me.

Regardless of the sometimes-sorry state of my finances, though, or of the recognition I so many times failed to find—and despite the shaky, shifting ground and the out-of-control mad-mouse ride I'd chosen as my life—I've always been blessed with the greatest opportunity of all: I get to spend the majority of my time makin' stuff up.

Through the years, at one time or another, necessity has had me toiling away at manual labor, data entry, mundane clerical work, courier deliveries, sales calls and such … among the many and varied enterprises I've tackled, for the sole purpose of feeding and housing myself and my family.

Conclusion: *THERE'S NO BETTER VOCATION ON THE FACE OF THE EARTH THAN ONE THAT ALLOWS YOU TO CREATE.*

I firmly believe that being creative is what we're *all* here for. Yet, sadly, so few of us ever recognize that a creative path is even an option, let alone a possible career. Being a writer, as difficult as it can be, surely beats layin' bricks (no offense to you bricklayers out there). Few would take issue with that.

Anyway, I'd just awakened, filled with that aforementioned glow of gratitude, when I received that fateful Monday-morning phone call. It was my frequent songwriting collaborator, Tim James, on the line.

Makin' Stuff Up

"Hey, Man," TJ began. "Just thought I'd let you know, we've got a 50-50 chance Toby Keith is gonna cut *My List* this afternoon."

"Cool," I responded—coolly. "Let me know if it happens."

As I'd been establishing an enterprise in the "straight" world—marketing legal plans to families and small businesses—I had no attachment whatsoever to any expectations of a show-biz nature. That evening, I attended a class on financial planning at Nashville Tech. Then, having heard nary a peep from my buddy, Tim, by day's end, I assumed that, like 99% of the "50-50 chances" in my lengthy music career, the Keith cut hadn't happened. Miraculously, though, I didn't feel a single smidge of remorse; I'd finally evolved beyond caring about those things over which I had no control.

Tim and I had written *My List* two years earlier, during a period of time shortly after both of us had been dropped by our respective publishers. The song, composed in the attic studio of my rented house on Natchez Trace Avenue, began as a seedling of an idea.

"I make a list of things-to-do everyday," Tim offered. "Let's write a song about that."

I started finger-picking my hand-tooled, circa-1979 Taylor jumbo acoustic. *Under an old brass paperweight...*—it just came spilling out—*...is my list of things to do today[i].*

AND THEY'RE OFF AND RUNNING, LADIES AND GENTLEMEN!

The song was 95% completed in that one session. The only major tweak was made the following day. After struggling over the phone to find a fresher way to say it, we finally succumbed to utilizing the old chestnut... *Why put off till tomorrow what I could get done today?[ii]*

Over the next week, I spent most of my spare hours striving to refine the musical and vocal parts to the home demo I produced and recorded on a Roland VS 880 hard disc. I added the mix of *My List* to a comp CD that included a dozen or so new tunes. Although several of those songs garnered flattering responses from artists, producers and publishers (and a couple even got cut), almost no music-biz professional or self-appointed "expert" seemed to discern anything exceptional about *My List*.

On the other hand, when I played the song out at the legendary Bluebird Café, or at any of several other songwriter-venues, I noticed that my fellow tunesmiths nearly always responded positively to that particular song. At one such gig, the audience actually burst into spontaneous applause at the end of the first chorus, after I sang its concluding line: *Start livin', that's the next thing on my list[iii]*.

At that time, I was writing for my life, amassing a new song-catalogue, and meeting with any publisher who'd listen, in my desperate quest of scoring a new writing deal. My savings—from my previous contract with Curb—had been decimated; I was working for Census 2000 as a crew leader, enumerating the jails, prisons and halfway houses of Davidson County, at a mighty 13 bucks an hour. (Tim James, meanwhile, was making his ends meet by breaking his back three or four days a week as a house painter.)

The turn of the new millennium had brought bleak days to Music Row. The Garth Brooks/Billy Ray Cyrus boom decade of the roaring '90s was a faint memory, and companies up and down 16th and 17th Avenues were shuttering up. There seemed to be another closure or merger nearly every week. "For Rent" signs lined the streets, and I expected sagebrush to blow by with the next stiff breeze.

My List was one of a growing catalogue of new Rand Bishop songs available to any publisher willing to make me a respectful offer. And, although I came a hair's breadth from inking two pacts—both with very successful producer/publishers—the deals somehow faded before coming to fruition. Once again, I had been forced to seek sustenance for myself and my family in the big, scary, alien world beyond the boundaries of show business. This time, at 50, I had decided I was bidding a fond, yet permanent, farewell to the industry that had offered me so many chances, and had been tossing me on the waves of its perfect storm since my teens.

However, although *I* had put my show-biz aspirations in past tense, Tim James was still out there in the trenches, heroically duking out the good fight: writing with any successful collaborator who was willing; playing his songs for every publisher and A&R person who would led an ear; determined to stay in the very same game from which I'd so unceremoniously (yet voluntarily) retired.

Tim deserves big-time kudos for his tenacity; because TJ became the first writer Toby Keith signed to his new Paddock Music venture, I was soon to enjoy the biggest success of my life (so far), and could set aside my card-file of leads, the stacks of brochures, bundles of promo DVDs, and folders full of enrollment forms. I hung up my grey flannel suit, and returned to the blessed enterprise I like to call "makin' stuff up."

Makin' Stuff Up

On numerous occasions, I've been asked this question: "Did you know that *My List* was a hit when you wrote it?"

The truthful answer to that remains, "No, I didn't."

I knew it was a pretty good song, well-written, with a wholesome, universal message. Frankly, though, I wasn't sure its message was particularly fresh.

Toby Keith, however—absolute genius that he is—felt strongly about the song from the first time he heard it. In fact, more than once, Toby, as the song's co-publisher, pitched it to other acts on his touring bill. And, just like with the rest of Music Row, the little, handcrafted *My List* demo I'd produced in my home studio fell on deaf ears. Toby got unanimous response from his peers—they *all* passed.

Finally, frustrated that no one else heard what he heard in the song, the stubborn, willful star decided he might as well record the dang thing his own dang self.

God bless you, Toby Keith. My family and I will forever be grateful to you.

Makin' Stuff Up

chapter one: The Song

How many metaphors have been employed in the attempt to sum up the elusive essence of the pop song? Who knows? Who actually cares? Regardless of that unknowable sum, I'm about to add to its tally.

A song can be a Polaroid snapshot that captures an image, a mood, a solitary, presumably meaningful moment in time. A song can be a short story—or, maybe more accurately, a screenplay—containing fully developed characters embroiled in a rich, engaging plot. A song can be an entire comedy routine, or just one cleverly constructed shaggy-dog tale. A song can be a wish or a prayer, a request or a plea, a letter to the editor, or a coach's pre-game locker room rant. More often than not, a song is a Shakespearean love sonnet, a Valentine card, or a suggestively smutty note passed across a classroom of hyper-sexed middle-schoolers.

All of those descriptions—and more—are certainly apt. The fact is, though, regardless of what you or I may set out to accomplish with each song, we only have a few hundred words, a dozen or so notes, and a very limited amount of time in which to pull off something magical.

Albert Einstein, a prolific and conscientious letter-writer, once wrote this to a friend:

If I'd had more time, I would have written you a shorter letter.

To actually succeed creatively at composing something as brief and succinct as a three-minute song is not the easiest of tasks. Given the innate restrictions and constrictions of the genre, it's amazing that we ever arrive at anything we can call fresh or original. But that's the very challenge that can make the process a fun one. The pop song is mainstream entertainment's idea of a Haiku poem. (Okay, we've got quite a bit more flexibility than a Haikuist—but I think you get my drift.)

≈   ≈   ≈

Makin' Stuff Up

Please allow me to take this opportunity to introduce and acknowledge the cast and crew, the various crafty contributors who will be conscripted to participate in the manufacture of your next masterpiece. This, my friends, is the very same, essential team that has endeavored to play nicely together within the often-cramped confines of every dwelling (whether airtight or drafty, neat or untidy) ever constructed along the seemingly never-ending, diverse and eclectic avenue of pop music.

I often tend to think of every song as a little piece of real estate. Some (perhaps you?) may consider this concept crass and unromantic. Bear with me for a moment, because the parallels (between songs and real estate) are several. Besides, let's be pragmatic here: While we all seek creative fulfillment in our writing (why else would we spend so much time and effort on so many songs that will never be heard by anyone aside from our collaborators, a select group of friends, and those blindly supportive family members?), ultimately we want to flip at least a few of these investments—in time, talent and resources—to receive some industry recognition and make a buck. Right?

So let's allow ourselves to imagine every composition as a structure, assembled wholly out of our individual or combined imaginations. We, the songwriters, are the architects and the contractors … as well as the taut, tanned, calloused crew wielding the saws and swinging the hammers.

Today's creative labors might yield a ramshackle lean-to, a cookie-cutter stucco box … or maybe (cross fingers), just maybe we'll luck out this time and erect an inspired, masterful innovation of contemporary design, one that provokes *oohs* and *aaahs* from gawkers on the street. Even better, we might effortlessly stumble upon a nursery rhyme for the ages—one that little girls will skip rope to and sing along with for decades to come. (You write a song that gets the kids chanting on the schoolyard and, believe you me, you've got yourself a lucrative copyright. That's a mansion with major square footage—in a very upscale neighborhood.)

That's the way, uh-huh, uh-huh, I like it, uh-huh, uh-huh…[iv] I couldn't have said it better myself, KC.

That's when this songwriting thing can become an even bigger blast than it already is. Smart song-craft, clever speculation and serendipitous timing can send six-figure checks winging toward your mailbox, making all those fallow years, all those myriad shortfalls, all those almosts shrink meekly into the shadows of your memory. *Good-bye macaroni days. Hello lobster-fest.* You're a land baron now!

Makin' Stuff Up

But we're getting ahead of ourselves. …

So you've set out to construct an impressive edifice. You think you're on the way to building that classic you've dreamed about, ever since the first time you heard Casey Kasem count down to number one all those years ago. Here's the catch: there's really no way of knowing whether you've accomplished your goal. As a songwriter, you can never gauge your progress until you step far enough away to gain decent perspective—which is virtually impossible, because you're always enmeshed *in* the process.

You came up with a relatively inspired vision. You crafted the piece with care and patience and precision. You disciplined it with tough love. You sought feedback from people you trust, squeezed it into your set list and received respectful applause from friends—and even a few strangers.

But even then, even when you've ironed out that final wrinkle and you're thinkin' the thing is just about as lovely as you're ever gonna make it, you can't be sure what you really have. What's more, even if you've accomplished work of which you're now truly and deservedly proud, there is no guarantee on God's green earth that your new tune is ever gonna make you a dime.

Ouch! Yeah, I know.

After all, you're not one of those tunesters whose name has become synonymous with "hit"—the handful of writers, at any given point in time, whose (please pardon the expression) "shit don't stink." Not yet, at least. All you can do is to try and build something so stunning, so appealing, so irresistible, so undeniably fantastic that its value is obvious to everyone who encounters it—from the very first gander.

Given all that, and assuming you're still determined to give it a shot, let's get down to the work at hand…

≈   ≈   ≈

The following materials are the lumber, nails, brick and mortar from which every song is fabricated:

* Verbal expression (words and/or nonsense syllables)
* Various tones (melody sung or text spoken)
* Phrasing (the relative emphasis of each, as well as the spaces between the syllabic tones)
* Harmonic context (chords, roots, modalities)

* Rhythm (groove, tempo, cadence … or the lack thereof)

Each of these essential supplies is free of charge and available to every single, living human being. So, why doesn't everybody just sit right down and build a big ol' hit—especially when doing so can be so doggone profitable? Same reason everybody doesn't just master the shake 'n' bake crossover dribble and lead the NBA in scoring.

Just like the song itself, the songwriter who wrote that little ol' thang must possess a number of requisite characteristics. Among these qualities are: (1) a modicum of talent, (2) a strong compulsion to write, (3) the organizational skills to set aside the required time, and (4) sufficient focus and patience to devote enough energy to see the process through—time, and time, and time-again. It doesn't hurt for our ideal scribe to be a little delusional (*read* "crazy") as well, because, as we've noted, this isn't even close to a level or stable field we're playing on.

Then, as the writer builds up his or her song catalogue, he or she would be well served to invest in an extra large pair of brass 'nads, to withstand the numerous, inevitable punches in the groin, while continuing to boldly initiate the contacts and maintain the relationships that can be key to his or her success.

≈   ≈   ≈

A song is an absolutely bizarre concept—doncha think? Have you ever wondered who it was that actually sat down and came up with the idea of combining the unique elements of poetry, melody and rhythm in this particular two-and-a-half to four-minute form? Why and how on earth did songs ever come to be in the first place? Well, whether or not you've spent a moment contemplating that head-scratcher, your author's about to do it for you.

It's my theory that there are two perfect reasons why songs exist:

Reason #1: Songs came into being, and have stuck around for thousands of years because (*drum roll, please!*) …

THE LITTLE BUGGERS ARE HOOKY.

Millennia ago—before laptop computers, Garage Band and Masterwriter software; before disposable ball point pens, yellow legal pads … or even #2 pencils; back before humans had even figured out how to jot down their inspirations and document their traditions and history (of course, nobody could have read their scribbles anyway, what with no kindergartens, pre- or otherwise)—some fragrant, stoop-shouldered, but very clever (and probably pensive) cave-dweller observed a phenomenon, one that's just as true today as it was 10,000 years ago.

You might wonder how that *eureka*! moment manifested itself in his (or her) lice-infested cranium. It certainly didn't take the cartoon form of the switching-on of a light bulb. (Remember, this was *way* pre-Edison.) Maybe a highly combustible torch was struck by imaginary lightning and burst into flame behind that furrowed, sun-and-wind-burned brow. Anyway, there was a spark of recognition, a realization, and the first, basic, fundamental rudiment of song-craft was born.

Here's what our brilliant *primitivo* figured out:

IF IT RHYMES, PEOPLE ARE MORE LIKELY TO REMEMBER IT!

And so, cultures began to store and pass on their folklore in the form of epic poetry. As time rolled on, over the centuries, our ancestors began to fine-tune (pun intended) the concept, which led to the next major discovery:

IF IT'S SET TO RHYTHM, IT BECOMES EVEN MORE IMPOSSIBLE TO FORGET!

The earliest John Bonhams now had a reason to lift their heads off of the mammoth skin in the morning.

Then, at last, when one of Cole Porter's distant great-great-great (etc.) granddaddies or grandmommies stuck a succinct little melody onto one of those repetitive rhymes and that irresistible groove, well, you can bet nobody in Cavetown could get a wink o' sleep—with those first choruses repeating non-stop between their ears.

RHYME + RHYTHM + MELODY. Now you've got yourself a big-time *HOOK*.

And that's how the first hit songs came to be—born of mankind's natural inclination to preserve its own history, tell its own stories and pass its own tradition from one generation to the next, in a virtually unforgettable way. With little or no competition (aside from some crude *knock-knock* jokes), these songs became the first, primitive forms of pre-Disney family entertainment, soon giving natural birth to their cousin arts: dance and musicianship.

Feeling the desire to create new, more appealing noises (and having loads of spare time on their hands), some of these clever dudes and dudettes began stretching animal sinew and strands of hide across gourds and hollow logs, thus inventing musical instruments. Others blew into blades of grass or conch shells. Accompanied by the twangs, booms and honks of these crudely constructed git-boxes, tom-toms and trumpets, the earliest versions of *Kumbaya* and *Louie, Louie* began to resonate down the canyons and up the riverbeds of that pre-historic, pagan landscape.

After Christians got hold of the idea, the satanic throb was muted from the mix and, for centuries, Western civilization was unable to move from the waist down. Then Gene Krupa came along, who passed his torch to Buddy Rich, then DJ Fontana (the guy who made Elvis' pelvis come unglued), then on to Ringo Starr—and Keith Moon, bless his immortal soul. Ever since, this eternal, rhythmic flame has had Conservative Christians and Moslems alike freaking out over the godless pounding that continues to propel the modern airwaves.

Today, you and I carry on the same process born in a cave those millennia ago, putting our best efforts toward coming up with engaging, memorable ditties, anthemic statements and poignant ballads we can only hope will make the masses lose sleep (as well as compelling them to part with a portion of their paychecks).

The only difference is: we're not writing about how Oooog killed a wildebeest with a flat rock and provided enough meat to feed his family unit for a moon. We're trying to figure out how to say (in a fresh, new way) "I love you" or "I'm gonna die, because you don't love me anymore," or ask, "How can I get you to have sex with me?" … or make the suggestion—if we've really got stars in our eyes—"Let's get together and create world peace and harmony now."

And that, my friends, brings us to **Reason #2** why songs exist (*trumpet fanfare*):

SONGS ARE EMOTIONAL!

The majority of songs are, to one degree or another, love songs, exploring themes of lust, passion, devotion and longing—all very emotional, uniquely human experiences. Other songs encourage us to dance and party (presumably a joyful experience). Some tell stories that touch our hearts, inspiring us and teaching us valuable life-lessons; those are the ones that go for the lump-in-the-throat, tear-on-the-cheek level of emotion. Some songs (particularly the big ballads from all those Broadway shows) stake a claim, stating a deeply held conviction: the *I-won't-let-this-cruel-world-defeat-me, I'm-gonna-make-it-on-my-own-terms, damn it!* formula, designed to push the right buttons and evoke standing ovations from sell-out crowds night after night.

Other songs are humorous, seeking mainly to provoke laughter and delight. Whatever the song is on its surface, though, its deeper intention is to communicate some kind of emotion. Without emotion, my friend, it just ain't much of a song.

When we look back at where we were and what we were doing during those iconic moments in our lives, more times than not, there's a song attached—one with the power to bring back everything we felt: every sight and sound, how hot or cold it was, whether it was breezy or still, how skunk-drunk or stone-sober we were, and so on. As Hugh Prestwood (*damn that gun-packin' scribe's brilliance!*) put it, ... *the song remembers when*[v].

So, when we hoist our guitars or plop ourselves down in front of our keyboards, determined to construct that elusive smash, we should know this much:

*WE'D BETTER HAVE A GOOD STORY TO TELL, ONE THAT RHYMES HERE AND THERE IN A MEMORABLE WAY ...
AND WE'D BETTER MAKE SURE THE THING HAS AN EMOTIONALLY RESONATING CORE.*

... otherwise, whatever structure we build will likely sit unoccupied, until it crumbles from neglect.

chapter two: Rock Garden

I was toiling away in the front yard of my family's house on Glenmorrie Drive in Lake Oswego, Oregon one warm, summer, Saturday afternoon. The year was 1965, and I was 15.

A few days before, after a particularly tragic plop-down in the barber's chair, I had returned home to catch a glance at myself in the bathroom mirror. Feeling devastated by the hopelessness of my botched do, I proceeded to hurl a hairbrush at my reflection. The resulting shattered glass doomed me to a weekend of hard, manual labor in my mother's rock garden.

As I endeavored to loosen a small boulder from its earthly trap, my portable radio was blasting out the latest release from a charming foursome hailing from the far side of the Atlantic. The echoey *chank, chank, chank* seventh chords played on electric rhythm guitar were placed on the twos and fours of the infectious vamp that began the record. Then young Paul McCartney rasped out that first line with unabashed commitment:

My love don't give me presents[vi].

She's A Woman by the Beatles has never been, by any stretch, one of my favorite songs. Most pop music aficionados would probably concur: this is not one of Lennon and McCartney's most exemplary compositions. Yet I remember exactly where I was and what I was doing the first time I heard it—mainly because I remember so vividly how crushed I felt that day, cursing my teenaged fate, while wiping the sweat from beneath my much-too-short-clipped bangs.

By that point in my life, I had already embarked on my own journey as a songwriter. I began my semi-professional performing career as a towheaded, baby-faced, 14-year-old folkie with a 50-dollar Harmony Sovereign strapped over my shoulder, warbling at Portland's Café

Makin' Stuff Up

Espresso for tips the audience generously tossed into a passed hat. By the summer of '65, I had assembled and established my first rock 'n' roll band.

An enterprising, entrepreneurial lad, possessing the audacity and presumptuous bravado of the Virgo first-born of five brothers, I had pooled my strawberry-picking earnings to take out a classified ad in the *Portland Oregonian*, seeking musicians to form an electric combo. The first response wasn't a musician at all, but a sportswriter employed by the very newspaper that published my ad.

Dan Yost, already in his early 20s, was looking for a band to perform the songs he'd been composing. Since, to date, I had completed a total of one original song myself (a folk-infused, two-chord love-drone entitled *If I Just Pray*), I cockily offered to collaborate with the elder writer, agreeing to meet with him to check out some of his lyrical ideas.

The first Bishop/Yost co-write was a Byrdsy selection we called *When I Give My Heart*. I was soon to discover that Dan's younger brother, Bob, was a hotshot electric guitarist. A rather surly, broad-shouldered, curly-headed blond, who smoked unfiltered Camels, Bob Yost and I conspired to team up to perform those original songs Dan and I intended to compose.

Adding Steve (Thumper) Williams on drums and Greg Lang on rhythm electric, we formed a group called The Turtles. By default, I took up the bass. The subsequent chart success of Bob Dylan's *It Ain't Me, Babe* by a California ensemble (who had the bald-faced nerve to use the same band name) necessitated a change in our group's moniker. So we eschewed our black turtlenecks and fake fur vests in favor of thrift-store tailcoats and top hats, re-branding ourselves as The Gentry.

By the summer of '65, we'd already weathered our first recording disaster, laying down crude, all-live, monophonic versions of three original songs—the aforementioned titles, along with a third that turned out to be an overt plagiarism of The Kinks' *All Day and All Of The Night*. The fateful session took place at the KHJ radio studio in downtown Portland, and was engineered by a gentleman whose only live recording experience was capturing a DJ speaking over a spinning 45. Needless to say, the results were less than sensational.

By then, though, I'd become hopelessly infatuated with the idea of becoming a rock star. (I also aspired to another equally unrealistic career, that of an actor—more about those dreams later.) Anyway, in order to become a rock star in the mid-'60s, you were well-advised to sharpen your songwriting skills. It didn't hurt to have a cool haircut, too. Even at that tender age, I considered myself well-qualified for rock stardom in most every way—with the temporary exception of the haircut.

The youth culture was coming into its own. The teens of America were being recognized as a viable demographic, possessing sizable disposable resources, cash we'd be more than willing to part with, in exchange for the right products. I rushed past the power tools and sporting goods at Sears into the Mod Shop. Perusing the knock-off Carnaby Street fashions (designed and priced especially for us pimply adolescents) made me feel like I mattered—like I was a real citizen of substance.

Another nascent phenomenon of the day was the Teenage Fair. These week-long, summer events were staged at Convention Centers and indoor Arenas, as a means of exposing the latest and hippest stuff targeted at the burgeoning youth demo. Booths lined these cavernous halls, hawking everything from clothes to candy bars to audio gear, and live bands played all day long. To your average adult, the constant mayhem and cacophony of these happenings must have been maddening. To me and my friends, this was Heaven on Earth.

The Portland Teenage Fair offered the region's most prestigious "Battle of the Bands." The prize that year for the winning local ensemble included a recording session at Northwest Recorders, produced by local legend Ken Chase. This was the very same facility and production mastermind responsible for the biggest hit by the area's most popular band. (In case you don't know, *Oh-woe, Babeee,* I'm talkin' 'bout *Louie, Louie*, by the Kingsmen.)

Bob, Greg, Thumper and I rehearsed our tailcoats off preparing for the competition. All that practice was well worth it; at the end of Teenage Fair week, The Gentry emerged as the victorious band-battler.

Ken Chase was a well-known, local radio personality, who also owned a popular teen nightspot located in the modest Portland suburb of Milwaukee, a party spot he modestly called The Chase. The DJ fancied himself as always being on the cutting-edge of the cultural curve. (At this point in time, Chase had shifted his primary focus, along with most of his liquid assets, away from music and into launching two slot-car tracks in the Portland metropolitan area. He was convinced that slot-cars would eclipse the success of another recent national phenomenon, trampoline centers.)

Makin' Stuff Up

Due to Chase's new obsession with toy racecars, our Northwest Recorders session lacked a guiding light. We were, however, graced with a visit by the young gent who had whined the shrillish lead vocal on the Kingsmen's aforementioned monster smash—prior to being given an unceremonious heave-ho by the band. Jack Ely (who pronounced his family name like Confederate General Robert E. Lee) saw fit to instruct Bob Yost on his amplifier settings.

"Ya need more distortion on that sound, man," the singer told our lead guitarist. "It should be dirtier."

The input I received from Ely had to do with my vocal style, which, according to the ex-Kingsmen front man, was too "on pitch," too "studied." The sum total of the guy's pop-music philosophy was his theory that the public was not interested in a pristine sound, or faultless, well-enunciated vocals. They wanted their rock 'n' roll raw and imperfect. (At the time, I had no idea how spot-on he was.)

The session didn't result in anything we'd have been proud to play for anybody. However, the next reward in our band-battle prize packet provided us with an experience I'm sure none of us will ever forget: The Gentry was placed on the bill of the Teen Expo in Vancouver, British Columbia.

Our quartet boarded the northbound train at Portland's Union Station. Along the route, we imagined ourselves as the Fab Four, replicating scenes from *Hard Day's Night*, in adenoidal Liverpudlian dialect:

Who's the old man?... Paul's Grandfathah... He's a clean old man... Mistah, can we have our ball back?... Ringo, what ya doin' readin' a bloomin' boooook...She's a drag, a well-known drag. We used to turn the sound down and say rude things... etc.

Arriving in sparkling Vancouver, we checked into the luxurious YMCA, which made up for its lack of frills by being tidy and centrally located. When we arrived at the Expo Center the following day, we were surprised and delighted to be greeted by dozens of screaming, teenaged girls. It was as if we'd just stepped into the Beatles' flick we'd been improvising on the day before. Here we were, an unknown combo, never having even released a record, yet being worshipped and fawned over as if we were on stage at the Ed Sullivan Theater.

We did four shows a day, signing autographs and posing for snapshots between sets. Our 48 glorious hours of superstardom provided a booster-shot for my already skyrocketing overconfidence. After our final show, we returned to the Y, our adrenal systems pumping with unrelieved aggression. A pillow fight in our jockey shorts escalated into a shaving cream skirmish, which, at some point, spilled into the corridor. Noticing that the case for the fire hose was unlocked, I mischievously unraveled its contents. Then, Bob Yost wrapped the hose around all the door handles down one side of the hallway.

We knocked on doors, and when each room's resident attempted to answer, the hose only became more taught, gripping tighter around each door handle. A number of colorful curses wafted from those poor, entrapped victims. We laughed our butts off, as we squirted shaving cream all over the place. All in all, it was a glorious night of authentic rock 'n' roll.

My first collaborator in song, Dan Yost, went on to further express his creative impulses by authoring the screenplay for director Gus Van Sant's breakthrough film, *Drugstore Cowboy*. Nearly 25 years after he and I made up those first few amateurish songs in the mid-'60s, I worked with Dan again, when he asked me to score the trailer for another low-budget, indie film he wrote called *Tunnels*.

chapter three: The Process

There are as many songwriting processes as there are writers, and as many nuances to those processes as there are songs.

What's important is that you discover the process that works best for you. Following *your* Muse, allowing yourself to learn by trial and error, keeping track of your creative results, observing your co-writers, and being hyper-aware of your own comfort level … these steps will lead you to the most efficient and fulfilling methodology for your writing. Then, once you've figured that out—especially if you plan on doing a good deal of collaboration—you'll still need to be flexible, because every writer has his or her own way of working, and every song wants to be written in its own, unique way.

The most common process is the approach many musicians take: jamming on some chord changes, noodling on a riff, la-la-ing or da-dee-dah-ing along until it sounds something like an intro-verse-chorus structure. Using nonsense phrases, the writer begins mouthing vowel and consonant sounds that seem to sing well with the music.

Somewhere along the line, the writer breaks out a piece of paper and bravely starts trying to get all that nonsense to make sense. Sometimes, with the music leading the way (and many times when melody, feel and phrasing get locked in early-on in the song's formation), it can be tough to wrestle those words to the ground, so they'll submit to doing their job satisfactorily. Often, using this method, a composer will end up with a song of obscure imagery and meaning, open for many, varied interpretations.

This is a great way to write for your alternative rock band or contemporary folk project. However, it takes a ton of discipline and patience—not to mention, a whole lot of skill and innate smarts—to create a seamless, entirely comprehensible lyric to an existing piece of music, regardless of how inspired that music might be.

Makin' Stuff Up

There are some incredibly gifted lyric-writers who specialize in writing words to melody. I had the privilege of a lifetime, when I was able to write a couple of songs with Cynthia Weil. Cynthia—with her husband, Barry Mann—has penned more than 30 top-5 hits, including such massive copyrights as *Just Once*, *Somewhere Out There*, *Here You Come Again*, *We Gotta Get Outta This Place*, *Kicks* and radio's most broadcasted song of all time, *You've Lost That Lovin' Feelin'* (which Mann and Weil co-wrote with mega-producer/madman Phil Spector).

Cynthia, whom I consider to be perhaps the greatest pop lyricist of my lifetime, requests that her co-writer compose a melody with accompanying chords. In other words, she orders up a virtually completed, fully structured song *to-go*—but, hold the language. She then listens to your melody over and over, as she formulates and refines her lyric.

Cynthia's work is absolutely respectful of every nuance of a composer's melody. One time, Cyn had completed the words to a Lionel Richie melody. Richie dropped by the Mann/Weil residence to check out Cynthia's new lyric. When he sat down at the piano to sing the song, he came to a spot where he said there was an extra syllable on the page.

"Oh, no," Cynthia insisted. "That's exactly what you sang on the tape."

"I don't think so, Cynthia," objected Richie.

"Okay, let's take a listen, and I'll show you," Cynthia volunteered.

As it turned out, Lionel had cleared his throat in time, between his la-dee-dahs, and Cynthia had attached a lyrical syllable to that guttural note. I don't know whether Richie chose to keep the extraneous wordlet in the finished song. I suspect he did, though, because Cynthia's lyrics are always not only immaculate, picturesque and emotionally precise, they also sing with ease, because the vowel-sounds are so perfectly placed.

I've heard that Don Henley often asks his collaborators to provide him with a mock-up demo track (no melody; just chords, groove and structure). Henley then drives around listening to the track until he begins to discover a tune inside the changes, which is then followed by lyrical ideas and fine-tuning. One could hardly challenge the viability and substance of such rock classics as *Boys of Summer* (w/ Mike Campbell), *The End of the Innocence* (Bruce Hornsby) or *Heart of the Matter* (Campbell and J.D. Souther). That process obviously works gangbusters for Henley.

Makin' Stuff Up

Although it's not my usual *modus operandi*, I wrote about 75% of the lyrics for the musical *Calamity and Wild Bill* to existing melodies composed by Jeff Silbar and Alan Jay Friedman. In this case, writing for characters with distinct voices and attitudes, and involved in specific situations—while having an encompassing plot to move forward—makes putting words to existing music a more unique challenge. However, it's one I thoroughly enjoy. When writing for musical theater, you don't have to dredge through your own life for emotional inspiration and storyline. The playwriting process gives you a chance to speak vicariously through fictional or historical characters, all coping with and commenting on *their* own exact circumstances.

I've met a number of wordsmiths who prefer writing a complete lyric before handing it over to a composer to set the words to music. For me, this is the most difficult way to write a song. It takes a one-of-a-kind talent to marry pre-existing lyrics to music in a way that really feels as if the words and melody were meant to co-exist. This process almost always drives me crazy, because something about the song usually ends up sounding awkward and clumsy.

Regardless of its relative brilliance, if a lyric doesn't sing to me immediately from the page, I have a tendency to pass on opportunities to compose with this process—unless the lyricist is willing to make substantial adjustments to the lyric, and/or accept my inevitable suggestions, as I endeavor to construct the musical environment for the lines on the page.

It's quite well known that one of the most successful and prolific songwriting teams of the last 40 years collaborated nearly flawlessly using the lyrics-first, music-second method. Bernie Taupin would send Elton John his completed lyric sheets, and was never in attendance when John sat down at the keys to put words to music. It seems evident, however, that Taupin gave John substantial liberty with the lyric, as the composer would often choose to repeat a single phrase numerous times in a way that would probably look odd on paper—yet makes perfect sense in the context of a pop song.

It's hard to imagine that Bernie specified and insisted on the exact phrasing of the "na, na, nahs" in *Take Me To The Pilot*. I'll bet you dimes to donuts, though, that *Your Song, Daniel* and *Candle In The Wind* were written pretty much verbatim, just as Taupin submitted them to John. There's a conversational nature to those lyrics that the music seems to emphasize effortlessly.

However, I can detect places here and there in the Taupin/John *opus* of pop masterworks where the melody seems to tussle a bit with the words. Oh, I'll admit that I might be completely off base in this estimation. Since I've attempted to pull off this minor miracle on plenty of occasions, though, I perceive a little bit of push/pull every now and then.

That's why, when it comes to process, the methodology that, through the decades, steadily rose to the top of my chart and has remained there for nearly two decades is (*another drum roll, Anton!*) … **let the melody and lyric grow together.**

Ultimately, your goal is to compose a piece in which the music and the words become one powerful, beautiful stream of story, music and emotion. You want language and sound to work dynamically in tandem, like a perfectly synchronized duo of *Cirque du Soleil* acrobats, to capture the attention of the audience and provoke awe and wonder. For me, the method most likely to achieve that result is raisin' melody and lyric up— from pups to champions—simultaneously, as a pair of fraternal twins.

≈ ≈ ≈

During my preferred writing process, there is an exact moment for me when an idea begins to have a real chance of becoming a song. I'm either listening to my co-writer share her list of titles or concepts, or I'm leafing through my own pile of scribbles. Or perhaps, during the course of everyday events, a few succinct words pass across the screen of my subconscious mind. Whatever. For me, the moment of conception comes when an intriguing, emotionally resonate, lyrical phrase suddenly latches onto a memorable series of notes and rhythm.

MELODY GRABS ONTO LYRIC … "THE ICON-PHRASE."

It doesn't necessarily have to be the actual title or even the hook of the song—although usually it is. It could be the opening line of a verse, a key refrain, or even a tag. However it presents itself, this amounts to a cutting from the great tree of mystery, a helpless infant for whom I've now accepted total responsibility, about to take root in the garden of my creative soul. I now feel obligated to place this seedling in the light of the sun, water it, fertilize it, nurture it—and bring it to fruition.

I have no idea where these inspirations come from. Many times, at first, I'm even reluctant to even share a newly arrived song-fragment with the other person in the room—assuming there actually *is* a someone.

> I'm going to describe this process as a co-writing experience. In the upcoming chapters—with your permission—I'm going to be writing a couple of songs … imagining that you, dear reader, are my collaborator.
>
> However, I think it's essential that every songwriter set aside time to write songs alone, regardless of how insecure you might be about it. Being able to write on your own sharpens your tools and keeps you in touch with your own intuition—and it's your intuition that makes you the unique writer you are.
>
> Meanwhile, here's a suggestion you can take or leave. (It may sound juvenile, but *what the hey*?) Whenever you're writing solo, place another chair in the room. Pretend there's a collaborator there with you—an imaginary partner who listens at every step of the way with a receptive and forgiving, yet critical ear. Listen to yourself as you would listen to a co-writer. You may be impressed with your own talent; you may even co-write a great song with yourself.

Okay, back to that seedling of melody, one that's just attached itself to those few words. Often, in my mind, this initial rendering sounds a little trite, maybe too derivative, or even completely plagiarized—as we say in the trade, *right on top* of another song.

Maybe my co-writer has a better idea, I think to myself. *I wouldn't want to impose mine or, even worse, squash hers.*

Despite all this, evidently, a spark reflects in my eye, or a certain grin of solemnity appears on my face, revealing that song fragment bubbling behind my brow—because, inevitably, the question comes…

"What are you thinking?" the other person in the room asks. *Yikes! This is it.*

So I take a deep breath and blush a little, preparing to pluck this germ of a song (up until this moment, only barely existing as an inkling in my imagination) and place it on display in the room, where not only my own ears will perceive it in real-time audio, but another talented, discerning, creative soul will experience it in multi-dimensions of reality. (No matter how many times one goes through it, this can be an intimidating proposition.)

Still insecure after all these years, I invariably apologize in advance: "This may sound completely stupid, but here it is."

Makin' Stuff Up

When I finally eke it out, the idea seldom quite sounds exactly like it did in my head. On rare occasions, it's much cooler than I imagined. Most times it has more than a taint of the ridiculous in it. But, let's face it, this is only the first of many—surely dozens of—times during this collaborative process when both of us will have to risk sounding like a proverbial song spaz. It's only the first toe in the pool. So, let's dive in. The water's fine. We've got a song to write and, at this moment, there's still every possibility that it could be a great one.

It's usually pretty easy to gauge a collaborator's response. By the way, always remember that:

BODY LANGUAGE SPEAKS MUCH LOUDER THAN WORDS.

Your collaborator's reaction could range from over-the-top ecstatic to recoiling disgust, but it's more likely to land somewhere in the range between tepid and reserved. He or she will probably consider it, readjusting to what is more than likely a new viewpoint, hopefully one that splashes a little more color on the horizon.

Once it's out there floating in the room like a giant, wobbly soap bubble, it's highly likely I'll want to repeat that proposed icon-phrase a few times … to oil the hinges, get my reticent voice accustomed to it and experiment with a few small (or large) adjustments on the fly.

≈ ≈ ≈

Okay, let's assume you've enlisted the enthusiasm of your co-writer, or that you've admitted to being wild about the bit-'n'-piece your partner just boldly volunteered. Anyway, no matter who was responsible for that initial inspiration, you both concur that *this* is the direction you're gonna be exploring—at least for now. By choosing that icon-phrase, you've just laid the cornerstone of the structure you're planning to build together.

My friend Billy Sideman—a New York guitarist/producer with whom I've written a number of songs—once used a wonderful simile, obviously culled from his day-to-day experience surviving in an urban jungle. This is how Billy described the moment when I, as his collaborator, took a few mutually-chosen words and connected them with a memorable series of notes:

"Man," Sideman said, "It's like you've just found us a reserved parking-space!" Owning a car at all in Manhattan is rare enough. Leasing a slot in which to park it is a major investment. Billy's analogy implies that the exploratory drill-bit of our collective imaginations just hit a vein that just might be filled with gold.

So now we're about to descend into the darkness—wearing those hardhats with the lamps attached. (Hope we remembered extra batteries!) What's more, we'd better be willing to get our hands dirty as we crawl through the mine-shaft, intent on unearthing and filling our pockets with the shiniest, rarest nuggets—the materials we'll be choosing to assemble our edifice of sound and language.

Here's another, perhaps even more apt comparison. That first icon-phrase of melody and lyric is like the key to a lock. You and your creative partner have now gained entrance into a long-abandoned mercantile market. By bravely letting that hooky little phrase resonate in reality, you've pushed open that squeaky old door, and the two of you are free to enter a mysterious new world filled with sights, smells and sounds. There, on the store's dusty shelves, lies every available word, alongside a nearly endless combination of note sequences and rhythmic patterns. You can use any of these supplies at your discretion—now, later or never.

You've been given permission to browse through the cobwebs for as long as you want, collecting as much of this stuff as you can use. However, here's the catch: you're only given one small cart in which to carry your selections.

So, you become a couple of newlyweds at Pier One, perusing the place for dishes, juice cups and napkin rings. Unfortunately, there are no helpful sales associates on duty to direct you to the section where you're likely to find the exact item you seek. You're just gonna have to try to do the best you can on your own.

As you eyeball and fondle the merchandise, every choice requires a discussion of the relative pros and cons, the practicality, the aesthetic appeal and, most of all, how (in your combined mind's eye) each placemat, doily and centerpiece fits into the scheme of the décor. All of this, you know, should flatter and support that swatch you brought in with you: your icon-phrase.

Now you kids are not always gonna agree on every item. In fact, you might just have a spat or two over this or that. (Should that happen, you'll both be relieved that no staffers are lurking behind the counter, sharing vicarious giggles over your squabbling.) Each of you will make your strongest case for why one thing or another works—or doesn't.

Makin' Stuff Up

There will probably also be a bit of competition over who actually discovered what.

In the long run—hopefully—together you'll have designed an inviting table setting for a festive dinner party. You might be preparing to serve the greasy ribs, baked beans and corn-on-the-cob of a drink-dance-'n'-party tune, or it could be an elegant, multi-course, gourmet story song with a poignant payoff. Whatever it is, you'd better put the right stuff on the table, or your carefully prepared meal will sit there getting dry and cold, and your guests will go home unsatisfied.

Some people, particularly those of the female gender, love to shop. (Some, I dare say, even *live* to shop—my mother-in-law, for example.) These people can spend a full six hours at Ikea and emerge with a reserve tank of fuel, ready and eager to hit the shoe-sale at Nordstroms.

I find shopping one of the most enervating, disorienting and, ultimately, exhausting experiences that contemporary life has to offer. Five minutes after I enter a department store, the overwhelm overtakes me. How can you possibly focus on any one particular thing when you're surrounded by all those vivid colors, potent smells, all that commotion and cacophony? In a matter of minutes, I start to get dizzy and my knees begin wobbling. I realize that I have no idea what to buy my Aunt Frieda for her 90th birthday. I'm toast.

But let's say I'm out to get a specific list of items for myself: a white dress shirt, a pair of boot-cut jeans, some boxer shorts, whatever. Now I've narrowed down my goals, and my task is at least accomplishable. With a good idea of what I'm looking for, combing the shelves of this establishment is a much simpler, and doable task. Not an easy one, mind you, but one that lives in the realm of possibility.

And so it is with songwriting. There are essentials you know you're going to need: a substantial (and we hope somewhat original) concept, a good story that flows on top of a supportive melody, and some dynamics. It's your job to excavate through the sale rack, find some bargains, smooth out the wrinkles, piece together an ensemble, and start your own parade.

≈　　≈　　≈

The "flow experience" is something that's been defined in a series of books by an author/researcher with a completely unpronounceable name,

Makin' Stuff Up

Mihaly Csikszentmihalyi. This Mr. C—who supported his theory by wiring up dozens of folks all over the world to gauge their relative moment-to-moment level of happiness—propagates the supposition that our optimal life experiences come when we somehow "find flow." We may think we are most contented when lying on the beach or lounging on the deck of a cruise ship sipping a Pina Collada. Don't get me wrong, I've got nothin' against lettin' a tropical breeze blow through the old brain every once in a while. Now and then (*now* usually being better) we all need a vacation from this hectic, stressful, modern rat race.

However, the greatest fulfillment in life (according to the unpronounceable author) comes when we are enmeshed in a task for which we have some level of expertise and preparation, one in which our progress can actually be measured, doing an activity that tends to make us lose all track of the passage of time. Most crafty, creative endeavors (painting, pottery or writing, for example) qualify as activities that can potentially put a person into flow. However, even such seemingly mindless chores as ironing, doing dishes, driving, or mowing the grass can accomplish the same experience: You're qualified to do the job. It's easy to gauge your progress. And time flies, even when you think you're not having fun. (Besides, dang it all, don't you feel great seeing that stack of neatly folded T-shirts sitting on the bed, or gazing at that perfectly edged front yard?)

At some point, every time you sit down to write a song, you should experience *flow*. I don't know on how many occasions I've been lost somewhere on the remote battle-zone of my imagination, jousting with a phrase or a musical passage, when a glance at the clock nearly made my heart stop. How that much time passed unnoticed, I'll never know. Then I look at my computer screen to see that I have a half page of words. For the last few hours, I've been whittling away at a song, each scrawl and mumble presumably bringing me an inch or two closer to the completed composition at the end of the path. At that point, I always have to admit, *I'm a pretty lucky guy*.

The greatest blessing of being a writer is this:

EVERY NIGHT, YOU GET TO LAY HEAD ON PILLOW, KNOWING THAT YOU CREATED SOMETHING THAT WASN'T THERE WHEN YOU WOKE UP THAT MORNING.

chapter four: Player Queen

"Why do you want to be an actor, when you can sing?"

I stood there for a moment in dumbfounded silence, probably with my youthful cheeks flushing pink, and certainly incapable of coming up with any reasonable response to the question the director had only just posed. This simple, very direct query summed up what was—to date—the most substantial quandary of my young life.

And so, at 18, armed with this proposition, I had come to see all-too-clearly the crossroads at which I stood: I'd have to make the difficult choice between two life paths—quite different, yet equally precarious—and the sooner I picked one road or the other, the sooner I could get a move on.

It was the summer of 1968, in the rolling, evergreen foothills of Ashland, Oregon. I'd had the privilege to be chosen as an apprentice in the acting company of the Oregon Shakespeare Festival.

Ever since preening across the stage of Lake Oswego Junior High, in the guise of the vain, foppish Captain Hook in the musical *Peter Pan*, I had been torn between two creative muses. On weekends—when I wasn't performing dramatic roles in *The Crucible*, *Beckett* or *Death of a Salesman*, or crooning and hoofing my way through *Sound of Music*, *Camelot* or *Oliver*—I was nearly always gigging with my high school rock bands: first, The Gentry, then Thundering Heard.

Here's an actual quote from the article published in my hometown paper, reviewing my portrayal of the egocentric Sir Lancelot in *Camelot*:

Randy Bishop looks good in tights. And, he can sing, too.

In retrospect, that blurb should have given me some clue to the hard choices I'd surely be facing in my not-too-distant future. At the time, though—like the six-year-old girl who naively professes her dream of someday becoming "a princess *and* a ballerina"—I fixed my sights on not one, but a pair of unrealistic, unpragmatic and completely improbable potential careers: actor *and/or* rock star. No back-up plan; that was my strategy, and I was stickin' to it. I grew up, preparing to make my grand entrance on the stages of the world, and presuming that I'd be greeted by my own personal follow-spot, as those twin gilded showers, fame and fortune, rained down on me after each and every curtain call.

The success of my high-school years only served to reinforce this presumed life path. A year before my season of Shakespeare, Thundering Heard had capped off our slow ascent to local renown by copping the most envied booking in the Portland area. The Crystal Ballroom is a magnificent, expansive, downtown venue, constructed in the bygone big-band era, featuring a wonderful stage framed in ornately sculpted wood, facing a ball-bearing dance-floor that actually bounces when you walk across it.

To give this engagement even more prestige, the Heard opened for Family Tree, an RCA act that held my highest regard. Although I admired everything about the Tree—from their cutting-edge fashions and hairstyles to their tight, melodic, harmony-laden sound—I was in extra-special awe of their sharp-beaked, quick-witted front man, Bob Segarini.

In the history of the world, there had never been, nor will there probably ever be, a more perfect time to graduate from high school and be playing in a rock band: 1967, thereafter celebrated as the "The Summer of Love." The hippie counterculture was in full flower-power bloom, certain that the Age of Aquarius had arrived (and along with it, peace, love and understanding for all the people of the world). We were turning away from the materialistic, militaristic dogma of our parents, and following Dr. Timothy Leary's new credo by "tuning in, turning on and dropping out."

Of course, for this 17-year-old, my "dropping out," for the most part, took place on weekend nights. After playing hippie, and submerging myself into that all-too enticing, alternative, fantasy world for an evening, I'd commute on back to my cozy, suburban bedroom and Mom's homemade chocolate chip cookies—a pretty soft-core demonstration of rebellion, I freely admit.

The afternoon of the big Crystal gig, my bandmates and I carried our gear across the trampoline-like hardwood, feeling our bellies fluttering with butterfly wings in anticipation of the night's 45 minutes on that splendid stage. A very appealing sonic blast was screaming from the huge P.A. speakers. The sound was fresh, but familiar, a multi-tracked vocal fanfare introducing someone called *Biiiillllly Shears*. Then the groove suddenly shifted to a lilting, two-beat bounce, motored by a liquid bass-line.

At that juncture, a rather bland voice asked the musical question, *What would you do if I sang out o' tune?*[vii] The vocal *was* actually slightly toneless but, nevertheless, it had a certain undeniable charm. *Sergeant Pepper's Lonely Hearts Club Band* was due to hit the record stores in a few days' time. The hippest guy on the planet, Family Tree's Bob Segarini, had scored a pre-release copy, and was sharing the Beatles' mind-blowing opus with the Crystal cast and crew.

Even though the Byrds and Jefferson Airplane were playing at Memorial Coliseum that same night, our show was well-attended, and we rocked credibly. After packing up our equipment, the Heard and the Tree trundled over the Burnside Bridge to the Travel Lodge next to the Coliseum, where members of the two chart-topping bands were staying. Still clad in our rock finery, we climbed a fire escape on the outside of the cinder-block building to an open third-floor door.

A young, bushy-haired (and relatively slender) David Crosby emerged from one of the rooms, carrying a portable stereo and dragging an extension-cord. The corridor began to fill with Portland scene-makers, and we all settled ourselves down, cross-legged on the carpeted floor. Joint after joint of potent reefer circulated, and everybody grinned and nodded to each other, as we held in our tokes as long as we could before finally exhaling—as if we were all acknowledging some unspoken understanding: that we were the generation fated to change the course of human evolution.

Crosby placed a 12" LP on the turntable, and several dozen extremely fortunate, pot-zonked longhairs sat transfixed, blissfully tagging along—in our minds, of course—with John, Paul, George and Ringo on the magical, musical excursion that was *Sergeant Pepper*. All in all, it was a glorious and absolutely unforgettable night of rock 'n' roll.

≈   ≈   ≈

Contrary to this blissful experience, my first year of higher education offered an experience that turned out to be far less glorious. In fact, it was a time of my life I'd just as soon forget—if only I were capable of deleting it from my memory.

Upon arriving at Oberlin, a liberal-arts college plopped unceremoniously on the stark flatlands of Northwestern Ohio, my first realization was that the beam from the follow-spot I'd fully expected to greet me was spread very thin—diffused, as it was, by a campus literally teeming with talent. Those two-thousand-plus students were the *crème de la crème* of North America. Not only was I not exactly standing out in this school populated by big fish from small ponds, I struggled to attract any attention at all.

During the first semester of my freshman year, I had to bust my can just to get C's. Having effortlessly achieved a 3.8 grade average in high school, being mediocre was not something I was accustomed to. My best grade for the year was the B+ I received for one particular assignment in Music Composition class. The trouble was, I'd plagiarized the whole piece—from Bob Segarini.

I kept *Miss Butters*, Family Tree's RCA rock operetta, to myself, as my own private discovery, like a secret, imaginary friend I hid under the bed in my dorm room. I listened to the album endlessly, memorizing every note of melody and line of lyric. Then (*Just to see what would happen, really!*) I stole one of Segarini's most distinctive *Miss Butters* melodic passages and turned it in as one of my own weekly compositions.

I wrote a laudatory fan letter to Segarini, praising the *Butters* album, confessing my theft, and congratulating him for helping me get such an exceptionally high mark. Mailing that letter would prove to be one of the most significant actions of my entire life.

The first floor of the Oberlin Conservatory was lined with practice rooms, each of which housed a perfectly voiced Steinway, harpsichord or pipe organ. As I spent so many idle hours sitting at those keys, improvising my little pop tunes, I couldn't help feeling seriously outmatched by my classmates next door and across the hall, whose fingers flew across those ivories with a dexterity that could only be the result of a lifetime of serious, dedicated study. (It wasn't all bad: At least my theatrical aspirations were encouraged, when I won supporting roles in two main-stage theatre productions—*A Streetcar Named Desire* and *Pajama Game*.)

I felt relieved when that interminably dark freshman year finally came to an end, and was very excited and flattered to be accepted into the company of the Oregon Shakespeare Festival. I was short and fair—

pretty, in fact—and I vied for parts with more mature, seasoned professionals, as well as other collegiate actors—all of whom actually looked their own age. I also had zippo stage-experience performing the works of the Bard.

As a result of my youthful visage and lack of classical cred, my parts for the season were relatively small. In an effort to give that season's production of *Hamlet* an aura of extra authenticity, the tragedy's director took full advantage of my feminine features, casting me as the "Player Queen" in the "play within the play." (In Shakespeare's time, female parts were actually portrayed by boys; in that tradition, I actually performed my *Hamlet* role in drag.)

With minimal attendance required at rehearsals, and oodles of spare time on my hands, I spent many of my afternoons plucking away at my acoustic guitar. Those private jams evolved into several new songs, most of which explored my current state of loneliness and alienation.

One of my company-mates seemed especially fascinated with my extra curricular tunesmithing endeavors. A buxom, outgoing, ginger-haired dancer/singer from the University of Texas, Amanda McBroom had also been making up a few songs on her own. "Mandy" approached me one day to share the rudiments of a folkie little ditty. Its melody was simple—and quite beautiful—while the lyric explored the idea of comparing love to a river, a razor, and a rose. I encouraged her to keep working on it.

Ten years later, Bette Midler would unveil Mandy's song, *The Rose*, in a hugely successful bio-pic inspired by the life of Janis Joplin. In completing that very same folkie little ditty (as I encouraged her to do) the gifted Ms. McBroom not only created one of the most perfect songs ever written, but accomplished one of the most often-recorded and most lucrative copyrights of the last half century.

There was a popular coffee house along the banks of Ashland's Lithia Creek. I approached the owner of the establishment with the idea of me pickin' and grinnin' a set after the play let out one evening. A number of the acting company and tech crew bucked theatre custom and, instead of bee-lining it to the pub, stopped by to check out my performance.

It was while retrieving a fistful of paper and coin from a passed hat, and accepting accolades from my fellow thespians, that I was challenged with the previously mentioned, crucial question, the one for which I had no answer:

Makin' Stuff Up

"Why do you want to be an actor, when you can sing?"

This is what that director was pointing out with his sincerely curious inquiry: Regardless of an actor's innate talent, training-level or resume-length, before he is ever given the green light to apply his craft, there are numerous factors—each entirely out of his control—that will more than likely come into play.

First, a writer creates the character, age- and race-specific, adding other defining traits, such as height, weight, relative attractiveness, etc. From that writer's template, the producer, the director and/or casting director all develop their own preconceptions as to the appearance, demeanor and other defining qualities desired for each available part. (The only trait that might ever overcome those pre-requisites is that of box-office bankability. Of course, if an actor never gets a chance to get on stage, he certainly has lttle chance of developing that elusive attribute.)

On the other hand, a singer/songwriter can sit down and write any time he damn well feels the urge. In doing so (for better or worse) he creates his own roles. He's his own playwright, providing star billing for himself in every song, presumably with a part ideally suited for his unique vocal and musical talents, his age and cultural perspective. In addition to the job of custom-penning, a singer/songwriter also functions both as the casting-director, who offers the role to himself … and the performer who accepts it. A very tidy and extremely self-serving arrangement—but one over which the performer has complete control.

A hopeful thespian might be destined to report for audition after audition, and still wait around for years for the opportunity to work. A singer/songwriter can do his thing 24/7/365 if he so desires. (He might, however—as we all know—still be waiting for remuneration as he expires his final breath.)

And so, enlightened by that director's astute challenge, my decision suddenly became an absolute no-brainer. Due to my baby-face, I'd likely have to be patient for years until I could score substantial theatrical parts, while that very same mug would likely be an asset to my pop-music aspirations. Why should I sit on my hands, waiting helplessly for some playwright or screenwriter to create the perfect role for me? I could seize complete responsibility for providing myself with the vehicles of my own personal expression—by writing my songs.

Makin' Stuff Up

It took me yet another year to extricate myself from school, and procure a draft deferment. By the following summer, I had joined the rock 'n' roll circus. Mere months after that, I was lucky enough to sign my first recording contract.

For many years, I didn't think of writing as "work" per se. Then, one evening, during a pick-up basketball game at the Hollywood High School gym, a lanky gent who worked in the film biz asked me if I'd been working.

"No, just writing," I answered.

"Well, that's working, " he instructed me.

"Hmmm, I guess you're right," I had to admit. I'd been writing songs for more than 20 years at that point. Maybe I was actually putting in an honest day after all.

I've said it before, and I'll say it again. Spending one's life makin' stuff up is a great privilege. To actually make a living at it? That's the greatest blessing I can think of.

chapter five: The Concept

I tell every burgeoning songwriter the same thing:

YOU SHOULD ALWAYS HAVE AT LEAST 100 SONG IDEAS.

Being a songwriter is a 24-hour, 7-day-a-week gig. You can't switch it on and off. Every conversation you have, every billboard you see, every newspaper article you read, every TV commercial, every movie, even every dream from which you awaken … they are all possible sources for that idea that could possibly become a huge hit song.

I'm not just talking song "titles" here. Don't get me wrong, a great song-title is definitely something to jot down, store and share with your co-writers. But the title itself, as far as I'm concerned, isn't enough. The words that make up that title need a concept, a special point-of-view, a way they can potentially become something more intriguing, something more special, extra-emotionally charged and, ultimately (and most importantly), something more memorable.

Over the years, I've amassed literally dozens of little notebooks, all filled with lyrical phrases, story ideas, characters and situations—every one of which dawned on me at some random moment while traversing through the mundane activities of my daily life. Admittedly, most of those ideas are fairly insubstantial; some are so obscure I often don't remember why I even wrote them down. Some of them *could* be amazing. But, for whatever reason, most will never become a song. You never know, until you sit down to work with your ideas—either alone, or with your collaborator(s).

But what's absolutely essential is this: when you *do* sit down to write a song,

Makin' Stuff Up

YOU MUST HAVE A SUBSTANTIAL CONCEPT.

My friend, Doug Johnson, illustrious producer, recording engineer, and president of Curb-Asylum Records—and no slouch as a craftsman of song himself—once told me that he thinks songwriters would be better served by spending their time mining for great song ideas, rather than banging their heads against the wall day after day, rehashing the same stale, overused concepts. If you don't have a great idea to write that day, he advises, go to the library or a museum, see a movie, read a book. Since I believe that a unique, highly developed concept is essential to a great song, I completely agree with Doug.

There have been periods in my life when I was so immersed in my search for that next great song-idea, I felt as if I was living a sub-human existence. I saw myself as a scavenger, a predator, a dumpster-diver, compulsively combing the known universe for a few words—and, ultimately, a concept that might just be the seed that would give birth to a gigantic copyright. To this day, I carry a file-folder in my briefcase, stuffed with scraps of paper, all covered with scrawled titles, quotations and rhyming couplets. Some of those scraps are more than 10 years old. But I couldn't bear to throw a song-idea away—not before it's had its opportunity to become a song … not for anything.

Most of the time these days, my collaborative presence is for the purpose of helping a young artist put something he or she has a strong desire to express into a more accessible and appealing frame. But on those odd mornings when we fail to concur on an idea that gets us both charged up, I break out that folder and leaf through those scribbles, while I quiz my partner about the things that matter most to him or her. Always listening, I select a few potential ideas and spread those torn paper fragments across the keys of my piano. I'm nearly always delighted when one of those inspirations is suddenly refreshed by the perspective of a new collaborator.

If you don't have a hundred song-ideas, you're not a real songwriter. If you don't carry a notepad, a writing implement and/or a portable recorder with you at all times, you're not a real songwriter. If you don't constantly scavenge for song ideas in every experience of your life and in the dusty corners of your every memory, you're not a real songwriter.

Having a few titles is a good start, but it's not enough. Great writers are always prospecting for gold, 24/7/365.

Makin' Stuff Up

≈   ≈   ≈

Jon Robbin is a delightful and gifted gent with a wandering eye (literally, you never know which one of Jon's eyes to look into) and an impish sense of humor.

Jon takes great joy in the songwriting process, and every song he writes (by his own humble estimation) is a masterpiece. Soon after arriving in Nashville from Mendocino, California, Robbin, a plumber by trade, co-wrote a tune considered by many Music Row mavens to be a perfect song: Lorrie Morgan's top-10 hit, *I Guess You Had To Be There*. He also scored a #1 in the spring of 2002, with Chris Cagle's *I Breathe In, I Breathe Out*.

At that point, Jon and I began collaborating on occasion. One day, he and I were confirming a co-writing appointment via telephone, when he happened to mention a song title he had a hankerin' to toy with. Robbin was puzzling over the enigmatic behavior of whatever woman he was dating at the time, wishing he hadn't gotten himself so involved with her impulsive craziness.

"Save me the trouble," he remarked. Then the inspiration dawned on him. "Hey, let's write a song called *Save Me The Trouble*."

"Save that title for me, Jon," I said. "I definitely wanna write that song with you."

When I heard Jon utter that common cliché, I envisioned a twist on the phrase that lent it a fresh, hopefully more playful meaning. Several months went by before Robbin and I finally got together to write. On the appointed day, as always, Jon began by spilling out several new and ingenious song-ideas—each one complete with title and concept. By that time, though, Jon had forgotten about the title we'd already agreed to pursue in our earlier phone conversation, and had no clue that I had a way to turn that forgotten phrase on its ear.

"I thought we were gonna write *Save Me The Trouble*," I reminded him. Never one to throw cold water on a co-writer's enthusiasm, Jon willingly agreed to join me in chasing down that idea.

Okay. Looking at the colloquialism, "Save me the trouble," as it's used in everyday vernacular, one might assume the song would amount to a request from a disillusioned lover to his or her unreliable and/or untrustworthy partner to break it off, thus, sparing the singer the anxiety of having to deal with all that *crapola* from henceforth. Yeah, that's what Jon thought, too.

But, no. The song we ended up writing became an enticing plea from a singer who confesses to being fascinated with the unpredictability, the on-again/off-again push/pull, of a beguiling, passive/aggressive lover's nature. The meaning of the phrase, which says in common parlance, "You're too much trouble," became "You're trouble. That's the thing I love most about you. So don't give your trouble to anyone else but me." This is the chorus we ended up writing:

Save me, save me the trouble
Give me both barrels, Baby, don't be subtle
I want all of the drama, the fights and the cuddles
Save me, save me the trouble[viii]

Save Me The Trouble has since become an icon-vehicle for an artist I've been developing and producing: young, sassy up-and-comer Hailey Stout.

So there, my friend, is a specific example of how a title can become a concept. Some of the best songs take fairly ordinary language and make those words speak a new truth.

≈   ≈   ≈

As I'll remind you emphatically—and often—throughout this book, songs are emotional things. Therefore, it seems to me that the folks who write those songs should have some actual heart-connection to (and true passion for) the subject-matter they choose to write about.

Maybe I'm an idealist—even somewhat naïve, if you will—after all these years: I actually believe the public can tell if a singer is sincere in his or her performance. When the vocalist latches onto the emotional core of the song, the audience can't help but connect to that performance. I think it's the same with the words and music of the song itself. Listeners can sense in their collective gut if the writer(s) really meant it.

When I sit down with a co-writer for the purpose of concocting a new song, he or she will more than likely have brought along a list of potential ideas. Some concepts, of course, will be more developed than others. Most times, I'll ask that my collaborator(s) share a good many of their ideas—not because I'm out to steal another creative soul's inspirations, but because I'm looking for the one that resonates most profoundly with me. If I'm about to invest a hunk of my time and skill into wrestling a song to the ground, I want to be relatively sure of two things: that *I* care about the idea; and that the idea has the potential for universal appeal.

I usually narrow my interest down to two, at the most three possibilities; then we discuss how we might approach each one conceptually—first lyrically, then musically. As we brainstorm over the "what-ifs" and fill in some blanks, I usually get a good feeling as to which idea is the one to which I can most effectively contribute on that particular day. This exercise might take as long as the entire first hour of our session, but, I always find it absolutely worthwhile: It insures my emotional commitment to the idea, thus providing me with proper motivation to give my best to the entire writing-process.

One of the professional wordsmiths I admire most, screenwriter/author William Goldman, applies a specific set of criteria when he considers accepting any job. His test amounts to asking himself two simple questions: *Do I love it?*... and *Can I make it play?*

If the answer to both of those questions is affirmative, then Goldman knows he should look seriously at the opportunity.

I borrow Goldman's simple two-part checklist, applying it to every song I write. The first question is simple enough: *Do I love it?* If a craftsman loves an idea, he'll certainly be more likely to put every bit of his heart and soul into its creation. If you can't put all of yourself into the process of writing—whether it be a song, an essay, a novel or a screenplay—then you're probably just wasting your time (and that of your collaborator).

And then, *Can I make it play?* Those five words present a more complicated proposition. A proper answer to that query requires some self-awareness and perspective, as well as a certain amount of experience—not to mention a good bit of hardy self-discipline.

A different way to ask the same question might be: *Am I the best man for the job?* Many times, as we've all been reminded on occasion, the best man for the job is a woman. As a matter of principle, I'm reluctant to write a lyric from a strictly female perspective without the input of a co-writer of the opposite gender. So, when a male co-writer brings me a concept (even a brilliant one) that comes from a woman's point of view, I almost always suggest that we invite a third writer to join us, one who possesses a pair of X-chromosomes.

That's not to say that a man can't write a great song for a woman performer; however, usually that same song would be unisexually truthful and, therefore could, with a tweak or two, be performed believably by either a male *or* a female artist. The aforementioned *Save Me The Trouble* is one such song: Although, as it stands, it seems custom-made for a young, haughty, country diva (like Hailey Stout), a male artist with just the right edge and attitude could perform it with conviction, too.

Your intuition will usually tell you if you're the right collaborator for any specific idea. Go with that feeling, whether it leads you to board the train, or inclines you to wait for the next one. There should be absolutely no offense in informing today's writing-partner, "Hey, that's a fantastic idea, but I think you'd probably get better results working on it with another co-writer."

I've heard multiple versions of that same beg-off, delivered by some pretty amazing writers. I'd rather save an idea I believe in for a collaborator who feels up to and inspired by the task. I take no personal offense to that kind of pass. I think most of your creative pals will also appreciate that same kind of honesty.

≈   ≈   ≈

Unfortunately, on the rare occasion, you might run into an awkward impasse—when a collaborator's eye just doesn't meet yours about how a concept should work. That can result in some very uncomfortable communication issues.

Say you've had a brilliant idea burning a hole in your notepad for some time. It's the one you've been saving up, hoping to spring it on the perfect collaborator. The day has finally arrived—an appointment with one of the hottest writers in the known universe. You do your best sales pitch, as you unveil your genius hook, along with its fully developed concept, including a brilliantly devised, heart-rending turn of events at its conclusion.

"I love that title," she says. Your little heart is going pit-a-pat. *It's a certainty*, you're thinking. *I'm about to spend the next several hours crafting a carefully conceived masterpiece, a song-of-the-year—with a big-time, hit tunesmith.*

You can hardly contain your excitement. Then she pops your bubble. "… but I wouldn't take that approach."

Her twist on the idea, in fact, isn't a twist at all. It's commonplace, crass; obvious, in fact. In your opinion, her approach sucks the heart out of the song.

Makin' Stuff Up

Yikes! What do you do now?

Remember those 99 other song-ideas? That's when you should suddenly recall one of those and get real enthused about it. *Quick, change the subject*!

If that doesn't work, and you can't seem to divert her focus on your golden calf, you only have two other options. The first (less risky, far more heartbreaking) is to bite the bullet and let her run roughshod over your dazzling inspiration. Second option, you could explain as honestly and sincerely as possible how you believe strongly in your slant on the idea, and that, if she doesn't share your vision, you'd prefer to save it for a collaborator who does.

Option #1 could result in a sacrificial lamb, a spark of revelation being doused before it had its chance to illuminate the sky. Option #2 could lead to your co-writer having a snit-fit, and/or giving you a pedantic lecture about how much you have to learn about writing hit songs. And it just might insure that you'll never, for as long as you draw breath, have another opportunity to write with Ms. Chart-topper.

Now keep in mind, there are a million great song-ideas waiting to be discovered. You may have to ask yourself, *What's more important?* Is it the potential of this particular, collaborative partnership? Or is it the possible wonder of this one, single song-concept? It's your decision. Whatever the case, should you ever be called upon to make it, it won't be an easy one. (I know. I've been there, and it was tough.)

My friend, Tim James, had saved a title he really believed in. It was quirky, catchy and unique, the kind of phrase that would effortlessly pique the imagination of nearly anyone who had the chance to hear it. Finally, getting an appointment with one of the most successful writers of the day, Tim put his title on the table, and Sir Success bit.

Unfortunately for TJ, the hitman had no intention of trying to make this idea into a commercially viable piece. Sir Self-Important seemed to be more interested in getting in, getting out, and moving on. The direction he took with the title was nonsensical and ridiculous. A couple of hours later, the result was something that might have been considered a novelty song—if it had only made a lick o' sense.

Why this hit songwriter would disrespect Tim in this way is anybody's guess. Maybe the guy thought the idea was so amazing that he simply wanted to quickly remove it from competition. Maybe he had a similar idea already underway. (More likely, he was just a sadistic, sociopathic egomaniac.) In this true-life scenario, Tim not only sacrificed a great song-idea, but never had a second opportunity to collaborate with Sir Success. Tragic … but we move on.

In my recent experience, I've had two occasions when butting heads over song-concepts resulted in long-term songwriting relationships being damaged. In both cases, the song titles and concepts were mine, and the co-writers were extremely successful. (One collaborator, in fact, was a Hall-of-Famer, and one of the nicest, most mild-mannered people on the planet.)

I'm a pretty stubborn fellow when it comes to being loyal to my own concepts (and not *just* my song-ideas, as some of the stories in the "memoir" sections of this book clearly illustrate). Unless a partner can offer what I consider to be a better approach, I'm gonna stick with mine. One of the songs in question was never completed; the second has been recorded a half-dozen times. Nevertheless, I've never written with either of those collaborators since.

≈   ≈   ≈

One of my pet peeves is the old-before-his-time songwriter who disdains the idea of writing from a more youthful perspective. This refusal usually follows a litany of belly-achin' about how all the artists are "so dang young these days that they couldn't possibly have any life-experience to sing about."

What an absolute crock *that* is!

There are several reasons why I say this. First and foremost, let's look at that very limiting attitude from a commercial point of view. The largest active group of music consumers is—and has always been—in their teens and early-20s. Why wouldn't you want to write for the demographic that's the most interested in and passionate about new music? We're in the music *business*, after all!

Secondly, what makes that aging curmudgeon believe that the experiences, concerns and passions of youth are in any way less valid or less meaningful than those of an older generation? No feelings are more fervent than those felt when we are young. Meanwhile, since songs are all about emotion, those youthful themes—lust, love, loss, mischief, coming of age, partying all night, loneliness, alienation and declaring independence—make absolutely perfect fodder for the songwriter's craft.

Makin' Stuff Up

Being a writer is about recollection and reflection. At this autumnal stage of my life, I welcome every opportunity to leaf through my life's scrapbook and re-visit my exhilarations, my longings and my heartbreaks … without having to actually relive them. I was there, I did all that stuff, and I lived to tell—why should I remain silent about it? My versions of those events, accompanied by a plethora of strongly felt emotions, are all stored in my sense memory. Now I get to make daily withdrawals from that overflowing memory-bank. That, my friend, is a true privilege!

≈   ≈   ≈

Let's assume that you and I have convened for our very first scheduled writing session. We've bantered a bit, getting to know one another. Now we're starting to toss around some song-ideas. You're a dutiful warrior with a kit-bag packed with worthy song concepts.

With my eyes closed, I listen and contemplate as you present ten, maybe even twenty of your titles or basic ideas.

"Go on," I encourage you. "What else have you got?"

You're beginning to feel more than a little insecure, assuming I hate every one of your best concepts. But all along, I've been absorbing, considering without prejudice, allowing all of these ideas to either bounce off or stick. Then …

"What was that third thing?" I inquire. "You know, the love ballad with 'everything and nothing' in it."

"She's everything, and I'm nothing without her," you remind me, repeating that tidy, emotionally charged icon-phrase.

"That's great," I say. "I really like that one."

But there's another idea that also rings my bell—definitely up-tempo, fun and energetic. This one already has a title: *Goin' Down Swingin'*. It's about a guy who's losing his girl, you've explained. But, he won't give up without a fight. *If he's goin' down, he's goin' down swingin'*.

Two very cool, fresh, solid song concepts. Both of these ideas resonate with me. The ballad, in fact, is already singin' a melody in my head … and I can feel the spirit of that swingin' up-tempo thing.

I love 'em both—*and*, I think I can make 'em play. These two proposals have passed the Goldman test. So let's write a song …

No, let's write *two*!

chapter six: Can o' Worms

My first opportunity to apply my craft as an actual "professional songwriter" came in 1971 on the lot of A&M Records in Hollywood, California.

I'd joined the band Roxy two years before, as a barely adequate (though colorful and kinetic) bass-player/harmony-singer. By the time '71 arrived, I was 21, and had emerged from a rigorous rock 'n' roll boot camp—more worldly and hard-nosed, but still starry-eyed and party-hardy. Roxy's debut album for Elektra had failed to find a substantial audience—in spite of our constant touring, opening shows for Creedence Clearwater, Jefferson Airplane, Eric Burden and War, Poco, Flying Burrito Brothers and other top concert acts of the day.

Our drummer had surrendered to the lure of returning to his hometown of Stockton to pack on the pounds while negotiating the higher mathematics of his preferred musical genre, jazz. Those insidious Scientologists had abducted our keyboard-player, as he walked ever so innocently down a Hollywood sidewalk. The focus of his existence had now shifted—from glissing up and down the keys of his Hammond M-3 to becoming "clear." Our gifted lead-guitarist seemed perfectly content playing solitaire in front of the tube, along with his constant companions, a bottle of Wild Turkey and a pack of Larks.

The still-motivated members of Roxy comprised the remaining duo. Undaunted, the two of us were pursuing our own ambitions. I'd been in awe of the talents and charisma of Bob Segarini for more than five years. Beginning back when I was a peach-fuzzed high schooler with dreams of fame and fortune, Bob had been one of the first legit music-biz personalities to give me the time of day.

A purveyor of tidy, well-constructed, pop-rock songs—and a friend of (and collaborator with) songwriting legend Harry Nilsson—Segarini had succeeded in placing his beautiful, country-inflected ballad, *You've Got A Lot Of Style*, on Jose Feliciano's gold-selling *Light My Fire* album. In fact, Bob was the first real pro songwriter I'd ever met. Professional for two evident reasons: first, he sat down at the piano nearly every day to write; and second, he actually received quarterly royalty-checks.

So imagine how I felt when my idol, this very same Bob Segarini, called in the late spring of 1969 to inquire if I'd be interested in playing bass for his new band. Even though it meant sticking my best friend with the lease to our rented digs, abandoning my own solo album-project and reneging on important commitments I'd made to my parents, my spontaneous, affirmative response required no special consideration whatsoever. Without so much as a second thought, I picked up and moved from the damp, cool, green Pacific Northwest to the dry, peat-dirt oven of California's San Joachin Valley.

Sleeping in the very same closet/alcove in Bob Segarini's parents' house that Nilsson had once used as a temporary bedroom, I applied myself to learning the Roxy repertoire, as well as increasing my capacity for cheap, jug wine—not necessarily in that order.

I was now two years later. Following the relatively quick flame-out of our band, Bob and I had tagged our side-act Segarini and Bishop. Two Seg/Bish tunes had found their way into featured spots on the soundtrack of *Vanishing Point* (a film destined for '70s-era cult status), and our reputation as a team of tunesmiths was bubbling under on the L.A. scene.

Bob and I were introduced to Jack Daugherty by our friend David Anderle, A&R exec and staff-producer at A&M Records. Daugherty's back-story was about as fascinating as any successful pop music producer in history. Working at NASA for years, Jack had attained his personal goal there when Neil Armstrong made that giant leap for all mankind across the dusty surface of the moon. He then abruptly retired from the space program, packing his bags for Tinseltown in search of fresh challenges.

Daugherty's next adventure turned out to be writing lead sheets for Herb Alpert. After winning the trumpeter/label-head's confidence, the ex-space engineer was introduced to a brother/sister duo from Downey, California, who had recently inked a pact with the A&M label. This fateful introduction gave Daugherty his second opportunity to send young Americans skyrocketing across the Milky Way, when he took Karen and Richard Carpenter into the studio to make their debut album.

"Do you guys have any songs that might work for the Carpenters?" Daugherty queried Bob and me at that first, amiable meeting. As we pondered that most intriguing proposition, the friendly producer proceeded to suggest that we drop by the studio to meet the talented Bro and Sis from the L.A. mega-burbs. When I first experienced Karen's firm handshake, she and brother Richard were working on their fourth Jack Daugherty-produced album.

No recording had ever had more impact on me than the lilting Bacharach/David composition, *Close To You*, the smash that launched the Carpenters into superstardom. I remember pulling up in front of Segarini's tiny Hollywood Hills cottage in my VW Beetle when that single came on the radio. I sat transfixed, unable to extract my ears from Karen's clear, resonate alto, a sound so rich it seemed to fill every square centimeter of air in the atmosphere. I listened until the final nanosecond of the fade, knowing I'd just experienced a perfectly crafted song, performed by what I surmised right then and there would become one of the greatest pop voices of its era.

Now, several years later, I was meeting the woman behind that voice. Boyish and unguarded, Karen smiled as she graciously welcomed Bob and me into the A&M Studio B control room. The ending to the humorous anecdote she was just finishing off seemed to me to be somewhat unusual for a female jokester:

"Hey! Who's got the schematic for this can o' worms?" This punchline sent Daugherty and his recording engineer into throes of sidesplitting laughter. Lacking the context of the story's set-up, Bob and I could only offer a pair of bemused grins.

Richard Carpenter was in the tracking room, on the other side of the glass, testing out his newly tuned Wurlitzer electric piano with a medley of classic bits and pieces—from Irving Berlin to Bach. Incredibly gifted, that Richard.

"How does that sound?" Karen's brother inquired.

"Sounds great," responded producer Dougherty, as he attempted to suppress one final chuckle over Karen's joke. "Let's cut it."

Richard executed his overdub with the efficiency of a skilled studio pro. In the process, Segarini and Bishop got a good sampling of the kind of material the Carpenters were looking for, and we headed off intent on custom-crafting the perfect piece to complete the sibling duo's work in progress.

We returned 48 hours later with a pop tune entitled *Won't You Be My Friend For Now*. I don't remember a thing about the song itself, only that I stood next to the Studio B Steinway offering a harmony here and there, while my more-experienced songwriting partner, Bob Segarini, rendered a lead vocal to his own accompaniment. I do recall that our three-person audience—Jack Daugherty, Richard, and Karen—responded very enthusiastically.

Several days later, Bob and I decided to drop by Studio B to say "hey." Once again, Richard was preparing to overdub a Wurli part. This time, however, seeing us in the control room, instead of indulging in Berlin and Bach, he checked his levels with a spontaneous rendition of *Won't You Be My Friend For Now*.

We were then informed by a beaming Jack Daugherty that Richard had come up with a fantastic arrangement for our song, and the Carpenters were planning to record it on the album's final tracking session scheduled for the following week.

Naturally, Bob and I began speculating on how we might spend the fortune that would soon be pouring into our bank accounts from our Carpenters cut. However, those damned fates had other plans; our song failed to make the session. Evidently, as we were later informed, Richard—who customarily hired A-list L.A. session guys for Carpenters' tracks—had promised his road band that they could play on this last recording date. Unsatisfied with the road ensemble's interpretation of *Won't You Be My Friend*, big bro Carpenter decided to replace our original with a standard that had been in the act's repertoire for years.

Such is the life of a songwriter: *great expectations crushed by harsh reality*. Get used to it, kids. The only part of the process over which we have any control is the creative stuff; if you can't thrive on that—and that *alone*—you're headed for some very unhappy days. You might consider pursuing a vocation that features an actual relationship between effort and reward—songwriting offers no such exchange.

That was the very first professional disillusionment for a very naïve and presumptuous young writer; but it was by no means the last. Since weathering that initial blow, I've learned that it often requires a convergence of miraculous serendipity for a song to get itself recorded in the first place, let alone somehow find its way into the exclusive gated community of tunes that have somehow earned an address on the Boulevard of Major Copyrights.

chapter seven: The Chorus

B y now, we've laid the foundation of each of our co-writes-in-progress, in the form of two solid concepts. In the process, we've fabricated perhaps the most visible feature of these potential architectural wonders with our icon-phrases: a few critically important words attached to a bit of memorable melody. This is where I suggest we diverge from the traditional process of construction.

You're sitting there in that chair. I'm sitting here in this one. Now is when I ask the question, "Okay, where do we want to go with the chorus?"

"Hold on a dang minute," you might respond. "We don't even have an intro or a verse. Why are we leaping ahead to the chorus?"

"Ah," I say, nodding my XL sized brain, wizened by years of song toil. "I'm so glad you asked."

There are several reasons why I almost always prefer to start the actual composition of a song at the chorus. This, of course, is presuming that our song is actually gonna have a chorus—there's no hard and fast rule that says it absolutely must. However, the majority of pop songs have choruses, as will the tunes we're about to collaborate on, so let's proceed to examine my justifications for starting there.

A chorus usually represents the highest dynamic of the song—in language, range and intensity. In other words, the chorus is almost always designed to contain the hookiest lyrical substance, which is probably sung on higher notes, and with somewhat greater intensity than the material that surrounds it.

If we begin by writing ourselves a satisfying, fulfilling chorus, we'll know later on what we're building toward with our verses—both melodically and lyrically. In most cases, we'll want to keep the verse somewhat more sedate and in a lower register than our chorus, so the already-written chorus will suggest where we'll begin our verse, both intensity- and pitch-wise.

Makin' Stuff Up

More than that, since we probably don't want our verses to use any of the exact verbiage we're saving for that climactic chorus section, we'll know what vernacular can or can't be included in the verse.

Make sense? I hope so. Actually, you may think this is rudimentary stuff—to a large degree, self-explanatory. I'm just enjoying thinking this through, so I hope you'll tag along with me.

Now we begin, by endeavoring to complete the most visible, eye-catching component of our edifice first. Then, after we're pretty sure we've got at least a good mock-up chorus, we'll set it aside for a time, before hoisting it up and placing it on top of its supporting pieces.

≈　　　≈　　　≈

A chorus can be simple and repetitive, or it can be wordy and complex. It can contain long, sonorous vowels that invite the big belt, or brief, rat-a-tat syllables (intended to be as rhythmic as they are amusing). Your chorus can sum up the message of the song, further its story or take the listener to a completely new place. It can be enlightening, or completely inane. It can be conversational, professorial … or a blathering, arcane bunch of nonsense.

The hint as to where to go with your chorus is probably right there in your icon-phrase. Most times, that little passage is going to be part of your chorus, and is more than likely your song's title and/or main hook. In any case, that select slice of words and music has its own mode, mood, cadence and melodic range, all built right into it. Let those syllables and notes tell you what your chorus is going to sound like, and the kind of character it will be assuming.

Kinds of choruses

THE BIG BELT:

All By Myself, by Eric Carmen (Carmen, Celine Dion)
Without You, by Pete Ham & Tom Evans (Badfinger, Nilsson, Mariah Carey)
A Broken Wing by Phil Barnhart, Sam Hogin & James House (Martina McBride)
How Do I Live, by Diane Warren (Trisha Yearwood, LeAnn Rimes)

Makin' Stuff Up

These ballads are built for power. They invariably include those extended, open vowel-sounds that long for a big voice to sustain them with passion. (Take notice of the appealing tone of those sustained sounds. Long *A*'s, *I*'s, *Oh*'s and *Ooo*'s. You won't find a whole lot of *Eeee*'s; they can be too *screeeeeeetchy* and grating.)

Great singers love these kinds of choruses, because they're pretty much guaranteed to bring down the house. If you're gonna write a ballad, you might as well write one that performers crave performing. Every one of the above-mentioned titles has been recorded and performed time and time again. Big melodies, big lyrics ... big copyrights.

However, with big ballads (or ballads of any kind) you're putting yourself up against a whole lot of extremely heavy competition from the get-go. Professional songwriters probably pen twice as many slow songs as they do up-tempos. *Why is this?* you may be wondering. I think it's mostly because, when a writer sits down at a piano, or pulls out an acoustic guitar, a more placid tempo is the more natural way to go. With a drummer absent from the room, sustaining a brisk feel for the consecutive hours it takes to carve away at your sonic sculpture can be physically exhausting.

Consequently, we see many more (and more superbly composed) ballads, collecting dust every day. You can see (being the obviously intelligent person you are), by contributing yet another passionate, big-voiced belter to the already abundant supply, you're in all likelihood merely adding another piece of unused inventory to the stockpile.

To make this reality even bleaker, most artists (with the possible exception of Josh Groban and singers of his classical-pop ilk) commonly record only two, maybe three, ballads on each album project. Even if a singer has consistent single-success with ballads, he or she certainly intends to put together an entertaining stage show, infused with real dynamics; as a result, the artist and producer are usually inclined to mix up the tempos on their albums. With only a few slots available—and a ton of competition—your big belting ballad has far less chance of finding an adopted home than your sultry mid-tempo, or that high-octane foot-stomper.

However, in the long run, there's nothing more satisfying than to finish off a huge, heart-ripping ballad, with a soaring chorus, a screaming guitar solo and a modulated breakdown. *Yeah, Man! That's the good stuff.*

Makin' Stuff Up

Back to more chorus types …

THE HOOKY REPEATER:

Johnny B. Good, by Chuck Berry
All I Wanna Do, by Sheryl Crow
You've Lost That Lovin' Feelin', by Barry Mann, Cynthia Weil & Phil Spector
Listen To The Music, by Tom Johnston (Doobie Brothers)

From these examples, it's clear that this style of chorus can be successfully utilized in your ballads, mids, *or* up-tempos. The most important common feature of these choruses is the repetition of the icon-phrase or hook of the song. Often, on the original hit recordings, these recurring chorus-lines continue into a lengthy fade, one that hammers the point home (to an absolutely absurd and, dare I say, mind-numbing degree).

Nevertheless, every one of these copyrights is massive—and has made its composers and publishers multi-millions—due to their easily relatable, ardent and unforgettable refrains. They all climax on a powerful emotional note, cling to it relentlessly, and then punch us in the heart with it until we surrender ...

Okay, Doobie Bros. Woe-oh-oh, I'm list'nin' to the music! And I have been since 1971! Are you happy now?

In 1981, after 14 years of spotty, erratic success, those brilliant purveyors of Philadelphia blue-eyed soul, Daryl Hall and John Oates, released a ditty entitled *Kiss On My List*. This song strayed from the R&B inflections of Hall and Oates' earlier charting records. A bubbly, lightweight record of nearly infinite redundancy, *Kiss* remained at #1 on the Billboard chart for three weeks and, at long last, established the deserving duo as consistent hit-makers for a number of years to come. There are thousands of examples of these somewhat tiresome, yet impossible-to-ignore hit songs.

When you're writing a chorus with this template, you run the risk of wearing out your welcome pretty quickly. It would thus serve you well to make sure that the key refrain you intend to repeat is actually worth repeating. (You know, something truly substantial, like … *Who Let The Dogs Out?*)

fact, I used to joke about the writing session that led to the
hat canine-themed dance sensation.

ve got a great hook," writer one reveals.

"Well, come on," urges writer two, "spill it!"

"Okay," says writer one, with that smirk that spells H-I-T all over it.
"Are you ready?"

"Yeah, Man! Let's hear it."

"Here it is." The first writer starts beating on his knees and shouting
on a high droning tone, "Who let the dogs out? Who? Who?"

"Who what?" asks his dumbfounded collaborator.

(I used to crack myself up picturing that imaginary scene. Then I
found out that Desmond Childs, co-writer of such classics as *Livin' On A
Prayer* and *Livin' la Vida Loca,* was partially responsible for that shaggy
little puppy. Oh, well. Genius dons many guises.)

Within this category of choruses also reside those rope-skippin'
nursery rhymes I mentioned earlier: *I Like It, I Love It*, by Mark Hall, Jeb
Stuart Anderson and Steve Dukes, *What I Like About You*, by Wally
Palmer and Mike Skill, and *That's The Way I Like It*, by Richard Finch
and the inimitable Harry Wayne Casey ("KC" of Sunshine Band fame).

Imagine how much labor went into constructing this refrain... *That's
the way, uh-huh, uh-huh, I like it, uh-huh, uh-huh*[ix], repeated without
variation, ad nauseum.

And while we're at it, just try to get *this* sharp-toothed little monster
out of your head: *Do a little dance, make a little love, get down tonight,
get down tonight*[x] ... over and over and over, utilizing all of two notes on
the scale.

Now let's imagine the checks that continue to land in Finch and
Casey's mailboxes. Talk about *nauseam*. But it's genius stuff; we
shouldn't kid ourselves about that.

Songs utilizing this kind of chorus define the term "hook." They are
as hooky, hooky, hooky as they are repetitive, repetitive, repetitive—just
as catchy and indelible as those first refrains repeated by the earliest
cavemen/composers. If you've got one, go for it, but don't expect
glowing reviews. Then again, if it somehow finds its way onto the
playgrounds of America, prepare to spend the rest of your days counting
your moolah.

Makin' Stuff Up

THE LIST CHORUS:

One Week, by Ed Robertson (Barenaked Ladies)
Fifty Ways To Leave Your Lover, by Paul Simon (Paul Simon)
Before He Cheats, by Chris Thompkins & Josh Kear (Carrie Underwood)
Daddy's Money, by Bob DePiro, Craig Wiseman & Mark D. Sanders (Ricochet)

This approach to chorus-writing really appeals to me—and not just because I've had some substantial success (literally) in applying it. List choruses are usually wordy (can't make a list without a good bunch of words), rhythmic (to make room for all those words) and somewhat playful and/or poignant.

In order to make a three-minute song into a playlet, a complete short story—with fully developed characters and a satisfying plot—a writer needs to be very, very economical with language. Making a list in a chorus enables the composer to cram more information into limited space. With this tidy packing technique, you're able to fit an extra couple of outfits into your suitcase as you head out on your jaunt to Hitsville. That's the first reason why I like list choruses.

Second reason: I love a challenge. Listing offers an opportunity to assemble a more complex puzzle, thus making the writing process that much more amusing for a writer who truly enjoys playing with language. It usually requires a heck of a lot more time and concentration to come up with the perfect set (or sets) of succinct phrases—ones that not only work, but make sense, and rhyme to boot. Of course, once you've composed your list chorus, you're likely to discover that a number of the best, high-scoring words are already on the scrabble board, and you're hard-pressed for raw materials to construct your verses. *Fun, fun, fun*!

Third reason: Most list songs respect the intelligence of the public. I almost always prefer the kind of writing—in *all* forms of media (movies, TV series, fiction, non-fiction, journalism, theater, *et alia*)—that doesn't pander to the lowest common denominator. Because a list contains a lot more detail than a repetitive chorus, the writer is giving the listener credit for the ability to absorb, comprehend and appreciate this presumably more sophisticated listening experience. It takes a smart writer to compose a great list song, and a smart public to embrace it.

Fourth reason: List songs can often sustain the interest of their audience for a longer period of time. These titles can bear repeated listenings, because the language is less redundant and therefore, at least ostensibly, stays fresher longer. These days, hit songs remain on radio playlists for six to nine months or more. Let's have some mercy on the battered ears of those millions of Top 40 fans, and give 'em somethin' they can listen to every 90 minutes for an entire year of their lives— without simultaneously giving them the overwhelming urge to barf! (Of course, there's no greater feeling than the guy next door complaining that he's sick and tired of hearing your song. That invariably means you can start making plans to move to a pricier neighborhood.)

List choruses are fun and challenging, and they give the writer an opportunity to stretch out a little bit more with language. Meanwhile (unless you or your collaborator happen to be one of those stream-of-consciousness geysers of instant brilliance), you'll labor long and hard over your list chorus, only to discover that your verses are equally, if not more difficult, because the good words left in your shopping cart are few and far between. Nevertheless, it's a very satisfactory way to go; take it from somebody who's been there and done that—*and* deposited the royalty checks.

THE SIMPLE (or SIMPLY **GREAT**) CHORUS:

Just Once, by Barry Mann and Cynthia Weil (James Ingram)
I Can't Make You Love Me, by Mike Reid & Allen Shamblin (Bonnie Raitt)
One More Day, by Steven Dale Jones & Bobby Tomberlin (Diamond Rio)
Both Sides Now, by Joni Mitchell

This, I believe, is the most commonly attempted style of chorus. In fact, this is what most readily leaps to mind when we tune-scribes think "chorus:" a few, succinct, intelligently constructed, rhyming phrases that begin and/or conclude with the icon-phrase or title of the song. Most times, the lyric sums up or hammers home the song's central theme or lesson; it certainly represents and/or strengthens the emotional core of the composition. As those lines float effortlessly atop a memorable melody they serve to make the message even more poignant ... or inspiring, heart-rending or exuberant. As always, they must be absolutely unforgettable.

The examples above demonstrate it well: this chorus-writing technique can yield a result that is virtually watertight, classic and iconic. With every one of those four exemplary compositions, songwriters have accomplished brief paragraphs of flowing sonic poetry, the perfect response to their verses' call. These are choruses you can't wait to get back to; each time they mercifully return, to grace our ears and rattle our hearts again, they affect us even more profoundly than they did on their first visit.

≈   ≈   ≈

As we writers are provided with limited usable vernacular—both lyrically and musically—we're bound to struggle to assemble choruses that are both simple and relatable, while at the same time being inspired and special. Ironically, it's often the most mundane phrase that cries out for a new voice, a new treatment, a fresh point of view. That's where true songwriting genius has an opportunity to reveal itself.

Just Once is exactly that kind of chorus. Ever since the first time I heard the Quincy Jones-produced original recording of this stunningly perfect song, performed with soulful sincerity by James Ingram, I've been in awe of how Cynthia and Barry took such a common, two-syllable phrase and co-opted it into an emotionally true, yet sweet-flowing plea for romantic reconciliation.

Who among us hasn't been at a loss to explain why a relationship that began with such blissful promise keeps turning so sour? How many times has a lover longed for a "time out," a few minutes of peace to try to find common ground? There's nothing new about the situation or the language used here, and the melody doesn't invent notes or chords that haven't been heard before. So what *is* it that makes this chorus work so flawlessly, thereby making this song so special?

As in so many of Cynthia Weil's lyrics, the situation in which the singer finds himself is universally relatable, and the lyricist's language is completely conversational. There's no effort to invent an original metaphor, coin a new simile or paint an image never before utilized in song. That's another reason why Cynthia is the best "pop" lyricist of her generation. She's able to speak the way people really speak, while hitting the bulls-eye with every syllable. At the same time, the words sound beautiful when they're sung, because she pays such precise attention to where the vowel-sounds fall into the melody, thus exploiting their natural, internal sounds and rhymes.

Meanwhile, Barry Mann's musical bedding provides reinforcement to all of those very crafty and appealing qualities. There's not a split-second where the words don't phrase the exact way they would commonly be spoken in everyday dialogue. For instance, the tidy pair of notes accompanying the title mirror precisely the way we'd articulate the phrase, if we were ever so unfortunate to find ourselves in the sad circumstance of this desperate lover. The composer takes a short jab at the word "just," then provides a longer, more emphatic note for "once."

Say "just once" to yourself, as if you were the lover pleading for another chance. See? That's exactly the way it should be, and so, it is exactly the way Mann and Weil make it work in their splendid song.

≈   ≈   ≈

On occasion, even though you've created a fantastic first chorus, you're going to need to consider changing some words in the choruses to come, in order to make them work for the verses that precede them, and/or to further the progression of the song. I usually resist this with every fiber of my being, and try every way possible to use the same exact words in every chorus.

I resist—not just because custom-crafting each chorus means a whole lot more time and labor for me. I'm also reluctant to make these adjustments because each change creates an additional challenge for the listener, who may just be struck with the inclination to join in and sing along with that second and third chorus. What's more, every new nuance makes the song more difficult for a singer to memorize; since established performers already often have a large repertoire already etched into their grey matter, some are bound to eschew test-driving a song, if it requires the additional concentration it takes to learn and retain several separate chorus lyrics.

That being said, sometimes you just gotta bite that bullet and tweak a second or third chorus so it can do its job. Suppose you've got a hook that you intend to speak on behalf of two or three different characters, or during two or three periods in time. Maybe the speaker of the first chorus is the singer's grandpappy, the second is the singer's pappy, and the third is the singer his own self—now having become a pappy and speaking to his own kid.

Here's my advice: try to change each chorus as little as possible, and *only* where absolutely necessary; re-use as many of the key words as you can; and (of utmost importance), if at all possible, make sure that icon-phrase or title always stays intact and works *verbatim*.

I strongly discourage you from changing tenses or gender in the actual hook-line of the song. After all, let's face it: every slight difference in the hook makes it a little less hooky. Our ultimate goal is to make that one critically important phrase remain constant, so that every time the song arrives there, the words are repeated exactly the same way. (Of course, you can experiment with inverting the melody and/or stretching out the phrasing, as the piece develops, at appropriate points, in order to create dynamics, dramatic effect and a song that offers more impact in performance.)

Both Sides Now is not only a perfect song, but a perfect example of a song in which the chorus changes every time it appears. The first chorus describes looking at clouds *from both sides now*, the second addresses *love*, and the third examines *life*; each chorus had to be different to accommodate these varied subjects. However, the icon-phrase of the song re-occurs at the very same rhythmic and melodic spot in each chorus; it is also unchanged in tense, thus enriching its meaning and maintaining its innate hookiness.

And then, Joni (*who does she think she is, anyway?*) Mitchell has the brass to slay us softly with her song, by reprising the language of the first chorus, while replacing the word *cloud* with the word *life*. Absolute genius. That a songwriter had that much skill, savvy and wisdom at a mere 24 years old … is entirely unfair to the rest of us tin-pan hacks.

Regardless of the style of chorus you feel compelled to write on any given day, you're striving to sum up the theme (or themes) of the song, using concise language and pleasing vowel sounds, while establishing what is likely the song's most intense musical dynamic. You want your chorus to be as hooky as possible, yet have the robustness to bear hundreds—hopefully thousands—of repeated listenings. Above all, you want that chorus to be the song's emotional high-point, and its most memorable section.

≈   ≈   ≈

I don't know how many times I've listened back to my own songs, and wondered how in the heck I ever accomplished them. I don't know how you and I did it, but here are the two choruses we've come up with.

First, sung with an upwardly moving arpeggiated melody and traveling in counterpoint to a descending chord pattern … is our ballad, which we've decided to title, *Everything and Nothing*.

She's everything to me
And I'm nothing, if I'm not crazy for the girl

Makin' Stuff Up

She's everything I need
And there's nothing I'd refuse her in the whole wide world
She's everything, and I'm nothing without her

It's direct and emotional, just like a love song should be. It has a fairly fresh twist as it plays on the words of the title, but not so clever as to blunt the song's sincerity. And it's pretty darn hooky, even if I do say so my own self.

Next, *Goin' Down Swingin'*, our fast-paced story-song, starring the guy who refuses to give up his girl without a fight (BTW, we've decided to name this stubborn lug Billy, and his ex-girl, Sally.):

Sally left Billy back in San Antone
He was past tense, 'least that was what she was thinkin'
But Billy was a boy with a jealous bone
If Billy's goin' down, Billy's goin' down swingin'

This chorus tells us a good deal about the characters and the situation. It packs some witty language. *He was past tense* has special appeal to me, and our icon-phrase is a really strong one.

Not bad. Now I'm feelin' like an expectant daddy. We've got a pair of fraternal-twin buns in the oven. Both of 'em are definitely worthy of our further attention, and will require a great deal more gestation before we can call 'em fully cooked.

Next, we're gonna hafta get down to some heavy lifting—by writing some verses.

chapter eight: Hoot Night

When we weren't on the road with Roxy during late-1970 and early-'71, Bob Segarini and I never missed a Monday Night Hoot at The Troubadour. For the Southern California acoustic music scene, the Troub bar was the place to hang out, imbibe a libation (or twelve), schmooze and wait for a turn on stage. Every week, the legendary club (which hosted the L.A. debuts of such luminaries as Elton John, Cat Stevens, Neil Diamond, James Taylor, Carole King and Steve Martin) provided a platform for denim-clad, shag-haired up-and-comers to try out a couple of original compositions in front of an attentive audience of scenesters and music-biz professionals.

Pumps primed with a pitcher or two of sangria from Le Figaro (a bustling restaurant standing a stone's-throw away, near the corner of Melrose and Doheny), Bob and I would lug our guitar cases into the dimly lit, cozy, stain-glassed Troubadour to sign up and stake out a stool at the heavy, hardwood bar. Once there, we'd greet and be greeted by our compatriots, the hoot-night regulars, like Jackson Browne and Bernie Leadon.

Segarini and Bishop's most obvious and direct competition came from another studly, fledgling duo calling itself Longbranch Pennywhistle, comprised of the craggy, red-topped J.D. Souther and a skinny lad with shoulder-length, straggly, brown hair from Detroit … by the name of Glenn Frey.

Frey seemed to consider himself the un-crowned prince of the Troub bar: for him, every female in the place, regardless of her current relationship status, was fair game. Glenn's dramatic Monday night entrance always included a pause, for a radar-like leer, as his eyes adjusted to the darkness and he prepared to survey the room for what he hoped would be his next likely female conquest.

Makin' Stuff Up

Frey wore the same pair of bellbottomed jeans every week. And every Monday evening, as those aging trousers became more threadbare, there'd be a new patch on the front of one of the legs.

One very rare week, my then live-in girlfriend, Melanie Bray, accompanied me to the Hoot. Arriving early, my lady and I commandeered a table by the stained-glass windows that paralleled the Santa Monica Boulevard sidewalk. We were engaged in playful conversation, when Prince Glenn silently announced his conspicuous arrival with his patented lust-filled gaze. Naturally, he lost no time in locating the comely Melanie. Then, without more than a cursory acknowledgment of me, Frey proceeded to sidle up lasciviously on her other side.

"What's your sign?" the prince inquired, in an oily, presumptuous tone.

Evidently, my girlfriend had heard this exact cliché come-on on several occasions in her brief, but eventful,18 years of life. She was locked, loaded, and ready to return fire.

"Asparagus," retorted Melanie, with a wry smile that told Frey he had less chance with her than an Eskimo Pie in The Congo.

Someday I'm gonna marry that girl, I promised myself (and I did). Mel's brush-off had me laughing so hard that beer spurted out of my nose, as the deflated future Rock 'n' Roll Hall-of-Famer slunk away to locate potential bimbo number-two.

$$\approx \qquad \approx \qquad \approx$$

During the course of Segarini and Bishop's frequent Troubadour Hoot-night appearances, I had occasion to get to know the venue's cherubic soundman. This friendship provided me with some extra-special privileges, including access to the club's private offices and dressing rooms, and an ongoing bar tab I successfully avoided paying—for months at a time. My soundman friend was also generous enough to add my name to the guest list for some incredibly memorable shows—including those of Cat Stevens, James Taylor and Carole King.

Troub owner Doug Weston, a gangling praying mantis of a man, with a head of crazed, unruly hair, was exceptionally proud of his latest coup—scoring the L.A. premiere booking of that extremely odd bird calling himself Tiny Tim. Weston was hosting a pre-show nosh at his house to celebrate the occasion. Through my roly-poly soundman-pal, I received an invitation to attend.

Makin' Stuff Up

Being barely 21, and committed to the lifestyle of a confirmed Bohemian, I had scant experience with such civilized social events. This evening, however, was unprecedented, in that it also turned out to be my very first all-male, gay dinner party. The colorful Weston was unashamedly animated as he bubbled over Tiny Tim's Troubadour appearance. In the middle of the meal, he suddenly remembered to call his mother and vociferously shared this moment of extreme pride with her via long distance.

Following his exuberant, five-minute conversation with Mom, as coffee and *aperitifs* were being served, Weston rolled a fat doobie and passed it around the table. It was pungent stuff, the finest Panama Red. So far, aside from some obvious, yet bemusing eccentricities, the evening seemed fairly normal. However, then the dinner train veered off the tracks into a very strange and (for me at least) heretofore-unexplored wilderness.

One particularly quirky feature of the Weston pad was the large, square, mosaic-tiled bathtub sunken into the very center of his living room—in direct view of our dining table. Our host strode across the room on his mile-long legs to stoop down and turn the spigots. He tested the steady flow of the water cascading into the tub, and adjusted the temperature until he was satisfied.

Then, wild-eyed and hovering over his dinner guests, at every bit of six-foot-six, Weston started unbuttoning and removing his shirt. His strip didn't end with a tease, but with his entire ensemble lying at his bare feet, his lanky frame fully exposed from head to toe. He swiveled and danced over to the steaming tub, and proceeded to lower his bony derriere into the luxurious water with a groan of pure pleasure. Leaning back, he kicked up his feet, and began bathing his extremities right there in front of the party.

"If anyone would like to join me, you're more than welcome," our gracious host invited.

There were no takers.

≈   ≈   ≈

I'd been a huge fan of The Dillards since my freshman—and only—year at Oberlin College. My roommate at the time, a bespectacled flat-picker from Wilmington, Delaware, had several of the exemplary bluegrass ensemble's albums in his collection, and I'd rapidly become a devotee of those tight, soaring Dillard harmonies and their superior musicianship. I found it a bit hard now to believe I was hanging out with Rodney Dillard himself, lead singer of the group he'd formed with his older brother, Doug, back home in Missouri's Ozark Mountains.

One particularly rowdy Monday night, that same older Dillard brother drove his Harley Davidson right into the Troub bar. The boisterous guffaws that greeted the banjo virtuoso's two-wheeled arrival were drowned out by the deafening roar of his souped-up hog's engine.

Gentleman/producer John Boylan was in the midst of collecting material for The Dillards' upcoming Elektra album. Boylan, one of the thirstier Hoot Night regulars, was well-known for capping off his weekly binge by hopping a ride home to Beverly Hills on the slow-crawling, westbound, midnight freight train that traversed the center divider between the lanes of Santa Monica Boulevard.

Just before he caught the choo-choo one particular Monday evening, Boylan was strolling through the Troub showroom on his way back to his bar stool—returning, no doubt, from a very necessary visit to the lavatory—when he was impressed by a certain high-energy number being performed by the duo on stage.

The title of the song was *St. Peter*. It was a sprightly, two-beat, gospel/bluegrass piece, in the tradition of *I'll Fly Away*. The pair pickin' and grinnin' this spirited composition was ... none other than Segarini and Bishop, the song's co-writers. After our two-tune presentation, Boylan approached us, inquiring about that particular song, and remarking that he thought it might be a good one for The Dillards.

Of course, I was beyond thrilled over the mere possibility that my bluegrass heroes might be at all interested in one of my songs. And interested they were: A week later, Rodney informed us that he and the band had worked up *St. Peter*, and went on to report that they were planning to include the song in their upcoming headlining appearance at—*you guessed it*—The Troubadour.

Dillards stage-shows not only featured lightning-fast chops and high-lonesome vocal excellence, they were also comedic entertainments, permeated with snappy repartee and down-home anecdotes. It would be no surprise when, a few years later, the group was drafted at-large to portray themselves, as recurring characters on *The Andy Griffith Show*.

On this occasion, Segarini and I sat through the 90-minute performance, thoroughly wowed and eagerly awaiting the unveiling of *St. Peter*. We were thus understandably confused and disappointed when the fivesome left the stage to a standing ovation—*without* getting to our song.

Makin' Stuff Up

On the heels of that recent, disheartening letdown with the Carpenters, I was beginning to assume that this was business-as-usual for a songwriter: great expectations dashed to the ground—time, and time, *and time* again. As The Dillards returned to the Troubadour stage, I was trying to keep a smile on my face, only half-heartedly contributing to the ongoing applause, hoots and hollers.

When the band kicked into their first encore, maintaining my grin suddenly became effortless. There, on the renowned boards of one of the world's premiere showrooms, less than 20 feet from where I sat (wearing a smile borne of authentic pride), my song was receiving a spirited interpretation by one of the greatest bluegrass bands of all time. It was the first time I'd ever enjoyed the distinct privilege of hearing a song I'd made up performed by another artist. The fact that it was The Dillards made this delicious experience even that much sweeter.

(A month later, The Dillards performed *St. Peter* on ABC TV's *Johnny Cash Show*, providing this young, apprentice tunesmith with another reason to feel real mighty good about myself. However, for whatever mysterious reason, the group never got around to recording the song.)

The only record-release of *St. Peter* was a version by Doug Dillard on one of his early solo albums. Years later, I ran into the elder, banjo-pickin' Dillard brother at Green's Grocery, in Leapers Fork, Tennessee. When I informed Doug that I was one of the writers of *St. Peter*, a broad, toothy smile spread across his cartoony face. He gave me a huge hug, and thanked me for the song.

Although I've never seen nickel one from *St. Peter*, that song was the source of some pretty big thrills back in those early days of my songwriting sojourn. Moreover, Doug Weston's Troubadour will forever live in my memory as a place where I encountered some of the most unforgettable experiences of my younger life.

chapter nine: The Opening Line

So now we've come up with a couple of excellent chorus-sketches. Each serves as the summation or reiteration of our two bulletproof concepts, and both take full advantage of those hooky icon-phrases.

At this juncture, many songwriting teams feel perfectly justified in taking a lunch break. This can be a risky proposition. We've got some real momentum now, and sending the blood supply from our active grey matter into our digestive systems tends to make us songwriters more than a bit lethargic. Since I'm starting to run low on blood sugar, though, and I get more than a little cranky when one p.m. rolls around and my tummy is growling … Yeah, come on, let's grab a sandwich.

"Besides," you suggest, naively. "We can work on our first verse over lunch." You even grab a notepad and a pen, along with your car keys. Aren't you adorable!

Mmmm, hmmmm. That'll never happen, I'm chuckling to myself.

Of course, we get distracted, gabbing about music, sports, politics, pets, spouses … you name it, everything *but* our song. Then we run into a few of our compatriots and get sidetracked, while we catch up on who just got a cut with whom, who signed where, and who's playing at what club when.

When we finally return to our womb of creativity, we'd better hope we remembered to store our chorus-sketches in some recorded fashion, because, for me, some chord inversion, or a riff, or a groove thing, a nuance of phrasing, or even the exact melody is likely to have evaporated into the ether—never to be retrieved in its original form … *FOR THE REST OF TIME.*

It's like pushing *Apple/s* on my Power Book every 30 seconds or so: Whether you're working in Word, Masterwriter, Garage Band or Pro-

Makin' Stuff Up

Tools, brothers and sisters, hear my testimony: *follow the wisdom of the prophet and "save, save, save."*

Meanwhile, unless you're one of those rare folks with absolute perfect recall—and I'm not sure that's even actually possible—record every potential musical and phrasing idea along the way. At some point, you're gonna thank yourself for doing that.

We return, with full bellies, and some kind of caffeine-laced beverage in hand to spark our now-numbed brain-cells. Our next mission is a daunting one, and we accept the challenge—with vigor. We're about to set that chorus up with a detailed, concise verse, one that captures the appropriate mood and makes our hook pay-off, big time.

Whoooeeee! You excited? I am.

It might bode us well—if we haven't done so already—to remind ourselves of the exact nature of the chorus we composed earlier, paying particular attention to its dynamic and musical range. Remember that we probably want our verse to commence in a tonal register somewhat lower than our chorus, and with a relatively gentler and more sedate demeanor.

It's also likely that we'll want to interject some contrast in the lyrical phrasing of our verse, as compared to the chorus. If our chorus-section hangs on long, sustained notes, maybe the language of our verse should be a bit wordier and more percussive, or vice-versa. Regardless of the challenge at hand, at the very least, we'll want the length of the lines (the number of syllables) to differ noticeably between our verse and chorus sections.

At this point in the process, a little bit of jamming on possible verse melodies and phrasing ideas would be called for. We're looking for the perfect "mode" for the verse. If the chorus begins on the tonic chord (the "1"), then maybe the verse kicks off on the "4," "5" or "6-minor." You might even try the "flat-7" or "2-minor." Any of those potential launching-pads might work. Remember, we're seeking to differentiate between the sections of the song—while creating a seamless and dynamic flow between them.

There have, however, been a plethora of hit songs that utilized the same (or a very similar) musical mode for both verse and chorus—sometimes even the exact same chord progression with a comparable melody. Usually, in those cases, phrasing is the main contrast between verse and chorus. *My List* is one such song, beginning both verse and chorus with the identical descending chord pattern. The verse is built on nine-syllable phrases—with sustained notes sung on long vowels at the end of each line:

73

Under an old brass paperweeeeeight
Is my list of things to do todaaay[xi]

Then the chorus accelerates into its list lyric, with a series of quick, four-syllable phrases—each one hanging on the same three repetitive notes, as the chords move underneath:

Go for a walk, say a little prayer, take a deep breath of mountain air...[xii]

Regardless of the mode we choose for our verse, its task will be to build to our chorus. Where does that build begin, musically and phrasing-wise? Keep noodling away until you find it.

I don't know how many more variations on *Three Blind Mice* (3-2-1 on the scale) we can stand to begin a verse melody. It seems that every other song commences in this mode. Give the world a break—at least *try* to find a fresher melodic start.

I also find it much richer harmonically to avoid singing the root-note of the chord in the melody. If your verse starts on a C-chord, try not to have your tune start *on* a C-note. Use another note in the chord (E or G), or a suspension (D, F or A).

Ah, hah! Eureka! You're a genius. But, of course, you knew that already.

Our ballad, *Everything and Nothing*, starts its chorus on a descending pattern, chords changing with every bar, beginning on the 1-chord. So, through experimentation, you've discovered that lingering on the 4-chord for two bars is an ideal place for our verse to begin. Then, we come up with a pattern of brief four- and five-note "*da-da-da-da-da's*" that float nicely over that four.

Goin' Down' Swingin''s chorus begins with two bars on the 5-chord. The verse mode we come up with for this one is a quick, three-chord, 1-5-4 vamp. A very conversational melodic phrase floats over the traveling chords.

We certainly won't forget to record those little verse bits and pieces, because now that we have modes and melodic ideas for our first phrases, we're going to be setting off on a safari with the purpose of capturing a true rarity: the perfect opening line.

Makin' Stuff Up

≈   ≈   ≈

Your song's opening line is often its second most recognizable and important lyrical component—next to your icon-phrase. How many first-verses have spun their wheels at the green light by beginning with such lackadaisical and mundane words as *I woke up this morning, I remember the first time I saw her* or *You are so beautiful to me*?

Wait a minute! That last one's a pop-standard. Maybe mundane can be the perfect way to jump-start your classic vehicle? For another example, our lyrical heroine, Joni Mitchell didn't do too badly with *Woke up ...* (when she followed it with) *it was a Chelsea morning...*[xiii] If mundane leads to greatness, even an every-day, hackneyed phrase might just do ... once in a while.

Actually, though, while on very infrequent occasions mundane might work fine, you're gonna find, 99% of the time, that more exploration, more originality and more imagination is called for, when mining for ear-catching verbiage to get your song off the starting-blocks.

But here's the deal: We're looking for descriptive language that creates even more atmosphere than the musical ambience in which it will reside. We want to seduce our imaginary audience of music-lovers, using precise imagery and/or action that will be sure to pique their interest, drawing them inextricably into our little three-minute mini-episode.

Think of the opening scene of your favorite film. It has impact, *pizzazz*, intrigue. Those visuals set the table for the delectable drama about to unfold. What the filmmaker has so deftly accomplished on the screen is the same thing we're gonna try to pull off with our opening line.

With the musical mode of the verse, and perhaps a phrasing concept—five, 10, maybe 20 *la-las*, representing the syllables of that first melodic passage—repeating in my brain, I sit and listen to the musings of my subconscious. I generally don't like to pound away on the keys or strum my six-string while I'm waiting for this inspiration. I want to be quiet, allowing my muses to whisper to me from the ethers. As my consciousness streams, I'll generally type away at two, three, perhaps four possibilities ... before I share them with my collaborator.

"What are you thinking?" he or she might dare to inquire, or...
"Whatcha got?"

If I'm ready to offer an idea, I do. If I'm not, I ask for some time, to allow my inspirations to percolate. To me, this opening line is all-important to the success or failure of this composition—both creatively and commercially. I'm gonna sit for as long as it takes for some valid dribs and drabs to trickle into my head.

"Okay," I finally say. "How about this?" Once again, just like that icon-phrase of lyric and melody we came up with way back an hour or two (or a few minutes) ago, this introductory-phrase might sound completely alien when it meets with the atmosphere of your writing-space. What's more, your collaborator's body-language will sing loud and clear in its response—or lack thereof.

I like opening lines that include "furniture." In other words, I almost always want something visual, tactile and/or kinetic—images you immediately feel as though you could reach out and touch.

Here's a great example, from the *grand opus* of the Mann/Weil songbook:

In this dirty old part of the city, where the sun refused to shine[xiv]

My Lord! How much do we know already? Cynthia has put us into a part of town that's obviously littered; it's decaying; it's probably crowded; and it's dark. All of those facts are provided in a perfectly composed and easy-to-sing fourteen words, which Barry sets into a gorgeously hypnotic musical environment. How could you not be fascinated to hear the next piece of info to follow? Incredible opening line. Mission accomplished.

Another Mann/Weil gem:

You never close your eyes anymore when I kiss your lips[xv]

Voila! We already know this much about the singer and his erstwhile lover: they've been intimate for some time; she's no longer returning his passion; and he's probably hurting because of it. More than that, Ms. Weil has planted those powerful, close-up visuals in our mind's eye—the skeptical, open orbs, as young lips meet. That adds some real gush to the scene. Inspired stuff.

I could pick virtually any opening line from the lexicon of Mann/Weil. For instance:

I did my best, but I guess my best wasn't good enough[xvi]

Makin' Stuff Up

Awesome! This line could be the beginning of a great American novel. It's *that* great! How many questions leap into your head when you hear these words? *Who is this guy? What was he trying to accomplish that he failed at? Who is he speaking to, and why would that person or persons be concerned or interested in his struggle?*

Okay, by now, you're painfully aware that I worship at the meticulously pedicured tootsies of Cynthia Weil. And, why shouldn't I? Study her work, and I'm quite certain you will join my cult, just as awed by her talent, grace and craft as I am.

However, I do have some other fave writers who have time and time again invited us into their three-minute scenarios with the consummate skill-set of the story-telling poet, Homer (not Homer Simpson, for crimany sake! The blind *Greek* dude!).

So please allow me to introduce you to a few of these gifted folks. While we're at it, why don't we indulge ourselves by imagining what they might have written, if they weren't so damned brilliant—just so we can appreciate their craft a little bit more.

In *Johnny B. Goode*, the illustrious Chuck Berry could have settled for this pretty decent opener: *Way down south, where the pine trees grow*

Instead, in his trademark rat-a-tat-tat, the lyrical mastermind gave us:

Deep down Louisiana, close to New Orleans
Way back in the woods among the evergreens[xvii]

In *I Like it, I Love it*, Mark Hall, Jeb Stuart Anderson and Steve Dukes might have chosen: *Last night, I took my girl to the fair/ And I spent every dime in my pocket ...*

Instead:

Spent forty-eight dollars last night at the county fair
Throwed out my arm, but I won her that teddy bear[xviii]

In *Sympathy For the Devil*, Jagger and Richards could have written: *Glad to meet you / I'm a rich and classy guy ...*

77

Makin' Stuff Up

Instead, the enduring rocker/composers gave us:

Please allow me to introduce myself
I'm a man of wealth and taste[xix]

In *I Can't Make You Love Me*, Mike Reid and Allen Shamblin might have lazily begun with: *I'm ready to make love, but I'm still confused ...*

Instead, we have:

Turn down the lights, turn down the bed
Turn down these voices inside my head[xx]

In *Loves Me Like a Rock*, Paul Simon could have commenced by informing us: *As I kid, I got in a whole lot of trouble ...*

The ever-original Mr. Simon wouldn't settle for that. So he came up with:

When I was a little boy and the devil would call my name[xxi]

Or, in *Sounds of Silence*, the same writer might have easily scribbled: *It's the middle of the night, and I'm lonely ...*

But, no. The always-fastidious Simon offers:

Hello, darkness, my old friend
I've come to talk to you again[xxii]

In *Across the Universe*, Lennon and McCartney could have written: *Everybody's talking at once ...*

Instead, they blessed us with:

Words are flying out like endless rain into a paper cup[xxiii]

In *Big Yellow Taxi*, Joni Mitchell might have compromised on her language: *What was green is now concrete ...*

Makin' Stuff Up

Instead, we have the unforgettable:

They paved paradise and put up a parking lot[xxiv]

Or how about this Joni choice? *Raised on Robbery* could have started this way: *The man sat in the bar with a drink in his hand ...*

But that wasn't good enough for our Joni. She came up with:

He was sitting in the lounge of the Empire Hotel
He was drinking for diversion ...[xxv]

I think these examples speak for themselves. Read them again, while imagining their accompanying melodies and musical atmosphere. I think, like me, you'll find admiration in how these choice words set the tone for each song and grab the listener by the ears. Like the first visual of a film classic, these opening lines are cinematic. Like the phrases that begin every great novel or memoir, these passages are literary. In every case, they offer an attitude, an ambience, a character and/or a situation that hooks our interest and makes us want to hear more.

$$\approx \qquad \approx \qquad \approx$$

In order to live up to the precedents set by the greatest pop songwriters, and to give our songs a chance at drawing attention to themselves, every time we set out to make up a new one, we must strive to introduce our story, our characters, our situation, our emotional state-of-the-heart to our listeners in the freshest and most evocative way. This is a task that requires vivid imagination, strong intuition and sense memory.

If this song is personal, and you're conveying its emotion from a currently honest place of private expression, then you already have a leg up. This is a song you and *only* you can write—or, perhaps with the assistance of a skilled co-writer. It may tax you to keep yourself in that place of ecstasy or that overwrought mood, while you simultaneously stand back and discipline your language into submission. Every time you have a lyrical idea, be brutally honest by asking yourself these two questions: *Does this describe **exactly** how I feel or felt?* If so, *is my language as novel, as colorful, as intriguing, yet as conversational as it can possibly be?*

Makin' Stuff Up

We want to use every means at our disposal to grab and keep the listener's attention: perhaps it's a visual image that evokes a vivid picture of time, location, characters and specific situation; maybe a phrase that ponders some provocative question the song will be willing to answer. Remember, we're setting a mood—both lyrically *and* musically—so the words and notes need to be like a pair of highly toned, beautifully choreographed synchronized swimmers (hopefully, without the nose plugs).

Whether this new song is intended to be fun and energetic, or somber and thoughtful, or whether it's a sensual hip-grinder or a glorious, passionate anthem ... that first line needs to be great. Work on it until you've set the table for the feast to come.

Although you might be tempted to settle for:

The first time I saw you, you won my heart

Or:

I'll never forget the first time I saw her

... ask yourself, what do those phrases actually say? Do they offer anything at all interesting or unique to the literature of song-lyrics? Why not be more specific, giving the listener some comfy furniture to sit on? Consider the scene in detail. What precisely was it about this enticing, alluring creature that might have captured your attention and made your little heart go pit-a-pat?

If it's a love song, like for instance our germinating ballad, *Everything and Nothing*, we might consider something like:

They were bright and clear and blue as the sky
My heart was no match for her laughing eyes

Hey, go ahead and have a good chortle. Yeah, this imagery is a little sappy. But it's a dang good start—one of maybe three or four pump-primers I might put out there to get us rolling.

For another example, let's say it's a fun, sexy, up-tempo romp, like *Goin' Down Swingin'*. Try this opener on for size:

Makin' Stuff Up

Her legs stretched from Dallas to Houston and back
I ordered two longnecks and sat down to chat

These two pairs of couplets each do the job. They provide solid information and ambience to our story by employing clear imagery. They're very singable lines over the music we've sketched. I think we're onto somethin' here ...

I hope you get my drift. Always endeavor to give each song an opening line that will reach out and grab your listeners by the ear lobes. Kicking your tune off with an imaginative, descriptive, succinct intro statement is never a bad idea. So go for it, and don't settle for mundane language, overused phraseology, cliché musical modes or hackneyed melodies.

chapter ten: Don't You Worry

The backhanded compliment my little song had just received was as inaccurate as it was embarrassing. In the brief, but seemingly endless (and certainly excruciating) silence that followed Norman Schwartz' absolutely inappropriate remark, my skin had begun to crawl, as I waited, anticipating a sharply barbed retort from Bob Segarini. But, to my surprise, my former bandmate kept his glibness to himself.

The year was 1974. Segarini—the man I'd once idolized, the guy who'd drafted me into the big leagues, my longtime-collaborator and partner on five Elektra Records albums—and I were paying a visit to the Manhattan apartment of our manager. Prior to co-opting our band, The Wackers, Schwartz' major management credit had been his handling of Oliver, the one-hit-wonder, mop-topped tenor. (Who could forget *Good Morning, Starshine* from the musical, *Hair*?)

The Wackers had been born with the convergence of three 20-something singer/songwriters, in the rustic, picturesque, seaside town of Eureka, California. Super-suave producer David Anderle had introduced Bob and me to Michael Stull. Anderle was, at that particular moment in time, in the process of putting the multi-gifted Stull under contract to A&M Records, while simultaneously making similar overtures to Segarini and Bishop. Bob and I had recently sung back-ups on Anderle's first Rita Coolidge LP, and we'd scored two coveted slots on the soundtrack of '70s cult flick, *Vanishing Point*. As a performing, songwriting duo, our post-Roxy stock was rising on the L.A. scene.

I can only imagine how peeved the ultra-cool Anderle must have been to observe his two fledgling acts merging and morphing into a group that had little resemblance, either sonically or visually, to its original components. The band Segarini, Bishop and Stull formed featured the tight, soaring harmonies of Crosby, Stills and Nash, combined with the androgynous image and punky energy of New York Dolls. After weathering the trial-by-fire of week after week of seven-set nights at a tavern called The Purple Haze, The Wackers were inked by Elektra Records and made our first album, under the auspices of songwriting and production wizard Gary Usher.

While the rock-press slathered praise on The Wackers, Top-40 radio and the general public pretty much turned up their noses, and we were reduced to applying for food stamps as we prepared to record Elektra album number-two. Our original manager had finally passed the brutal California bar exam, thus segueing into the unenviable role of acting as our attorney. The task of managing our band of ne'er-do-wells was passed onto one Mr. Bill Siddons. Bill, who was also handling The Doors, had very little empathy or patience for the befuddling, gender-bending image of The Wackers, or for our frequent rock 'n' roll shenanigans.

Siddons deigned to throw our band a bone by booking us in the opening slot for a Doors tour—the campaign that Manzerek, Densmore and Krieger had misguidedly engaged upon after Jim Morrison's death. While the billing did offer us Wacks some semblance of prestige, the two acts on the bill had such divergent appeal that our colorful, highly kinetic sets probably earned us as many enemies as they did new fans along the way.

As the Doors tour unwound, my bandmates and I grew more and more frustrated by a distinct dearth of attention from our manager. In his defense, Siddons most certainly had his hands full, trying to gain and sustain the interest of the press and the public for a legendary act left widowed by its infamous, self-destructive, superstar lead-singer. To our constant chagrin, though, the sum-total of Siddons' Wacker career-shepherding amounted to handing each of us an envelope of *per diem* cash at the beginning of each week, with the following instruction: "Don't have too much fun." (An absurd suggestion, if I've ever heard one.)

Our frustration came to a head on the eve of our scheduled appearance at the shrine of all performance venues: Carnegie *bleepin'* Hall. Holed up at the staid, midtown Wellington Hotel, surrounded on all sides by high fashion, and dispirited by the increasingly disheveled state of our thrift-store, bargain-bin and/or hand-made wardrobe, we demanded a powwow with the man himself. Siddons relented by scheduling a confab in a conference room just off the Wellington's starched main lobby.

There we sat, the most unlikely looking corporate board in New York history. CFO Siddons called the meeting to order. Without waiting to be recognized by the chair, lanky, pock-cheeked bass player Kootch Trochim piped up:

"So, Siddons, are we gonna get some money for some cool clothes, or what?"

Siddons's negative response resounded succinctly in the shape of a single syllable ..."No."

As our moans and groans of dissent crescendoed, peach-cheeked roadie Steve Wood poked his head into the room, alerting our manager to an incoming phone call. *Doors business, no doubt*, I thought to myself, resentfully. During the next 10 minutes, while Siddons tended to this urgent matter, we determined insurgents conspired to impress him with our wardrobe-woes by way of a much more visual form of protest.

Bill re-entered, marching myopically to his place at the head of the table. He then took a deep breath, preparing to weather the next expected gripe from his recalcitrant charges. At that point, Kootch rose from his chair, revealing that he was wearing not a single stitch of clothing—aside from the slender tie around his neck.

The bassist's genitals bobbling at the edge of the mahogany conference table, he repeated his earlier query: "So, Siddons, are we gonna get some money from some cool clothes, or what?"

"Yeah!" we all chimed in, as we stood in unison, expressing our solidarity, while simultaneously revealing our common nudity.

Our manager's face was blooming valentine-crimson, as he rose from his chair. Without uttering a word, he strode out of the room, leaving only the echo of the slamming door behind him. At the tour's end, Bill Siddons resigned as our manager, demanding that we repay him the $900 he claimed we owed him. Not being a band of deadbeats, we settled our weighty debt with nine boxes, each containing 10,000 pennies.

Ironically, now residing in Montreal, and without the assistance of established management, The Wackers' next single hit the Top-40. *Day and Night*, a Segarini/Bishop composition, was a rhythmic, Caribbean-inflected sing-along, punctuated by a Lady-Madonna sax section. It finally looked as if our hard-working ensemble, now on its third Elektra album release, was poised to break into the big time. That was when new manager Norman Schwartz swaggered like Buzz Lightyear onto our loopy space station.

Schwartz, a handsome, swarthy New Yorker (with an impressive apartment, an even more impressive—and substantially younger—wife and an obligatory bleeding ulcer), led us through the next year like a field general. Following Norman's always jam-packed itinerary, we got a taste of what real celebrity must be like, rising at the crack of dawn for drive-time radio interviews, and scooting from one record retailer to the next for in-store promotional appearances. Now we had a good idea of what it's like when a manager actually pays attention to his act.

Our friend, Elektra-founder Jac Holzman, had thoughtfully left his favorite little combo, The Wackers, with a renegotiated seven-album commitment—just before selling Elektra Records to Kinney Corporation and resigning his long-held label-head post. Shortly thereafter, we were deeply disappointed to get the bad news that our fourth album, *Wack And Roll*—a half-live, double disc—had been rejected by the new Elektra honcho, David Geffen.

On the band's behalf, Norman Schwartz gave Geffen a jingle—presumably to sort out this unfortunate misunderstanding. I'll never know what our manager said to the Napoleonic executive, but it failed to yield the positive outcome Schwartz had hoped for. All I heard was that Geffen responded to Schwartz by slamming his phone down on his desk, and screaming across the room to his assistant: "I don't know who that asshole represents, but I want his act off the label *NOW*!!!"

Sure enough, the crack Elektra legal affairs squad found a way to wiggle out of that seven-album commitment, and the group *Creem Magazine* had once branded "the greatest rock 'n' roll band in North America" suddenly found itself out on the street, languishing label-less and record-less in *Provence de Quebec*, Canada.

The Wacks' wild reputation and our chosen city of residence already amounted to two strikes against us. Our inability to procure the rights to the *Wack And Roll* masters from Elektra was the third.

We were opening for Alice Cooper's *Billion Dollar Baby* tour, when I began to realize that every self-abusive week on the road was shortening my life—measurably. Since I wasn't exactly willing to commit a slow suicide while going down with a sinking ship, I informed Bob and the rest of the lads that I planned to leave. The Wackers' final show took place at an Ottawa hotel ballroom. As always, we rocked our hearts out for those two hundred or so die-hard fans.

As one door closes, another opens. My pal, Doug Pringle, Montreal's most popular bilingual FM radio personality, had signed a record deal with Gamma Records—the label responsible for launching the career of French Canadian superstar Robért Charlebois. Pringle inquired as to my interest in co-writing some songs for his project and producing his sessions. Ever since I'd manned the production chair a few years before—for a demo that led to my brother Bart's band, Providence, getting their deal on Threshold Records—I'd entertained a strong desire to take on the producer role again.

Baby Face, the first Pringle/Bishop collaboration, shot to number-one on the Quebecois charts. Soon, Gamma's Dan Lazare had me busy helming sessions for a Pringle follow-up, as well as for a debut LP for Anne Anderssen, a sultry Parisian chanteuse with a Swedish moniker.

During our co-writing sessions, Pringle and I came up with an English-language ditty, too—a little tune I decided to save for myself. *Don't You Worry* was a Todd Rundgren quote, mixed with elements borrowed from Spooner Oldham and Dan Penn's *I'm Your Puppet*. The lightweight, all-acoustic recording even featured percolating *pizzicato* strings. The listener would have been hard-pressed to identify the gender of the vocalist, as I crooned reassurance to a fictional "friend," who seemed to be having a tough time dealing with some unusually strong emotions.

Don't you worry. You're in love, and that's all right[xxvi], I comforted in my smoothest head-voice.

In The Wackers, I'd always worn my rock rebelliousness with pride. As a band, we'd cultivated an attitude and an image designed to shock and repulse parents, while simultaneously exciting and (hopefully) stealing the defiant hearts of their teenaged children. With songs like *Juvenile Delinquent* and *Rock and Roll Circus*, we connected strongly and directly with the angst of pimples and alienation.

With *Don't You Worry*, I was consciously striving to make a much more universal, non-controversial connection, one that would be received equally well across generational divides—and, more importantly, one that might be embraced by radio programmers.

So there we sat, Bob Segarini and I, ex-partners in rock-rebellion, in that Manhattan apartment, both equally bewildered by Norman Schwartz' assessment of my new, safe, (one might even say innocuous) solo single, *Don't You Worry*.

"If The Wackers had written songs like that," pontificated Schwartz, in his Brooklynese snarl, "you'd still have a record deal."

I have no idea how Bob held his usually acidic tongue in check after hearing those pedantic words, spoken so carelessly by the very man who had been responsible—with one phone call—for getting The Wackers dropped like a radioactive stone from our long-term record contract. Bob's discreet silence demonstrated his respect for me as a fellow creative soul. I will always appreciate every opportunity and every encouragement that Bob Segarini gave me back in those wild and wooly days of the early-'70s.

While *Don't You Worry* subsequently climbed into the top-five on the Canadian national charts, it was not by any means a career-breaking song. The record received a ton of airplay—probably more because of its lack of distinction than for any special, defining personality or statement. One program director defined my first solo single as a "palate cleanser," meaning that it was a song that wiped the airwaves clean between records with more identifiable character and substance.

To this day, *Don't You Worry* receives regular spins on Canadian radio. The song was also (appropriately) licensed as the theme for director Sharon Hyman's *Neverbloomers*—a feature-length documentary film about a generation that refuses to grow up.

chapter eleven: The First Verse

O kay, my friend, we're pickin' up speed, with construction fully under way, and our concepts and choruses-to-die-for (including those provocative, ear-catching icon-phrases). We've introduced both of our little musical dramas with colorful, furniture-filled opening lines. Let's take a deep breath and allow ourselves to feel a wee bit o' pride 'cause, with proper nurturing, both of our songlings have an excellent chance of growing into real champions.

In track and field parlance, if we were in the midst of tackling the grueling mile-run, we've just finished the first lap of four. We've found our groove—but we'd better pace ourselves, because there's a whole lot more race yet to run.

Then again, writing a song is not a race. In fact, it's perfectly okay for these little creations to take their own sweet time. It's even likely that we've already completed an entire day's work by now. Maybe we've used up our final, fresh, creative thought for this session—or you may be looking at your watch, discovering that it's high time to pick the kids up at school, or hit Whole Foods to supply that dinner party your spouse sprung on you this morning. You've got a life, for Pete's sake (*and who the heck is Pete?*).

Anyway, if our session is over for the day, we've probably set up a return engagement, or at least exchanged email addresses, promising to check our respective calendars at a later time. (I'm also going to presume that every essential component of our works-in-progress has been documented in some recorded fashion. *Duh!*)

Whether we're still in the middle of an exceptionally productive Day One, or we've reconvened for round two, it's now time to finish off our first verse. From the phrasing and mode of our opening line, we already have a good idea of the melodic flavor of the verse. Now that we've accomplished those provocative first lines, we'll need to sketch out the rest of the verse melody over a basic chord-progression.

Makin' Stuff Up

By "sketching out," I mean mocking up a direction within our chosen musical mode and dynamic range, along with a certain rhythm and syllabic pattern, without getting completely and irrevocably locked into an *exact* melody—or even an absolutely fixed chord progression, for that matter. Having a basic, pliable verse-shape to work within will give our yet-to-be-written words and the notes they sit on a good opportunity to meld together like peanut butter and crackers (or celery, bananas or mayonnaise. *Hey, some folks love it!*)

Remember, nothing is written in stone. (Until, of course, it *is* written in stone; *I only just now realized how incredibly morbid that expression is.*) It's a good idea to remain flexible during the early stages of song-formation, allowing the music and words to grow togcthcr, as we encourage them to fuse into one mutually cooperative expression. However, there *will* soon come a time when you have to be decisive. (Writing is ultimately a decision-making process; as far as I'm concerned, chronically ambivalent, namby-pamby writers can be a pain in the *keister*.)

Invariably, one of the writers in the room is acknowledged as being the stronger musician, so that partner is more likely to assume the lead role in this "verse sketching" part of the process. However, if you've got bit of a brainstorm when it comes to music or phrasing, regardless of your relative level of musicianship, never shy away from tossing your *"how 'bout this?"*-es out there.

Most times the simplest concept is the best. Yet, on occasion, the most unconventional, unusual or intuitive and unschooled inspiration is exactly the contribution that can make the song incredible. Either way, keeping your ideas to yourself doesn't make for good collaboration, nor does it lead to a fulfilling creative experience for you. Just don't take the sidelong glances or disdaining headshakes personally; even accomplished musicians can be snooty, sometimes.

We all have different imaginations springing out of our creative little craniums. Listening to each other is critical. We writers (I'm as guilty as the next guy) often have a tendency to bully each other, by ignoring each other's offerings and repeatedly making noise with our own. While it's positive to have a conviction that your own ideas are good ones, collaboration requires, at the very least, being respectful of your creative partner(s). And who knows? He or she just might shed some new light on the picture—the exact, unique perspective that will end up making this song a much better one.

Makin' Stuff Up

In actuality, I have to admit I get very bored with the musical ruts I fall into. So I'm *always* keeping my ears open for other choices, other places to go. Many times, I find it tough to actually capitulate to my co-writers' point of view; I don't always feel inspired by the direction he or she is inclined to take. In those cases, I do lobby to steer the thing in the direction of my own intuition. However, every step along the way should make for, to one degree or another, a malleable, two-way process.

So now 20 minutes of jamming yields a basic few passages of verse melody that we're both liking, over a simple, but supportive, chordal base. (And we've recorded it. *Come on! Do I have to remind you?*)

≈ ≈ ≈

Now let's talk rhyme scheme. Remember what our pre-historic ancestor discovered back in 8,000 BC? That's right ... *If it rhymes, people are more likely to remember it*. Now, after all these millennia, and eons communing with ethnic chants, folk ditties, and finally pop songs, we actually *expect* them to rhyme. It literally stuns us when they don't.

A verse that doesn't rhyme can be like a stalled escalator undergoing repairs at the mall. You step on, expecting to scoot ahead, but no! Your entire body goes through that lugubrious sensation of losing momentum. Your eyes lose focus and your knees get all wobbly, and you have to look away from the stationary stairs as you climb them, because your head can't wrap itself around their lack of movement.

Maybe somebody should have relayed that old rhyming axiom to David Byrne of Talking Heads, because on occasion he's completely defied our expectations in that regard. Don't get me wrong; I think *Life In Wartime* is a very catchy, genuinely inspired tune. Still, couldn't the enigmatic composer have thrown in a few sound-alikes here and there? After 25 years of listening to those jagged, dangling phrases, that *Wartime* lyric still messes with my mind. But then again, Mr. Byrne has been known to gravitate toward weirdness on occasion. I think maybe it's kind of "his thing."

We, on the other hand, tend to be more traditional in our song-craft. Wouldn't you agree? I hope so, because I love to think about and sound off about this stuff. I'm a bit of a rhyme-scheme freak. It's kind of "*my* thing."

Let's begin by discussing what actually qualifies *as* a rhyme. In the libretto of a Broadway musical, or the lexicon of pop-song-genius Jimmy Webb, a rhyme must be a hard rhyme, a perfect rhyme. In other words, the words that end the rhyming phrases have to end with the *exact* same sound. This is the songwriting philosophy that gave birth to such overused clichés as *moon* and *June*, *college* and *knowledge*, *love* and *above*, etc.

On the non-cliché flip side, for hard-rhyming perfection, look no further than the most phenomenal Broadway musical in the history of the stage (*I'm not prejudiced. Really, I'm not.*). Of course, I'm referring to *My Fair Lady*. Within the boastful text of the misogynistic, self-congratulatory *You Did It*, Alan Jay Lerner blesses our ears with the most creative hard-rhyme ever. Imagine the delight Mr. Lerner must have felt when he came up with a rhyme for *Budapest* in the insulting description ... *ruder pest.*

You may object, because the second syllable of "ruder pest" doesn't sound exactly the same as the second syllable of Budapest. Don't leap to conclusions, my friend. When enunciated with the proper, upper-class, British inflection of phonetics professor Henry Higgins, *ruder* becomes *rudah*. And thus, the three syllables of *ruder pest* arrive at our ears as an absolutely perfect rhyme. Every time I hear those lines, I laugh my fanny off—and curse my own pedestrian rhyming skills. (*I'm not worthy, Mr. Lerner, Sir*. May you rest peacefully in Songwriter Heaven.)

In the craft of pop songwriting, however (thank our lucky stars!), we're not required to use perfect, hard rhymes. If it sounds good, it's allowed, and so I encourage you to be as creative as you can be in your rhyming endeavors.

Country-music writers are the most liberal of all tunesmiths in this regard. (In fact, rhyming is probably the only issue many of them are at all liberal about ... *but that's another book, altogether.*) In Nashville, "ee" rhymes with "ing." I've lived in Music City for 13 years, and I still can't figure that one out. A lot of what is considered a rhyme on Music Row depends on how it's pronounced in indigenous Southern-speak. That's where Alan Jackson and Professor Higgins find some common ground—enunciation can make all the difference.

KINDS OF RHYME SCHEMES:

There are a number of rhyme schemes to consider. The first, perhaps the most common, is writing in couplets. In this technique, each pair of consecutive lines rhymes with each other, as in the following:

Da, da, da, da, da, da, deeee
Ta, ta, ta, too, ta, ta, ta, teeee

This would be called an "a-a" rhyme (the first rhyming-sound introduced in the song is labeled with the first letter of the alphabet). The first part of your verse would probably contain two pairs of rhyming couplets, each pair ending with a different vowel sound, the second rhyming sound being logically labeled with a "b." A four-line section is called a quatrain, the verse pattern is called an "a-a-b-b" rhyme:

Da, da, da, da, da, da, deeee
Ta, ta, ta, too, ta, ta, ta, teeee
Dip, dee, do, dah, skip to mah loo
Just let FedEx ship it too

The first alternative to this rhyme structure is an "a-b-a-b" verse, in which every other line of the quatrain rhymes:

Da, da, da, da, da, da, deeee
Da, da, da, da, da, da, tahh
Ta, ta, ta, too, ta, ta, ta, teeee
Dipsey, doo-doo, doo-doo, dah

This pattern can also be modified with the "a-b-c-b" form:

Da, da, da, da, da, da, deeee
Da, da, da, da, da, da, tahh
Ta, ta, ta, too, ta, ta, ta, too
Dipsey, doo-doo, doo-doo, dah

I quite like the "a-a-a-b" form, in which three consecutive, usually shorter phrases rhyme, and the fourth introduces a new sound.

Da, da, da, da, day
Da, dee, da, dee, tay
Da, da, doo, doo, say
Tah, dah, tah, dee

The new sound (the "b" rhyme) would either rhyme with the fourth phrase of a matching section to follow, representing a "c-c-c-b" scheme:

Makin' Stuff Up

Tee, tee, tah, tah, tie
Tee, tah, tee, tee, die
Tee, tee, tah, tah, bie
Tay, day, dah, tee

Or, it might rhyme with the channel, pre-chorus or build section to come. On some rare occasions, the "b" rhyme can even be left hanging on its own, eventually to be rhymed with the last syllable of a matching quatrain in a second verse.

Contemporary pop phrasing allows for some pretty inventive rhyme ideas. Everything doesn't have to be exactly proportional. An "a-a-b-b" or an "a-b-a-b" verse could be constructed with lines of slightly or very different lengths. If it sounds conversational, then it's worth a try.

≈   ≈   ≈

Another rhyming technique you might want to pay some attention to is the internal rhyme—hard rhymes or sound-alikes within lines that please the ear. While internal rhymes are not essential to great lyric writing, they can make a song that much more appealing—both to the singer and to the audience.

Just as a fashion stylist might use a certain shade of belt to compliment the color of a pair of shoes, our vowel-sounds (and where we place them) combine to create a sort of "color palate" in our songs. Internal rhyming is the subtle trim of a tastefully designed room. Everybody won't necessarily take notice, but to the most discerning eye, those touches can make the difference between pedestrian and elegant.

Some writers apply this cunning craft intuitively. I once complimented my dear friend, Amanda McBroom (*The Rose*), on her internal rhymes in a certain lyric; she wasn't even aware that they were there. Meanwhile, other writers labor over them.

When I first began writing in Nashville, I felt extra pride in bringing my internal rhyming skills to the co-writing table. More than once, my natural inclination to utilize this technique would tend to irk my collaborator.

"Yeah," I might point out—while deliberating the relative pros and cons of two possible lyrical phrases—"but I like this line, because the word *lie* picks up the sound of *right* from the line before."

Makin' Stuff Up

After receiving more than a few squinted daggers—and even some overt chortles—it became painfully obvious that most Music Row pros have far less interest in toying with internal rhymes than they do in creating a lyric that is succinct, to the point, literal and conversational. Meanwhile, my years of experience inform me that, with a bit of extra care, and maybe a bit of dumb luck, craft and story can co-exist very well in the same song.

Two pointers: first, never let the clarity of the lyric suffer from a stubborn adherence to craft. Secondly, if you *do* establish a scheme that employs internal-rhyming, try to make that pattern as consistent as reasonably possible. Let's say, in your first verse, lines three and four each contain a sound-alike vowel on the fourth syllable. If so, it's a very good idea to place a pair of matching sounds in the third and fourth lines of verse two, as well. Having heard it the first time, the listener's ear tends to expect the rhyme-scheme to repeat itself, and will likely miss it if it's not there the second time around.

≈ ≈ ≈

Now we've got a quatrain of verse-melody sketched out, with a proposed rhyme-scheme to follow our opening line. Where do we go from here? How do we cross that seemingly unfordable chasm standing between our opening line and our chorus? We know we want our verse to build to our chorus, both melodically and in its narrative. We want our words to reveal the perfect amount of information so that our chorus has a chance to pay off big time when it arrives—but with not so much detail that we have nowhere to go with that second verse.

To that end, let's remind ourselves of those lovely opening lines we've already so cleverly invented …

Our love ballad, *Everything and Nothing*, begins…

They were bright and clear and blue as the sky
My heart was no match for her laughing eyes

(If you've identified this couplet as the start of an "a-a-b-b" rhyme scheme, congrats—you might just be a songwriter!) As we know, the chorus to which we're building goes something like this:

Makin' Stuff Up

She's everything to me
And I'm nothing, if I'm not crazy for the girl
She's everything I need
And there's nothing I'd refuse her in the whole wide world
She's everything, and I'm nothing without her

What do the existing lyrics tell us so far? The opening couplet explains that the lady has a pair of welcoming baby blues, and indicates that our singer was in over his head from the get-go. The chorus reveals that this is not a one-night-stand. In our singer's heart of hearts, this is a relationship to which he is unashamedly devoted.

What critical info do we *not* know? How long has this thing has been goin' on? What's the status of *her* feelings at this particular juncture? Here's one critical decision we'd better make right now: Are we gonna put this romance in jeopardy, or are we about to make this a wedding song?

By wedding song, I mean a devotional love-ballad that might someday, if we're really, really lucky, become a wedding standard. That could mean scads of sheet-music sales, not to mention a song that gets covered several times a year and licensed over and over for films and commercials and … But hold on just a second.

> Devotional "one-on-one" love ballads are among the hardest songs to write. Why? Because the available language is extremely limited, so the lyric often ends up sounding hackneyed. You wanna say what you wanna say with total sincerity—but almost everything feels incredibly saccharine and cliché. So beware. You'll probably only write one or two good ones in your lifetime.

Even though this song wouldn't be *"one-on-one"* (it's really a testimony of love to the world, from a man who feels moved to make such a declaration in song), with that thought in mind, I express my jaded opinion that relationship jeopardy is the way to go. I'm thinking we might have much more potential in describing a relationship that may be on shaky ground as the song begins, but has enough survival skills to come out stronger on the other end of this difficult, yet temporary, rough patch our singer and his love-interest are going through. This proposed scenario gives us the opportunity to build to a climax that has a real heartfelt pay-off for our singer. He's obviously determined to make it work. Besides, what pop music fan couldn't relate to a stressful, heart-rending stall for some lane repaving along the highway of love?

With that goal in mind, we decide to use the next couplet as a way of providing some additional information about that day our gallant, stud-muffin singer first cast a gaze at the blue-eyed girl of his dreams. This, we agree, might also offer us the chance to slip in a little more detail about how long they've been together.

We brainstorm and contemplate, throw a few phrases back and forth, express our concerns, discuss a few "what-ifs" and maybe have a laugh or two at some ridiculousness. We're keepin' it loose, but closin' in on a pretty decent pair of lines to complete this initial quatrain. And this is what we come up with:

> *They were bright and clear and blue as the sky*
> *My heart was no match for her laughing eyes*
> *Since that steamy June Sunday in Riverside Park*
> *When I first held her hand, she's held onto my heart*

Now we have some details to work with: we know when this flashback took place, where the young lovers were, and even what the weather was like on that auspicious day he fell for her. We also know it's been at least a year ago, probably longer. Excellent! (Except for one glaring flaw that's slipped right by us. *Can you find Waldo in this picture, boys and girls?* More on this to come …)

For now, let's set our love-song aside for a moment and address our sexy, up-tempo number: that spirited little piece called *Goin' Down Swingin'*. Remember our opening couplet:

> *Her legs stretched from Dallas to Houston and back*
> *I ordered two longnecks and sat down to chat*

And the chorus we composed earlier:

> *Sally left Billy back in San Antone*
> *He was past tense, 'least that was what she was thinkin'*
> *But Billy was a boy with a jealous bone*
> *If Billy's goin' down, Billy's goin' down swingin'*

Makin' Stuff Up

It's pretty clear that our singer/narrator has got himself in a bit o' trouble. The opening couplet explains that he's in a bar, putting the make on a leggy—presumably available—Lone Star babe. The chorus suggests that "Sally" is not quite as single as she might have thought she was, a fact that may put our hero's square jaw in some peril. So now we set out to fill in the detail between the moment he bought her a brew and pulled up a chair, and the entrance of the jilted, distraught, yet still-determined boyfriend, this fellah we've identified as "Billy."

This, we agree, might be a good time to use some conversation to further the plot. After some more collaborative give-'n'-take, we complete our "a-a-b-b" quatrain thusly:

> *Her legs stretched from Dallas to Houston and back*
> *I ordered two longnecks and sat down to chat*
> *I said, "I've never seen you 'round Waco before"*
> *She said, "I'm new in town, Honey. Name's Sally, what's yours?"*

Now, we know a lot more about these two people and where they are: He's a Waco local. She's a fresh face in town, and a friendly sort who encourages his advances with enough curiosity to ask our cruising dude his name.

≈   ≈   ≈

Okay, it's time to consider the next portion of the verse. In Nashville, we call this "the channel." (In the past, I've referred to this as the "B-Section" of the verse; some writers call it the "sub-chorus" or the "build.") Whatever label you pin on it, it's a separate piece of music, most times one or two lines long, that acts as the ramp to launch the verse into the chorus. Some songs need one, some don't. We both agree that *Goin' Down Swingin'* does.

We want our channel to function in the following ways: first, it should offer some brief, musical relief from the chordal mode we've established in the first quatrain of the verse; second, it should apply itself to a slightly different phrasing pattern and/or rhyme scheme; and third, it should give us language that helps the chorus speak loud and clear, enhancing the core emotional impact of our song.

The *Goin' Down Swingin'* verse has been hangin' on a 1-5-4 chord pattern, basically changing every two beats. We also know that the chorus begins on the "5." The channel offers our first chance to get into a fresh musical mode, so we begin this section with the 6-minor.

Purposefully, for variety's sake, we come up with two melodic phrases over these new changes that are slightly longer than the first couplets of the verse. The first line comprises 13 descending syllables, the last of which—the rhyming syllable—is sustained. The next line needs slightly more length for its arpeggiated build to the chorus. We jam on it, until we arrive at this channel-lyric:

Then I saw the rock she was wearin' on her left hand
And over her shoulder stood a very tall, strong, and angry man, yeah...

Drama ... imagery ... intrigue. We now have a great set-up for our chorus, one that leaves us numerous plot-possibilities to come. We play the first verse and chorus to see how it hangs together. Lo and behold, this is starting to actually sound like a real song. *Yeehaw!* And we just made it up!

Regardless of what happens for the rest of the day, you and I can drift off to our separate dreamlands tonight with the knowledge that we created something that wasn't there before.

As Martha Stewart often informs us, "It's a good thing."

$$\approx \qquad \approx \qquad \approx$$

Don't worry. I didn't forget our now-forlorn love-ballad—the one we left waiting for its channel a couple of pages back. Upon a review of that lovely little thing, we discover two significant issues we're gonna have to deal with. First, we've used the word *heart* twice (the *Waldo* in the picture): once at a strategic point in the second line; then, again, as the conclusive rhyming-word at the end of the quatrain. It would be best if we did some re-thinking about that, and tweak one of those phrases.

It's almost always advisable not to re-employ featured nouns or verbs within the context of a single song. Sometimes it works to repeat a fairly generic noun like *love*, or a verb like *feel*, in adjacent verses and choruses. Usually, though, a reprise-visit dulls a word's edge, and even somewhat clouds its glimmer. (*Exception*: As we'll discover later, in a certain type of bridge, repeating a strategic word or two from earlier sections of the song can be very effective. But we'll table *that* discussion for our chapter on The Bridge.)

Makin' Stuff Up

We spend some time trying to find a way to replace one of the *hearts* in the first quatrain, but nothing we've come up with so far seems satisfactory, and our engine is losing steam. While we both recognize the necessity to eliminate this unintended redundancy, we decide that, for now anyway, we're gonna move on. We don't want to get completely bogged down over this one issue. At a later time, with some fresh perspective, I'm trusting that a light bulb will switch on, and one of us will come up with the perfect solution.

For the moment then, we decide to point our creative attention to another even more substantial challenge: we've got a heck of a lot of information to cram in before our chorus, if it's ever gonna hit that emotional bulls-eye. There would probably not be enough available space in a channel-section to fully describe this precarious state of affairs, in order to set up the singer's plea to the universe that this shaky relationship be spared by the Grim Reaper of love.

A major decision is called for: our solution is to adjust the structure of the song from single-verse/chorus to double-verse/chorus. With this double-verse (A-A-B) form, we also decide to do without a channel altogether. Our proposed double-verse will function best without a channel-section for two reasons: first, adding a channel would make the entire double first verse too long; second, the verse music we've written seems to set up the chorus quite nicely already.

The question is, what do we need to accomplish with this second quatrain of our double-verse? Quite obviously, we'll have to connect the past (the first quatrain) to the present (the chorus) somehow. We also want to explain why the girl is dissatisfied enough that she's willing to put this relationship—the one that started with such innocent promise on that hot, summer day—in jeopardy.

Examining the words we've written so far, I suspect the clue to this little mystery lies in the chorus lyric, *there's nothing I'd refuse her.* I wonder if maybe our singer has been unaware of something his girl needs from him, something he *hasn't* been giving her. Yep, my friend, *that's* the detail we should set out to reveal in this double-verse quatrain.

But what exactly is it that's been lacking?

Aha! Here's an idea. What if he's been assuming that she needs "things?" He's obviously a good guy, so he's been spending all his time and energy earning money to buy her stuff. But, what she really wants is the attention, the affection, the intimacy he hasn't had the time or energy to provide for her.

Makin' Stuff Up

Assuming that's the route to take, how are we gonna do that? When there's a choice between "showing" and "telling," I'll go for "showing" every time. As far as this writer is concerned, imagery, action and dialogue almost always tell the story far more effectively than just coming right out and saying how a character feels. There are exceptions, of course, but for now let's consider:

I worked double shifts to buy her that ring
Proposed in the fall, planned a wedding next spring
Been out slavin' away, savin' up for our life
Guess that wasn't enough, 'cause now she's sayin' good-bye
And I realize...

She's everything to me, etc.

Wonderful, even if I do say so myself!

chapter twelve: High Harmonies

H ow could I have possibly ended up with *two* half-full cans of
Coors sitting next to my lyric pad?

Well, it had everything to do with the lovely Mrs. Clarke's
unexpected entrance to the room, and the supposedly on-the-wagon Mr.
Clarke surreptitiously scooting his beer in front of me. And now, there I
was, looking like the proverbial two-fisted town drunk, packin' away the
suds at two in the afternoon on a typically shiny Southern California day.

As I stood to shake the delicate, outstretched hand of Mrs. Clarke, I
noticed her pretty, brown eyes suspiciously traveling to the twin
brewskies that sat conspicuously within her husband's reach. Thinking
quickly, I sat back down and picked up the closest one of those cans.
Bringing it to my lips, I guzzled the remaining four ounces in one long
gulp.

Setting the empty down on the table, with a hollow "cank," I wiped
my mouth with my forearm, and exclaimed, "Man, I don't know why
I'm so thirsty today!" Then I picked up the second can, toasted the air,
and grinned as if this was my everyday routine.

By now, Mrs. Clarke's apprehension seemed to have been
temporarily allayed, and her relieved hubbie looked at me from across
the table and secretly winked one of his very grateful eyes.

The year was 1977. I had returned to L.A. two years before, after
living and working in Montreal, Quebec for four years. Having written
two self-produced, Canadian, top-five solo singles, and with seven of my
productions reaching the top of the Quebecois charts—performed by
artists of the French-Canadian persuasion—I fully expected Hollywood
to welcome me back as a burgeoning musical *auteur*: songwriter, artist
and producer.

With the assistance of my highly connected lawyer, John T.
Frankenheimer, Esq., I was able to meet with a number of the most

important cogs in the L.A. music machine. However, after dozens of such meetings, a U.S. record deal had not been immediately forthcoming. (In fact, it had taken a full year for the first offer to materialize, and when that proposition finally peeked over the horizon in '76, it had carried with it none of the creative autonomy I'd assumed would be mine upon my So-Cal reentry.)

Kip Cohen must have sensed that this young singer/songwriter, accompanying himself on the A&M office spinet piano, was a pliable piece of clay. The youthful, roly-poly A&R man played me as Paganini worked that one-stringed fiddle, praising my songs and my voice, then offering to finance some piano/vocal demos of my tunes. While I was more than pleased and encouraged by his interest, similar exercises—at Capitol, and with Mike Curb—were fresh in my memory, and had failed to bear fruit. I dared not be overly optimistic. This time, alas, a recording-contract was in the offing.

The good news was, the proposition was from one of the most prestigious imprints around: A&M Records. The bad part, however, was that it was not what one might call a major commitment. In fact, it was a "singles deal," which meant the label would only be on the hook for recording six Randy Bishop sides in that first year, and wouldn't be in any way contractually obligated to produce or release a full album—at least not until such time as I had achieved a certain level of chart-success with a single.

To oversee my piano/vocals, Kip had paired me with Michael Gore, baby brother of Lesley (*It's My Party* and *Judy's Turn to Cry*) Gore. By that time, the young Mr. Gore, a well-schooled keyboardist, had composed scores for a number of Jacques Cousteau TV documentaries, but he was champin' at the bit to get into the pop production game. Michael brought some excellent arrangement-concepts to the four original tunes we recorded, in the same, cozy A&M studio where David Crosby had produced Joni Mitchell's debut *Clouds* LP. Those four demos, produced by Gore, sealed the deal.

Michael Gore logically assumed that, having helmed the sessions that successfully got the artist signed, he would be producing my A&M masters. I was under another, equally erroneous impression: that my songs had passed muster, and that one would be selected to be my first single release. Puppet-master Cohen, however, had his own agenda.

I entered Kip's office for a scheduled meeting, only to receive a surprise introduction to one Mr. Spencer Proffer. The tall, blonde, effusive man pumped my hand and, in a surprisingly high pitch, uttered, "I'm really looking forward to working with you, Randy."

"Spencer brought me an incredible song," Cohen elaborated, "... and I think it could be a huge hit for you."

Kip proceeded to play a demo of *Daybreak*, a tune Proffer had composed with David Pomeranz, the hot, young tunesmith responsible for Barry Manilow's *Tryin' To Get The Feelin' Again*. (Pomeranz, a Jewish Scientologist, later went on to pen *It's In Every One Of Us*, which has curiously become an anthem for a number of alternative church-gatherings and spiritual retreats.)

Daybreak was indeed a beautiful piece, and it didn't take much imagination to see why Kip found it perfect for the marketplace, while suiting my pure, in-between-gender vocal style. In fact, it sounded very much like a song I might have written myself.

So even though I found it devastating to be faced with the shocking realization that not one, but two of my triple-threat talents would be going un-utilized by A&M, I forced a smile and faked enthusiasm about my upcoming Spencer Proffer-produced recording sessions.

Meanwhile, being iced out of my project, Michael Gore was deeply disappointed. The broken-hearted fellow picked himself up, dusted himself off, and went on to win himself two Academy Awards—for his score and title song from the mega-smash movie *Fame*. From there, Gore went on to work on the offshoot TV series.

(In 1981, when Michael was developing the *Fame* TV pilot, the then-recent Oscar-winner gave little ol' me a call. He had a brainstorm of hiring me to sing a sort of "fantasy voice" in the echoey imagination of the songwriter character, Bruno. Unfortunately, by that time, my vocal-instrument had ripened considerably; I was no longer capable of emitting that clear, innocent sound Gore remembered from five years before. I failed to get the job, and Gore scuttled his "fantasy voice" concept altogether.)

Anyway, back in '76, Kip Cohen was looking like a genius, as my initial, Spencer-Proffer-written-and-produced A&M single, *Daybreak*, began picking up stations. The label's promotion staff responded to the activity by taking out trade ads to capitalize on a Randy Bishop buzz that seemed to be crescendoing across the nation's airwaves.

As it appeared for the moment like I might just have myself a stateside hit my first time out—thus meeting the criterion to warrant finishing up an album—Cohen sent me back into the studio with Proffer to cut some more sides. Two out of those four new songs were my own originals. The third was written by my namesake, Stephen Bishop (who was, at the time, managed by Proffer's first wife, Trudy Green), while the last on the session was another Pomeranz tune.

Then, as fate would have it, Bette Midler heard my record of *Daybreak*, and rushed into a New York recording facility intent on cutting her own rendition. The release of Midler's single shot my ascending hit out of the sky like a heat-seeking rocket.

Although I was writing prolifically, Cohen looked everywhere but to the artist for that next likely hit. What he found was a song that had been kickin' around for a few years, but had yet to demonstrate its chart-topping appeal.

Barry Mann and Cynthia Weil's *Here You Come Again*, as perfect a slice of pop *strudel* as has ever been baked up, had originally been custom-composed for BJ Thomas, as a follow-up to *Raindrops Keep Fallin' On My Head*. Thomas' version missed its mark. Then Barry Mann, his own royal self, cut it on one of his many albums. The recording Kip Cohen played me in his office was an unreleased arrangement by the Carpenters.

(*Déjà vu* all over again. My single of *Here You Come Again*, recorded in 10CC *Things-We-Do-For-Love* style, and backed by an all-star L.A. studio band, drew the attention of another notorious female singer of the day. Dolly Parton covered the song, making it a massive hit and, in the process, crossed her recording career over from rhinestone-country to platinum-pop. Ironically, though, it was the divine Ms. M's label, Atlantic Records—the imprint that had headed my first bulleting A&M release off at the pass—that gave me the opportunity to author my next U.S. single release.)

Anyway, here I was, at the Benedict Canyon home of Spencer Proffer—right next door to (*Get this, Grandma!*) Mary Tyler Moore and Grant Tinker—sitting at a table, guitar in lap, co-writing a song with a man who possesses one of the most recognizable voices of the late 20th century.

During the '60s and '70s, Allan Clarke, as lead singer of The Hollies, pulsated radio speakers everywhere, with such classics as *Bus Stop, Carrie Anne, Look Through Any Window, Air That I Breathe, He Ain't Heavy (He's My Brother)* and *Long Cool Woman In A Black Dress*. The craggy-cheeked Clarke, who had grown up in working-class Manchester, England, has a vocal tool that could effortlessly slice through concrete. (And yet, the man himself is as gentle, gracious, and giving as a rock star could possibly be.)

Makin' Stuff Up

I was privileged and delighted to provide whatever assistance Allan might need in his quest for solo success. On this particular afternoon, as he compiled the material for his Atlantic project, I was not only his co-writer, but the smokescreen for his closeted thirst, the surrogate alcoholic in residence.

At that very table, lubricated with cold, Rocky Mountain brew, I had the honor of collaborating on the song that would become Clarke's first solo Atlantic single, *Shadow In The Street*.

I then acted in the role of a substitute Graham Nash, singing those requisite high harmonies on the album's background-vocal sessions. My various contributions to the Clarke project inspired Atlantic's West Coast A&R hotshot, John Kolodner, to say some very supportive and flattering things about my writing and singing talents.

Some years later, the infamous Kolodner would take those compliments back.

chapter thirteen: The Second Verse

We have permission to give ourselves a little pat on the back. Both of our songs are really taking shape—becoming more realized, clearer in vision and more substantial, as we cruise through each stage of this mysterious process.

With completed first verses and choruses, we're over the hump now, and ready to coast to the finish-line. It seems like a proverbial piece o' cake from here—what with only a verse waiting to be written, to music we've already composed. A few choice, new words over existing music … I mean, what could be difficult about that?

Don't kid yourself, Ducky. Second verses are hard, hard, HARD! And did I mention how incredibly difficult it is to write a great second-verse?

Here's the challenge: we've already said a whole bunch, and there are about a dozen directions we could take from here. We're like conjoined-twin Alices, standing at a Wonderland crossroads, staring dumbfounded at a signpost that points left, right, forward, back, up and down all at the same time. It's also likely that each of us has a different opinion, or is perhaps equally confused about which pointer is the correct one to follow.

If that built-in conundrum isn't enough to make your head spin, we also have *this* little bit of reality to face: we need to maintain our listeners' interest, *and* give our second chorus a bigger emotional pay-off than it had on its first visit. *And*—get this, my friend—we have to do all this with a smaller supply of words—as we've been greedy little piggies and cherry-picked a brimming basket full of choice verbiage already.

Okay, since we're not re-writing *Henry the Eighth* (*Second verse, same as the first!*), we've got our work cut out for us. In all likelihood, this won't be as easy as we might have thought it would be, when we gave ourselves that congratulatory back-pat just a moment ago.

Makin' Stuff Up

Thought it would be a breeze to write the second verse
The same ol' melody with different words
But as I'm findin' out, it's harder than it looks
To find a single line
That you ain't heard a million times[xxvii]

If you're coming down with a case of vertigo, as you look up at our very confusing, intimidating Wonderland signpost, please allow me to be your tour-guide/translator.

Second verses can be assigned many varied functions. It's up to us to give our two verse-twos their marching orders, and make sure they carry out their specific assignments obediently, with aplomb and vigor.

≈ ≈ ≈

Like a screenplay or a novel, a song normally has its own chronology: it depicts or describes scenes, and/or expresses feelings that happen (or happened) over a period of time. A song can also exist quite well as less than a movie, and more of a snapshot—better yet, a richly textured oil painting, one that strives to capture a single moment (usually the present), in which the singer feels the overwhelming desire to express something painful, or joyful—or to make a profound (or humorous) observation.

Regardless of whether the storyline of any particular song moves forward or backward in time, or clings to the here-and-now, the shape of that composition can usually be defined with "calendar terminology." For example, the exquisite *You've Lost That Lovin' Feelin'* stays in one anguished moment: the very instant when the singer comes to the realization that his love-interest isn't all that interested in him anymore. Therefore, in calendar terminology, its verse-chorus-verse-chorus structure could be described as *today-today-today-today*, because the lyric never departs from this single, poignant place in time: the present.

The same section of another song could be summed up in *yesterday-today-today-today* terms, or maybe *today-tomorrow-yesterday-tomorrow*. *Yesterday*, of course, would either be a chapter of the story (or an entire tale, for that matter) told in past tense, or a flashback that describes what used to be. *Yesterday* verses can often be used to help give the characters and the situation some background and/or explain why things have arrived at their present state—a condition worth singing out loud about.

107

Makin' Stuff Up

Tomorrow might be represented by hopes and dreams of a better life or a perfect love: wishes, projections into the future (*Wouldn't it be nice if we were older, and we didn't have to wait for love?*[xxviii]). Other leaps forward in time could describe a sad, regrettable fate, due to some kind of loss taking place in the here-and-now, that may have happened before, or that is bound to happen—unless better choices are made soon.

A difficult song to describe in these "calendar" terms would be a song that works on a chronological, linear storyline, but expresses every scene in present tense. A perfect example of this approach is one of the greatest and most recorded rock 'n' roll classics of all time, *Louie Louie*, by Richard Berry:

In verse one, the singer tells us about the girl he's obsessing over— the one who waits for him *across the sea*—and goes on to tell of setting sail and risking his life so he can be with her. Verse two depicts our determined singer surviving those three precarious nights and days on the Caribbean, all the while fantasizing about the fragrance of the flower in her hair. This second stanza follows the first logically, in traditional, sequential, story-telling fashion. A third verse completes the voyage, and he takes her in his arms again. However, throughout the song, the lyric always keeps the singer's narration in the present tense; even though the verse structure could be described as *daybeforeyesterday-yesterday-today*, it reads as *today-today-today*.

Lots of story songs assume a *yesterday-yesterday-yesterday-yesterday* structure. *The Good Stuff*, by Craig Wiseman and Jim Collins, recorded by Kenny Chesney, is a superb example. It's a linear, "guy goes into a bar" narrative, all told in past-tense. Chesney (the guy) has just had his first serious fight with his girl and bellies up to drown his sorrows by downing a belt or two of *the good stuff*. Instead of serving up an aged, single-malt Scotch, however, the wizened bartender informs Kenny that *you can't find that* (i.e. the good stuff) *here*. In the brilliant chorus to follow, the barkeep goes on to list a few of the simple things in a relationship, things that truly qualify to be categorized as *the good stuff*.

Then, in verse two, the writers really lower the emotional boom. Over a couple of glasses of milk, the cross-generational duo chat, as the older gent reveals how when his wife, Bonnie, succumbed to the "Big C," he spent five years clutching a bottle. Three years of sobriety since have led him to realize there are things in life *stronger than the whiskey*. This leads to a second chorus list of brand-new, even more powerful *good stuff* images.

Makin' Stuff Up

Wiseman and Collins are a hard-working pair of songwriters. The plot-construction, the gradual revelation of information, the imagery and the detail of this song add up to incredible emotional impact. (That may explain why the record hovered at the top of the country singles-charts, week after week after week.) Meanwhile, if you take a look at the rhymes in the verse, you'll notice that unique *a-a-a-b* pattern I mentioned earlier.

≈   ≈   ≈

We left our love ballad, *Everything and Nothing*, with a double first-verse and a chorus:

They were bright and clear and blue as the sky
My heart was no match for her laughing eyes
Since that steamy June Sunday in Riverside Park
When I first held her hand, she's held onto my heart

I worked double shifts to buy her that ring
Proposed in the fall, planned a wedding next spring
Been out slavin' away, savin' up for our life
Guess that wasn't enough, 'cause now she's sayin' good-bye
And I realize…

> *She's everything to me*
> *And I'm nothing, if I'm not crazy for the girl*
> *She's everything I need*
> *And there's nothing I'd refuse her*
> *In the whole wide world*
> *She's everything, and I'm nothing without her*

We've set up our chorus with just enough info to make it heartfelt and sincere, while tantalizing the listener for specifics that we'll cleverly expose in our next verse-section. I'm sure you've noticed that we've added an extra bar of music to accommodate the additional rhyming phrase at the end of this second verse, *And I realize*. This makes our double-verse rhyme scheme *a-a-b-b-b*, with the last *b* phrase containing five syllables instead of 11-to-13. This extra line may or may not be necessary, but for now we'll try it out as an extra propellant into our chorus. [Note to self: *should we choose to keep this short, extra "b" rhyme at the end of the first verse, we'll probably want to match that a-a-b-b-b shape in our upcoming second verse-section.*]

When writing a ballad, we do have to be aware that slower songs tend to be overly long—especially when they indulge in eight-line choruses. Our chorus is five lines long. Even so, you'll find that it's often a challenge to pull off a *verse-chorus-verse-chorus-bridge-chorus* ballad in under three minutes and thirty seconds—the optimum length for a radio-single. So we need to be very economical with our language and structure. (One thing's for certain: to avoid exacerbating the length-issue, our next verse will need to be a single one, not the two-for-the-price-of-one verse we've employed the first time around.)

This particular ballad does have one advantage: it employs some fairly brisk phrasing in its verses, enabling us to cram in more bang for the bar. We also haven't built in a lot of pauses between lines. Not to say that busy-ness is the best way to go, emotionally or composition-wise. Since that's the shape this song has taken, though, we've succeeded in giving ourselves more notes and syllables with which to work. That may just help us out as we try to furnish our love-story with adequate information.

There's an interesting combination of tenses in the second half of our first verse. The first two lines cover *yesterday*, while lines three, four and five arrive at *today*. This functions as an excellent connector to our *today* chorus, in very much the same way a well-written channel would. Goes to show ya, there's more than one way to peel a tangerine. (*That cat-skinning thing never really appealed to me.*)

We now know that our singer has been hopelessly devoted to this comely lass since the first day he took hold of her hand in the park. They've been betrothed, and he's been toilin' his tail off to give her what he thinks she wants: stuff. But she's become so unfulfilled in the relationship that she's actually ready to break it off. This circumstance has our boy testifying to one and all that his world would be less than that of a cockroach if she should follow through with her departure plans.

So far, our singer seems like a really decent guy: hardworking and devoted. His lady, on the other hand. comes across a little bit like a spoiled brat, demanding more than her knight in shining coveralls could ever possibly provide her. How do we humanize her and give this fellah more justification for being, as he declares, so dang *crazy for the girl*? That's a primary question we'll certainly want to address with our second verse.

Makin' Stuff Up

We already know that she's physically beautiful (at least *he* thinks so—remember those baby-blues he describes in the first verse). What if he hasn't been taking notice of the beautiful contributions she's been making to their little corner of the world. Is she a great cook? An inventive interior designer? An artist of some kind? Maybe she's like Snow White and loves furry little woodland creatures.

Regarding her culinary expertise, it'd be hard for any man to ignore his woman's skill in the kitchen, but us guys do have a tendency to take homemaking for granted. Supposing we have our singer look around, and notice the environment his lady's been creating and nurturing for the both of them. He could see her effort, her loving touch, her own personal aesthetic … through eyes newly opened now, by the threat of her leaving. That observation would also serve to reinforce the emptiness she'd leave behind. Taking this approach, our hero would be missing his water *before* his well runs dry. Very interesting, indeed!

It's usually those little things that add up to love, doncha think? (Once again, a song pops into my head from that flawless musical, *My Fair Lady*: *I've Grown Accustomed to Her Face*. A somewhat similar sentiment would work well in this second verse.) After discussing these ideas, this is how we decide to solve the issue of the character of our singer's love interest, while simultaneously giving more detail and additional reasons for this love-struck fool to cry out desperately in favor of keeping that lady around:

Now I look around at how she's fixed up this place
That bunch o' wild flowers in a thrift-store vase
And that cat she rescued, (that's) always hissin' at me
I'd even miss him, too, if she should pick up and leave
Gotta make her believe

She's everything to me…

In principle, it's usually not a good practice to use the same rhyme sound for the last couplet (or tuplet, in this case) as the first rhyme of the chorus. For some reason, though, this seems to work well here; rules are, after all, breakable, so we disregard that one in this instance.

And now we've created the essence, the fundamentals of our *verse-verse-chorus-verse-chorus* to *Everything and Nothing*:

Makin' Stuff Up

They were bright and clear and blue as the sky
My heart was no match for her laughing eyes
Since that steamy June Sunday in Riverside Park
When I first held her hand, she's held onto my heart

I worked double shifts to buy her that ring
Proposed in the fall, planned a wedding next spring
Been out slavin' away, savin' up for our life
Guess that wasn't enough, 'cause now she's sayin' good-bye
And I realize…

>*She's everything to me*
>*And I'm nothing, if I'm not crazy for the girl*
>*She's everything I need*
>*And there's nothing I'd refuse her*
>*In the whole wide world*
>*She's everything, and I'm nothing without her*

Now I look around at how she's fixed up this place
That bunch o' wild flowers in a thrift store vase
And that cat she rescued, (that's) always hissin' at me
I'd even miss him, too, if she should pick up and leave
Gotta make her believe…

(repeat chorus)

Of course, we'll be returning for whatever tweaking might be necessary, after we've pondered this lyric for a day or two. Then, when we feel "finished" with the song, we'll be seeking the kind of feedback (i.e., constructive criticism) that helps us refine our composition even further.

≈   ≈   ≈

For the time being, we'll take our leave of this leavin' song, and get back to that peppy cliffhanger we abandoned in the bar—with the leggy lass from San Antone, our on-the-make singer … and Billy, Sally's hotheaded, never-say-die ex-boyfriend.

Makin' Stuff Up

Her legs stretched from Dallas to Houston and back
I ordered two longnecks and sat down to chat
I said, "I've never seen you 'round Waco before"
She said, "I'm new in town, honey. Name's Sally, what's yours?"

Then I saw the rock she was wearin' on her left hand
And over Sally's shoulder stood a very tall, strong and angry man,
yeah…

> *Sally left Billy back in San Antone*
> *He was past tense, 'least that was what she was thinkin'*
> *But Billy was a boy with a jealous bone*
> *If Billy's goin' down, Billy's goin' down swingin'*

We know that our singer's feeling more than a mite threatened by the sudden, unexpected appearance of the possessive (and presumably *p.o.*'ed) Billy. All of us (the singer and the writers) assume that, by declaring that he's willing to *go down swingin'*, fisticuffs are inevitable. Sally's ex- seems ready to get it on—right then and there.

But wait! There's more than one meaning to the term *swingin'* (and more than one to "gettin' it on"). They *are* in a nightclub, or at least a tavern. Let's presume it's a weekend, and there's music playing. Maybe Billy isn't such a Neanderthal, and it crosses his mind that he might-could win Sally back *without* resorting to violence. With that thought in mind, here's what we come with as our second-verse quatrain:

Just when I thought I'd have some hell to pay
He asked her to dance, I didn't stand in his way
His sneer told me that he'd just soon I was dead
Soon they were cuttin' up the hardwood, just like Ginger and Fred

Now we've cleverly set up a new meaning for our icon-phrase in the upcoming second chorus. Shortly after slappin' a high-five over that inspired bit of song-craft, though, we realize we've completely removed our singer from the action, making him a passive observer. We need our second channel to bring him back to the emotional core of the story:

My eyes scanned the room for the nearest exit sign
Was thinkin' I got lucky once, I'd better beat it while my life is still mine

I suddenly wonder if maybe we need to adjust our second chorus to accommodate this two-steppin' twist in our plot. We certainly don't need the existing third line to remind us that our singer's nemesis is prone to jealousy. I suggest an alternative line-three to refer to Billy's newly revealed proclivity for dance, and his willingness to let his boots do the talkin' in his efforts to reclaim his girl:

Sally left Billy back in San Antone
He was past tense, 'least that was what she was thinkin'
But out there on the floor, the boy's right at home
If Billy's goin' down, Billy's goin' down swingin'

I'm not sure whether this particular alternative third line works as well as it should. We bat around the pros and cons, and finally decide it's a good idea to change the line to move our plot forward and emphasize the new meaning of our icon-phrase. Even though the language might not be the absolute ultimate, for the time being, we choose to keep it as-is, reserving the right to revisit and reconsider this line at a later time.

> I don't like to get bogged down on one particular passage for too long; that can be a complete momentum killer. Two hours later, after contemplating a single word or phrase from every possible angle at least a couple-dozen times, our minds will have turned to mashed potatoes—yet there we are, still stalled. It's better to refresh our creative spark by going on to another section of the song, with the implied pledge that, in the long run, we're not gonna leave any stone unturned in our quest for perfection.
>
> However, as long as we're making progress and keeping our focus on the prize—writing the very best possible song we can write—I'm pleased with our process. We can always return as many times as might be necessary to any specific area of the song, if it should demand our renewed attention.

Like *Everything and Nothing*, *Goin' Down Swingin'* is taking shape. We play it through, and it sounds like we're a mere bridge away from one of the rarest commodities on Music Row: a quality, up-tempo, positive number, with a lot of lyrical detail (some interesting characters) and an engaging plot, riding on a spunky groove. We can be very proud of ourselves.

chapter fourteen: A Sudden Chill

The air in the room had dropped at least 40 degrees in the last split-second. On this typically arid Southern California afternoon in 1977, I swore I could see my own breath exhaling into the space between my chair and the distinguished, bespectacled, senior executive facing me—the man who was, and arguably still is, the most powerful individual in the entire music business.

Clive Davis was sitting there a mere 12 feet away, red-faced, jaw clenched, shaking his head in evident befuddlement. What was beginning to dawn on me, as the instigator of this sudden chill, was the gravity, the absolute finality of the casual remark I'd only just spouted—three glib words that seemed to reverberate over and over off of the walls of this private bungalow at The Beverly Hills Hotel.

Then, in the next moment, the hollow echo of my offhanded rudity was drowned out by the sudden sobbing of the blonde-haired woman sitting to my right.

I had met Clive Davis for the first time approximately two years prior to this inauspicious day— shortly after he formed Arista Records. With his background as president of Columbia Records for five momentous years, there was no single person in the music world who possessed a more comprehensive knowledge of the industry.

Davis is fully capable of fixing the coffee, stocking the warehouse, negotiating the most elaborate and convoluted contract, unearthing a surefire hit song, selecting album photos, promoting a record to radio, and charming the talent over a gourmet dinner. That, in a nutshell, might be a typical Clive Davis day at the office.

Even at this writing, as he approaches 80, Davis remains a hands-on executive, who never seems to tire of working closely with artists, songwriters and producers. While I've never exactly seen eye-to-eye with the man on a creative level, and despite what he probably thinks of me today (if he thinks of me at all), I have the ultimate respect for Davis and remain in awe of his résumé of illustrious accomplishments.

Clive was generous enough to set aside some of his valuable time for me during several of his frequent New York to L.A. jaunts. My first audition for the Arista starmaker took place in a small ballroom at the Beverly Hills Hotel. I sat on the bench of that grand piano, with my eyes closed, my fingers trembling and my voice wavering, as I played a handful of my newest songs for this music-biz icon. Afterwards, he kindly offered some gracious compliments and a few pointers. He also indicated what seemed to be sincere interest in my career development.

We'd repeat our routine a few more times: Beverly Hills Hotel. Piano. Me nervously rendering a few fresh compositions. Clive politely and attentively listening and giving his feedback. After the third such private concert, Davis invited me to meet with him and A&R rep, Roger Birnbaum, at the West Coast Arista headquarters. Some flattering words were spoken, with Clive equating me and my talent to Arista singer/songwriter (and ex-Raspberry) Eric Carmen. (Being an ex-Wacker and a pop-rocker at heart, I appreciated that comparison very much.)

Then, Clive fastidiously pulled a 45 RPM disc from its paper sleeve and placed it on the turntable. "This," he advised, his tone suddenly turning toward aloofness, "is the kind of song you should be recording."

Barry Manilow's voice was unmistakable. To me, though, this particular song—due to be released on the Arista imprint in a few weeks' time—was insufferably pompous and self-important, and the record's production was laden with ludicrous overkill.

I had no idea that *I Write The Songs* had been penned by Beach Boy Bruce Johnston—a very nice man, and a very talented one at that. I only knew that I absolutely disdained everything that Manilow's saccharine, bombastic rendition represented.

Just months before, I'd returned to the murky, precarious swamp-waters of L.A. from Montreal, the island city on the St. Lawrence, where I'd been living and working for more than four years. There, I had kicked off my record production career, cranking out seven chart-toppers in the French-Canadian market. I was very impressed with myself, cocky and self-assured. I was also more than familiar with those overblown Euro-pop records, with their double-tracked vocals bathed in reverb and dwarfed by heavy orchestration. Moreover, being a compulsive wise-ass, I felt no compunction to restrain my editorial comments, as the Manilow recording faded redundantly into most appreciated (by me, anyway) silence.

Makin' Stuff Up

"Clive, I'm sorry," I remarked. "But that song should've been sung in French,"

It suddenly became abundantly clear to me that, in spite of my comparable marketability to Eric Carmen (who was, BTW, given full license to write his own material), Davis saw Randy Bishop merely as a pretty face with a pretty voice, a vehicle for whatever syrupy ballad he might choose for me to record, with whichever producer he might select as my puppet-master.

Having recently scored two top-5 Canadian singles as a self-produced singer/songwriter, I was not at all prepared to sacrifice my artistic autonomy to that extreme—not even for a legend like Clive. And so, Bishop and Davis had arrived at their first creative impasse.

However, after 12 months, and two other close-but-no-banana record deals—with Capitol and Curb—my resolve to retain total creative control of my career had somewhat weakened. Those thwarted efforts had led me in 1976 to A&M Records, under the auspices of Kip Cohen, ironically a protégé of the illustrious Mr. Davis. Cohen's equally iron-fisted A&R style resulted in two failed single-releases—both of them composed by other writers and produced by the gregarious Spencer Proffer. That experience had only served to rekindle my determination to once again be the *auteur* of my own fate.

Yet another year later, I'd formed a duo, partnering with the aforementioned blonde woman—the one weeping at my right side. Marty Gwinn has one of the richest alto voices in all creation. I first heard her honeyed tones in the fall of '75, as I entered St. Charles Place, a cavernous music venue/restaurant that once austerely sat adjacent to the boardwalk/zoo of Venice Beach.

Wife-number-one had found herself a new, more adoring boyfriend, and my tender heart was impaled by Ms. Gwinn's performance of Irving Berlin's *What'll I Do*—as perfect a song about lost love as has ever been written. There she stood, regal and patrician, in a long, black gown, fronting an old-timey orchestra of rag-tag, hipster musicians.

I became reacquainted with Marty's talent when I saw her in *Keepin' 'em Off the Streets*, a music review that showcased monthly at the Roxy Theater on Sunset Strip. The simple sincerity of her segments always exemplified the classic style of the greatest pop singers, with impeccable phrasing and effortless technique, rendering understated arrangements that conveyed every gram of the emotional truth in her material. When I heard that this attractive diva was seeking a producer and songs, I tossed my hat (and my catalogue) into the ring—without so much as a single qualm.

I arrived at the Gwinn domicile, a tiny cottage near the Hollywood Bowl, with a mutual friend, drummer Chris Castle. After an oddly civilized conversation over cups of perfectly steeped DarJeeling, I obligingly shuffled over to the piano to demonstrate a few of my original tunes. As I hit the second chorus of the second song, Marty felt compelled to chime in—in unison.

The noise our voices made together was unworldly, creating a natural flange that quite literally wrinkled the air in the room. At the song's conclusion, I turned to Marty and Chris, wearing what I'm sure was a mask of wonderment pasted across my bewildered face.

"Did you hear that?" I asked. Both of their expressions confirmed that they had borne witness to the same heavenly resonance I had just beheld.

The Bishop and Gwinn vocal blend was special. I'd experienced a similar vibration singing *Wake Up, Little Susie,* Everly-style, with my own brother, Bart; however, Marty's and my timbre together created a sound that was well beyond filial. It was logo-rhythmic, two voices that multiplied each other into a virtual choir of gorgeously woven harmonic textures.

Even Clive Davis agreed that our blend was something extraordinary. Having heard some demos I'd produced at Lyon Recording on Balboa Island, Clive invited us to do our thing live for him at the old same place—his expansive, private bungalow at the Beverly Hills Hotel. As always, Davis was extremely gracious and complimentary, and this time a contract offer from Arista was in the offing.

A follow-up powwow was scheduled to discuss the possible parameters of our creative and business arrangement. The Bishop and Gwinn camp was represented by the *artistes*; our manager, Harvey Markowitz; and our lawyer, John T. Frankenheimer. Clive and his new West Coast A&R rep, the red-haired bombshell Carol Childs, were there on behalf of the label. A third person—a rather reserved gentleman with dark, thinning hair—sat with Davis and Childs. I only assumed that this unknown, perfectly silent fellow was from business affairs or marketing, or maybe promotion.

Clive began the conclave with some very positive remarks about our duo, our songs, and the rosy potential of our future at Arista. Marty returned my grin with a toothy smile of her own. We were both genuinely excited about the idea of recording for Davis' imprint. Then

Clive decided it was time to reveal the identity of the mystery man sitting to his right. "I'd like to introduce you to your producer," he said. "This is Harry Maslin."

Although I'd never laid eyes on the man, I certainly knew Maslin's name. As the engineer/co-producer of David Bowie's *Young Americans* and *Station To Station* LPs, this guy had established himself, in my estimation, as a monster of the control room. I idolized Bowie, and anyone the Pale White Duke enlisted into his brigade had big-time status in my little world.

However, my admiration for Harry Maslin (by way of Bowie) didn't prevent me from asking the following question—in a rather presumptuous tone, I might add.

"You mean *CO*-producer, don't you, Clive?"

"I'm sorry?" Davis responded, not quite catching my drift.

"You know *I* produced the sides you liked so much," I reminded him.

"That wasn't production," Clive took issue, a distinct hint of professorial condescension coloring his response. "Those were *demos*, not masters."

(This was where my youthful pride grabbed the steering wheel and drove me right over the cliff. Some of my friends and family, who are painfully familiar with my history, consider this to be my most regrettable moment of self-destruction. As numerous nefarious decisions from my checkered past could contend for that particular crown of thorns, I'm not so sure I'd agree with that evaluation. I'll have to admit, though, this has to be right up there with the worst—and most unforgettable—moments of my life.)

"Well," I insisted, digging in my heels, and in so doing, digging an even deeper hole for myself, "I can't make records if I'm not involved in the production."

Clive then removed his signature specs and began cleaning their windshield-like lenses, giving himself time to pick his next words with ultimate care. He cleared his throat, before looking me directly in the eyes, proclaiming:

"… And I can't make records with an artist who has your attitude."

Okay. I *could* have offered up a contrite apology to the most powerful man in the music business. I *could* have swallowed the jagged pride that had spoken those defiant words, so foolishly and so ill-conceived. I *could* have made a last-ditch effort to salvage this once-promising creative partnership—already plummeting into premature disintegration.

But *NO*; I chose not to do that. In fact, the devil-ego whispering in my ear urged me to take another, completely opposite tact.

This is what I actually said—with all the self-righteous flippancy of the presumptuous ingrate I occasionally was back in those days:

"That's show-biz, Clive."

Mmmm, hmmm. I'm not kidding. In the past, on occasions when my first ex-wife has felt compelled to recount this family myth, she's made the claim that I "told Clive Davis to F*** OFF!" Not true. I simply disrespected the man with a brief statement, casually tossed off the cuff, with absolutely no regard for the dire consequences of my words and the youthful arrogance that gave them air.

The consequences were far-reaching for me: The legend of my verbal dissing of Clive Davis spread quickly and far, traversing telephone lines, wafting up and down corridors, from the roots to the tips of the music-biz electric grapevine. Some of my ex-bandmates considered me a hero—for defying the formulaic Clive Davis pop machine. To many if not most of my other industry acquaintances, however, I became *persona non grata*, punk-ass poison, for years to come. And the venerable Mr. Davis still keeps his distance—even after these 30 years have passed.

"That's show-biz, Clive."

Wow. I still find it hard to believe that I said it.

What followed my remark was that aforementioned moment of chilly silence. Then, my duet-partner Marty burst into tears. Mere minutes later, Bishop, Gwinn, Markowitz and Frankenheimer were standing in the hotel courtyard, recalling the good old days, when we had had an offer from Clive Davis and Arista Records.

After contributing to three feature-film soundtracks—all of which I produced—Bishop and Gwinn signed to a start-up imprint, Infinity/MCA Records. Once again, the label chose to opt for outside production, only this time I didn't object. Our album, *This Is Our Night*, produced by Fred Mollin and Mathew MacCauley, stiffed. (Irony of ironies: that label called Infinity only lasted a year.)

chapter fifteen: The Bridge

"This song doesn't need a bridge, does it?"

For at least the first five years of my stint as a professional Music Row tunesmith, I'm pretty sure I heard a version of this question at some point within the context of every single writing session. However, this wink-and-a-nod plea for bridge-clemency was rarely, if ever, initiated on my side of the writing table.

The bridge, in fact, is often my favorite part of the song. Invariably, I look forward to taking a whack at writing one, and I'm generally disappointed when—due to excessive length, or for other structural reasons—a bridge actually isn't called for.

Nashville writers, as great as they are, are (dare I say it?) a pretty lazy breed. The majority of Music City song-scribes put in about a five-hour workday—if you include that 90-minute lunch/schmooze at the Sub Stop, Tin Roof or Broadway Brewhouse. As a result, it's usually about three p.m., just as the end-of-shift whistle—the one only song-dogs can hear—starts blowing in their heads, that the question of "to bridge or not to bridge" typically comes up.

Some Nashville cats—Toby Keith's frequent collaborator, Scotty Emerick, for instance—even have a blanket "anti-bridge policy." These writers are like housekeepers who refuse to do windows. (I have to confess, though, that possibly my very favorite song of all time from the Music Row lexicon is perfect as-is in its bridge-less-ness. I'm referring to the gorgeous, heartrending, richly textured *I Can't Make You Love Me*, by Mike Reid and Allen Shamblin.)

Regardless of the success (creative and/or commercial) that many writers have had—without ever so much as writing, crossing or even burning a bridge—I consider it a privilege to be faced with the opportunity to pen a great one. I welcome that option with open arms. And it *is* an option. However, with few exceptions, writing a bridge is almost always at least worth considering. How else are we gonna know if our song can be enhanced with a new section, unless we toss the idea around a little?

I think the seed of my passion for bridges was planted eons ago—in my Paleolithic childhood, when I was just beginning to awaken to the rudimentary sounds of that fresh, new genre of cave music called "rock 'n' roll." In those long-ago days, rock 'n' roll meant almost any and every brand of music that was embraced by the youth culture—from New Jersey doo-wop to Texas rockabilly, to records by Hollywood TV-star crooners (like Ricky Nelson), to country-western journeymen (like Johnny Horton).

One of the first times I remember a bridge hitting me directly in the center of my boyish heart was Skeeter Davis' record, *The End Of the World*. The way that new section of music and lyric arrived, taking an already hopelessly sad lament and bringing it to an even more heartrending place, just nailed me. I loved that song, and the quiet cry of desperation in the girl's voice. Every time the record came on the radio, I couldn't wait for the absolutely pure melancholy of that simple, brilliant bridge to come around again.

It still kills me to this day.

As far as I'm concerned, though, the absolute masters of the bridge were a pair of fledgling, intuitive, mop-topped composers from Liverpool, England—John Lennon and Paul McCartney. John and Paul referred to each of these little slices of genius as "the middle-eight," implying that the sections usually comprised approximately eight bars and happened somewhere around the center of the song.

Even in their earliest compositions, the Lennon and McCartney team demonstrated a knack for coming up with inventive and inspired bridges—both musically and lyrically. The song most Stateside fans remember as The Beatles' breakthrough hit, *I Want To Hold Your Hand*, is a perfect example. Who could ever forget this part of the song? I know I couldn't.

And, when I touch you I feel happy inside[xxix]...takes the listener to a refreshed musical place, while the lyric reinforces the song's unsophisticated, hormonally charged theme. Then it culminates in a three-peat of the phrase, *I can't hide*, which adds—*Surprise!*—an additional hook to the song, and gives human voice to the tension-building *four-four-fiiiive* chords that we heard in the record's intro.

Amazing stuff—especially coming from a couple of lads just emerging from their teens.

In examining their catalogue, we discover that, when the song called for it, John and Paul never shied away from coming up with a splendid middle-eight—and they seldom missed the center of the bull's-eye with their attempts. *And I Love Her*, *Eight Days A Week*, *I Saw Her Standing There*, *Please Please Me*, *Things We Said Today*, *Ticket To Ride*, *We Can Work It Out*, and *You Can't Do That* are just a few Lennon/McCartney compositions containing superbly composed bridge sections.

Of course, one of the most recognizable and flawless bridge-sections of all time glistens in the middle-eight of McCartney's *Yesterday*. What would that classic have been without the musical question, *Why she had to to go, I don't know, she wouldn't say…?*[xxx] This bridge completes one of the most perfect songs ever written. It takes the contemplative, yet transcendent remorse of the piece to a new place, providing the proverbial icing on the cake, the *a la mode* for that scrumptiously sad slice of angelfood.

Actually, one of my favorite Beatle-bridges is tucked into the relatively obscure *No Reply*. In this section, the musical atmosphere is suddenly changed from the minor-key mode of the song's *I nearly died* refrain to a more cheerful, optimistic, major disposition. At this point, singer Lennon gives his unfaithful, unresponsive girlfriend some *If-I-were-you* advice. This well-conceived middle-eight serves to provide a break from Lennon's detailed description of virtually stalking the girl, as she carries on her wayward ways.

One particular non-Beatle bridge tickles me no end, and could possibly be—by its quirky inventiveness—my favorite of all time. This one was concocted in the early-'80s by a young Brit New-Waver by the name of Thomas Dolby. A herky-jerky love sonnet from a fictional research scientist to his beautiful (presumably Japanese) lab assistant, Miss Sakamoto, Dolby's verses wax poetic in their praise of the young woman's most positive qualities, employing a sly interweaving of Shakespeare-speak and academic jargon. Then, suddenly noticing that his workspace has been altered, he complains remorsefully:

I can't believe it, there she goes again
She's tidied up and I can't find anything[xxxi]

Makin' Stuff Up

This bridge is as grounded in reality as it is hilarious. And the irony of Dolby's unexpected exclamation is not lost on yours truly. Having been married for more than 30 years of my life, I'm very familiar with the dramatic tidal change of dreamy-eyed goo turning into flashing rage in a split nanosecond. That's a truth about love and relationships we seldom get to hear in popular songs. A tip of the hat to Doctor Dolby for this dazzling bridge.

≈   ≈   ≈

Assuming that I've now convinced you to consider the challenge of tackling one, let's talk about what bridges do. What can we expect from these usually brief, but critically important sections of music and lyrical information?

Decades ago, some song-scribe decided to name this part of his or her pop tune "the bridge" for a very good reason: to one degree or another, it gets us from "here" to "there"—"here" usually being the end of the second verse and/or chorus, and "there" almost always being the final, conclusive chorus, refrain and/or tag.

We want to go out on our chorus or refrain, because this is where we've inserted the most memorable and intense melodic and lyrical elements of our song—including our icon-phrase. The chorus is where our payoff resides. It's the money-shot, the part we want the audience to be humming as they exit the theater.

It would probably be unsatisfactory to the listener—not to mention illogical—to return to a third or even a fourth verse-section. Although, in rare cases, another verse might be called for, doing so would in all likelihood make our song too long—especially if we followed every verse with an additional chorus. Meanwhile, an additional verse could make the song sound droney, samey.

If we've just doubled up our second chorus, the final one's likely to sound redundant—"same-ol' same-ol'"—unless we write a whole new lyric for it, and/or modulate to a new key. Maybe we have a little more story to tell, or we feel the need to hammer the point of the song home. That's where that courageous, self-sacrificing Samurai warrior, the bridge, steps up to volunteer for combat.

Bridges can function in several ways. First and foremost, a bridge is a musical "palate cleanser." We use our bridge to depart from the mode of the earlier sections of the song just enough that, when the chorus comes back around one final time, it appears, tastes and sounds fresh again. By the time we've passed through the chord-changes of our bridge, the listener should be primed for a third helping of chorus melody. The bridge is a bit of gentle rain before the sun comes out again, or a brief pause in the shower, harkening the deluge's return.

Lyrically, there are several styles of bridges. Some offer the most critically important information of the entire song—possibly a twist in the story the writers have craftily set up with those previous verses and choruses, a plot-point cleverly concealed for its revelation at this select place in time. In another form, it could just be a snippet of new information that serves to push the plot forward, helping to make that last chorus even more meaningful than the ones that preceded it. To these we could apply the label, "informational" bridges.

Many bridges amount to philosophical statements that, for the moment, step outside of the personal feelings of the vocalist, to articulate some platitude about life that applies to the song's specific subject-matter. While it's often tempting to take a bridge lyric in this direction, it's a potentially precarious route. When you stray from the passion, desire and/or angst of the song, you're in danger of losing a grip on the emotional core so important to maintaining that heart-to-heart connection you're always striving to make with your audience.

When I'm flirting with the idea of writing a "philosophical" bridge, I always ask myself how the singer—who's so moved to wail about some state of affairs with such urgency—suddenly became so wise as to make an objective, rational observation about this situation. There has to be a justification for this unexpected insight. In short, philosophical bridges can sound pretentious and emotionally removed, but every once in awhile, they can be very satisfying.

Another common—and often effective—style of bridge lyric recalls and/or reinforces the text of the verses and choruses that preceded it. This technique succinctly reiterates the basic theme of the song, thus strengthening its message and making its emotional cry even more poignant. This kind of "summation" bridge even has permission to reuse strategic language from earlier sections, because reminding the listener of those key words or phrases can actually reinforce the emotional impact of the song's conclusion.

Regardless of the lyrical approach we take in our bridge, we know we want to take this part of the song to a fresh musical landscape. Ideally, our verse begins on a certain chord, our chorus commences on another, and our bridge introduces a third. If a beginning bridge-chord is repeated from an earlier section, it should probably be played with a changed inversion or voicing, while the melody should explore a somewhat different modality. Meanwhile, in almost all cases, the bridge melody should start on another note from the verses and choruses. Finding that precise place to go often requires a good bit of experimentation (jamming).

You'll probably want to play what you've written so far all the way through a time or two, to be certain that you've found the ideal location to build your bridge. The ultimate chord will give that needed uplift and free the ear temporarily from your established musical mode. There are scads of possibilities—but only a few of them offer real potential. Just make sure you play it a few times in context, to make sure this new starting-place follows the previous section seamlessly, while simultaneously straying just far enough away to make it satisfying.

(You'll also want the vocal range of your bridge to be within the realm of possibility for most singers. It would be a shame, in your quest to find that fresh musical landscape, to erect an inspired bridge section … only to find that 95% of singers are incapable of reaching the notes.)

Do understand this, however: you've got a lot more freedom musically with your bridge than in any other part of the song, so knock yourself out. You've also got some big shoes to fill. Listen to all those inventive middle-eights by the boys from Liverpool—for inspiration … and/or intimidation.

Once we've found that perfect new chord, the spot where we want to launch our bridge, and perhaps a basic mode and melodic structure, we ask ourselves the following question:

WHAT HAVE WE NOT SAID SO FAR THAT NEEDS TO BE SAID?

Sometimes the answer is as obvious as the middle C on the keyboard in front of you. More often than not, though, you're gonna have to give this query some thought, and indulge in a bit of brainstorming to figure out the best lyrical statement you can make with your middle-eight.

≈   ≈   ≈

Let's return to our ballad-in-progress, *Everything and Nothing*. We've left our singer and his girl with their relationship hanging perilously from the thinnest of threads. She's about to walk out the door, because the guy hasn't been fulfilling her need for his real attention—either physically or emotionally. After the first verse looks back, reminiscing about falling for her on that day in the park, the second realizes the exact ways she enriches his life and his home. In each chorus, he gives voice to the conclusion that his life would be meaningless without her in it.

First, we need to put our bridge in context, and clock what we've written so far to make sure we've even got time for a bridge. Very often, ballads will be three minutes or more by the end of the second chorus— particularly if, like ours, they open with a double verse-section.

Amazing! We discover that, even with our extended first stanza, our *verse-verse-chorus-verse-chorus* only amounts to approximately 2:20, even after a brief instrumental section played over the first four bars of chorus-changes. This song not only has plenty of acreage to accommodate a bridge, it actually expects us to build one.

What's more, after all that earlier talk about creating a fresh musical mode for our bridge, we also discover that our short instrumental section replicating the first part of the chorus lands us comfortably on the root of the 4-chord—the same bass note on which the verse begins. We play it through a few times, and the four seems to be the logical place for our bridge to kick off. And so, with a slightly altered chord-voicing and modality, that's where we begin our bridge.

The first lyrical idea we come up with amounts to a "summation," with the first line waxing "philosophical," while the second line reinforces the song's core emotional theme:

A job is just a job, and a house is just a house
But all that would be nothin' if she left me now

It's a good bridge, we agree. The question is, is it a great one? More important, does it make the upcoming final chorus even more meaningful? If we're honest with ourselves (*and we are, aren't we?*) we'll have to give a reluctant, but definitive "no" to each of those questions.

This bridge would be adequate for your average pair of writers, eager to congratulate themselves and head on down to the Flying Saucer to toast a couple of hopsy beverages. For us, however, as parched as we might be (and even though a pint or two would hit the proverbial spot right about now), we decide to ponder this bridge-lyric a little while longer— while hoping our mutual muse hasn't already packed it in for Happy Hour.

Makin' Stuff Up

We ask ourselves: *what could our forlorn singer do and/or say to give this crux situation a little more hope; to possibly change the girl's mind; to show her a side of himself she may have never seen before?*

"He could cry," you suggest.

"Hmmmm," I mumble. "That's true." I have an aversion to guys crying in songs, though—it kinda creeps me out.

"After all," you persist, "women have been getting out of speeding tickets for decades by shedding tears. She's been waiting for him to show his love for her in some other real way—you know, other than just working hard."

"When you're right, you're right," I have to admit. (I also know from personal experience that letting out a few sincere tears can work magic on the woman you love.)

So we agree that a strategic demonstration of genuine emotion might just be the ticket for our leading man. He's desperate, so radical measures are definitely called for—especially when it's only natural for him to feel more than a little vulnerable at this juncture. This is the bridge we arrive at:

I'm gonna take her in my arms, and let my tears flow
Whatever she wants, I'll give her, if she'll promise not to go
I just hope she knows…

She's everything to me, etc.

Even though we've got our big, masculine, hard-laborin' singer prepared to weep and beg like a little girl, I think we've hit the precise emotional chord the song calls for. Tears and pleading probably give him his best chance at saving himself from sleeping alone in a cold, empty bed tonight—and perhaps for many nights to come. And, this emotional plea sets the plate for our last chorus to soar higher than ever before.

≈ ≈ ≈

Now let's get back to *Goin' Down Swingin'*. When we left our singer, he was headed for the parking lot, relieved that Sally's jealous ex-boyfriend hadn't resorted to fisticuffs in a last-ditch attempt to reclaim that erstwhile lady. Meanwhile, Billy and Sally are puttin' on a pretty impressive display of boot-scootin' out there on the dance floor.

Makin' Stuff Up

What concerns me is this: I'm wondering if we should have waited until the bridge to reveal the second meaning of our icon-phrase—the first definition of "swingin'" being "fightin'," the second being "dancin'." *Maybe*, I'm thinking, *we gave away the twist too early. How*, I ponder, *are we now gonna keep our singer involved in the story, while making our final chorus work*?

That concern stated, we move on to our bridge, first looking for an initial beginning chord that satisfies our need to go somewhere new musically to offer that requisite bit of musical relief—while at the same time feeling natural and not overly shocking. We play our song from the top, through the second chorus and the refrain that follows, discovering that we haven't used the flat seven yet—the flat seven chord sounds like an excellent platform for kicking off our bridge.

The middle-eight we mock up comprises at least three consecutive seven or eight-syllable phrases with a descending melody. It sounds very bridgy and builds nicely to what will be our last chorus section.

Our lyrical challenge now is to turn our singer around before he hits the exit, thus keeping him involved in the story, while setting our final chorus up in such a way where our title phrase, *goin' down swingin'*, has a third meaning … or is at least substantially refreshed.

We joke around about Sally and Billy actually revealing that they, as a couple, are indeed "swingers." In that imaginary scenario, they might invite our singer to join them in a *ménage à trois*. This approach would certainly add that third meaning to our icon-phrase, not to mention an intriguingly naughty nuance to the words, *goin' down*.

Given country music's place as "family-friendly" entertainment, though, we quickly jettison that idea (after indulging in a tongue-in-cheek riff on it, of course), mop the tears of laughter from our eyes and get back to reality.

> In the course of almost every song, we'll hit a spot where irreverence will take over, threatening to make our train jump the rails into the valley of black-humor. Don't worry about it; it's a healthy thing. Let it happen. A good, cleansing laugh could even free your subconscious to meander into more appropriate creative territory.

In our first two choruses, we've applied two separate meanings to the word *swingin'*: "fightin'" … and "dancin'." We'd probably be reluctant to put Billy on a backyard tire-swing, or move our location from the bar to a creek bank, with a rope hanging from a branch over the ol' swimmin' hole. The only other meaning for *swingin'* we've come up with so far isn't particularly wholesome. Perhaps we might also consider a new implication for "goin' down" (other than the salacious one we joshed about only a few minutes ago).

Up until now, "goin' down" has essentially meant "losing Sally." However, we haven't used the most obvious, literal meaning of these words: as in *when gravity does its thing and something or somebody tumbles to the ground.*

There's Billy out there on the dance floor, shakin' his Wrangler-clad posterior and showin' off his fancy steppin'. Why not trip the cocky dude up? Seeing Billy take a fall would certainly stop our singer in his tracks. Meanwhile, maybe our narrator is even such a good guy that he runs to his rival's rescue. We decide to pursue that direction. Here's the bridge we come up with:

> *A piece of ice on the dancin' floor*
> *That boy's not dancin' anymore*
> *I gave 'em a ride to the emergency room*
> *Now I'm holdin' Sally's hand, sayin' "He'll be good as new"*

This bridge-lyric pushes our plot forward and sets up meaning number three for our icon-phrase, which we'll use in our final chorus to follow. However, we *have* left some questions still unanswered. We're gonna have to give that final chorus some pretty stern marching orders to fill in those blanks and tie up those dangling loose ends.

Songwriting—a never-ending source of fun!

chapter sixteen: Herman's World

As the man with the unmistakable, broad-faced smile rose from his chair to accept my handshake, an involuntary reflection flashed through my mind:

My God! He's so much taller than I thought he was!

I had seen Peter Noone perform—in the guise of his alter-ego, "Herman" of Hermits fame—way back in 1966. That year, Noone was actually the best-selling pop star on the surface of planet Earth—no small feat for a working class kid from dank, dismal Central England.

From my folding-chair on the floor of Portland's Memorial Coliseum, "Herman" had looked small—*tiny* even—standing on tiptoe to reach the microphone. As he rendered his repertoire of chart-toppers—*Mrs Brown, You've Got a Lovely Daughter*, *I'm Into Something Good*, and *'En-ery the Eighth, I am, I am* among them—the predominantly female crowd had worshipfully wept and wailed, in awe of the Brit popster's impossible cuteness.

Now, standing over me at about six feet, Noone appeared equally as striking as he had on that long-ago evening—although much more slender, statuesque and, at 35, considerably more mature. I realized that, along with those of millions of my peers, my long-ago teenaged perceptions had been manipulated. *Very clever, those image-makers!*

By dressing Peter in a suit that looked as if it was borrowed from his father's closet, raising the mic stand to nose-level, and keeping him several feet away from his bandmates at all times (so there would be no point of height-comparison), they made the singer appear miniscule from the audience's perspective—though he was actually slightly taller than average. A huge part of "Herman's" appeal was that all those girls wanted nothing more than to take care of the cuddly little fellah. They remained unaware that their favorite teddy bear of a superstar would certainly have dwarfed the lot of them.

I was introduced to Peter in 1982, during what was possibly one of the most contented periods of my life. (I had no clue at the time that those six months or so would actually turn out to be only a brief calm, before the devastating and nearly fatal storm called my second marriage.)

I was an unusually happy camper for several reasons. First, I'd only just recently extricated myself from the bitter end of my 11-year first marriage. Secondly, I was shacking up with my exotic, sexy, nine-years-younger girlfriend, in an upstairs duplex in the flatlands of West Los Angeles. Most importantly, my best friend, Tim Sadler, had asked me to store a baby grand piano he'd picked up at a yard sale. Sitting at those 88's, poised next to the picture-window of that resonate, masonry living room, I had at long last discovered the genuine fulfillment of passing my days as a full-time songwriter.

After 15 years of chasing after dangling carrots, myopically fixing my sights on that elusive mirage of stardom as performer and producer, my life was now consumed with exploring song-concepts and pounding them into reality on those keys. I had unwittingly discovered what would, decades later, be defined as "flow activity," as well as the core, personal satisfaction of creating something new, each and every day.

My mornings invariably began with that first cup o' coffee and a bowl of fresh fruit. Then I'd commute—all of a dozen baby steps—from the dining room to the piano bench to clock in at the office. Sitting there, hour after hour, I picked new melodies out of the air and attached those notes to words, scribbled on a yellow legal pad with a number-two pencil.

When I began to feel stiff, or found myself stumped over a rhyme, I'd rise and shake out the cobwebs by tossing a few Nerf jump shots into a toy basketball net hanging over the inside of the front door. Those were solitary hours, but extremely rewarding ones; I could also sense my songs improving, day by day.

By three o'clock in the afternoon, or thereabouts, my daily supply of creative juices was usually pretty much all squeezed out. I'd strap on my jock, a pair of shorts and some high-tops and drive over to the cement court at Plummer or West Hollywood Park for some pick-up games of three-on-three.

Makin' Stuff Up

I'd only recently rediscovered a passion for roundball that defied my five-foot-eight-inch stature, the pallor of my skin and my advanced age—at this juncture, I was closing in on my 33rd birthday. In spite of my obvious shortcomings (pun intended), I'd won a bit of a park-court reputation for my deceptive crossover baseline drive and my quick-release 17-foot jumper. I habitually wore a red bandana around my head, to keep my long hair and the voluminous perspiration out of my eyes.

One day, while picking sides, a broad-shouldered Kurt Rambis-wannabe pointed to a tall, lean, dark-skinned high-schooler and said, "I'll take you." Then Rambis' finger traveled in my direction to complete his squad. "… and I'll take the old guy in the headband."

It took a lot of stamina to keep up with those younger, considerably better athletes. But the competition always gave my mind temporary freedom from its obsession with words and music, and the vigorous exercise enabled me to indulge in food and booze to my heart's content—without so much as gaining an ounce. After three or four games, I'd return to my digs to nurse my blisters, shower and pour the evening's first glass of jug Chablis. It was a great life.

Meanwhile, taking full advantage of my long-term relationship with Pasha Studios, I scored some off-hour spec time with whatever eager second engineer was available, and recorded some skeletal piano/vocal demos of my new material. After rough-mixing that batch of tunes, I left a cassette compilation on Spencer Proffer's office-chair.

About two days later, I got a call from my old friend and frequent creative and business partner. Spencer's high-pitched voice sounded even more exuberant than usual.

"Randy," he exclaimed, "do you know how *good* these songs are?"

I knew I'd made some real progress as a writer over these last few months of nose-to-the-grindstone wood-shedding; I didn't expect this gush of praise. Spencer then proceeded to invite me down to his office to meet an artist with whom he was preparing to make an album. As it turned out, that artist was none other than the taller-than-I'd-imagined Peter Noone.

After releasing my handshake, Peter said, "Randy, Spencer just played me a couple of your demos. I love *Grace* and *Gone With the Wind*. I'd really like to record those two. And, if you're into it, I'd like to take a shot at co-writing some tunes for my album."

I was particularly flattered by Pete's selection of those two titles. As far as I was concerned, he'd picked out by far my very best songs—each of them personal, poetic and, in its own way, uncompromising. It's always gratifying to receive kudos for a song of which you're especially proud. Of course, Peter's suggestion that we get together for the purpose of collaboration was met with no resistance whatsoever.

Noone's most recent musical incarnation had been singing for a new-wave power-pop combo called The Tremblers. This ensemble had released an album with four singles, and toured with The Beach Boys, garnering some very positive notices from the snooty rock press. Nevertheless, the outfit had fallen somewhat short commercially.

The folks at Johnston Records, an RCA subsidiary owned by my old acquaintance, Bruce Johnston (of Beach Boys and *I Write the Songs* fame), were hoping that this proposed solo project would bring our boy, the superstar formerly known as "Herman," back to the top of the charts.

For several weeks thereafter, Monday through Friday mornings, Peter Noone climbed the exterior stairs to knock on my apartment door, reporting for our daily writing sessions. Peter's brother-in-law owned *La Orangerie*, a saucy, upscale, French eatery on La Cienega Boulevard—just a few blocks away from the place I shared with my French-Moroccan girlfriend. More often than not, Pete would arrive with his pores emitting a pungent, residual aroma of garlic, still escaping his system from the previous evening's gourmet repast.

On those particular mornings-after, he would invariably apologize for the olfactory offense. Seeing that I could hardly keep myself from recoiling from the heady aura that surrounded his body, wearing his signature broad grin, he'd say, "Hey, man. Sorry 'bout the stench."

My Brit partner-in-song revealed himself to be a delightfully cynical cuss, often applying a wicked and rather indiscriminate tongue to any person or situation he felt was deserving of his commentary. Our sessions invariably commenced with a caustic editorial, directed at whatever or whomever was on Pete's mind that particular day. This would more often than not lead to a protracted discussion. Before we knew it, it was close to lunchtime. We always went out for our midday feed—usually at the nearby Old World Café—and the ever-gracious Peter insisted on picking up every check.

As it had been more than 15 years since the peak of Herman's Hermits success, Pete was carrying on the "lifestyle to which he'd become accustomed" by selling off his collection of fine art and collectables—one piece at a time. When his bank accounts dipped low enough, he'd place a call to Sotheby's in London and instruct them to put another oil painting, priceless antique or vintage automobile on the auction-block. Noone had a light-hearted attitude about liquidating his assets.

"Those are just things," he explained. Life in the here-and-now, Pete strongly felt, is meant to be lived to its fullest—even if it also meant stinkin' up the entire L.A. basin with last night's garlic.

After a lengthy linger at the Old World, we'd return, sated, to the apartment, promising to get down to some real songwriting. Like his fellow hometown British invasionist, Allan Clarke of the Hollies, Peter was inclined to grease his creative hinges with whatever alcohol might be easily available.

In my household, there was always a plentiful supply of that cheap, California, jug Chablis on hand. Far be it for me to be an ungracious host—and, to be perfectly honest, I required little excuse or arm-twisting to break out the vino. We poured the amber liquid on the rocks. The ice cubes, we claimed, made our libation more of an "afternoon beverage."

Needless to say, these writing sessions failed to yield a prolific output of potential tunes for Pete's project. The flow, the discipline, the productivity I'd cultivated over those previous months … all dwindled to a mere trickle. Seeing so little progress being made, Spencer Proffer interpolated himself into the process and, together, the three of us dashed off the composition that would give the LP its rather effete title, *One of the Glory Boys*.

I was fortunate enough to end up with five cuts on the disc—the two solo-written tunes mentioned earlier, and three co-writes with the artist. However, despite receiving credit as the album's "Associate Producer," I was inexplicably not invited to attend the lead-vocal sessions. Hearing the playbacks, I was more than pleased with Pete's performance on *Gone With The Wind*. He definitely captured the song's essential phrasing and core emotion. When I heard his vocal on *Grace*, though, I felt like I'd been kicked in the gut by a mule.

Evidently, the artist and producer had decided somewhere along the way that the chorus needed a bit of a boost. So they inverted its melody to what was actually a harmony above the tune I'd originally, so caringly concocted. Instead of giving the song more power and gusto, as they'd hoped, this on-the-spot melodic re-draft diminished the piece to an unmusical fraction of its former self.

Beware, my fellow mamas and papas of song: When you set your children free out there in the world to meet new friends, you may find yourselves not exactly loving the folks your babies end up hangin' out with. In other, more-direct, words, if you're lucky enough to have your creations find other voices, there *will* be times when those interpretations are not exactly to your immediate liking. (At the very least, they may take some time to warm up to.)

As for you artists and producers, please be reminded that we tunesmiths take great care in the application of our craft. We choose our words and melodies with purpose—after deliberating long and hard over every possibility we can think of. More times than not, by making impulsive, wholesale changes to our songs, you'll have undone something integral to our work.

(Immediately after completing recording the *Glory Boys* LP, Peter Noone was spirited off to the sparkling lights of the Great White Way. The old cat found a new life and a new career, replacing Rex Smith in the surprisingly successful Broadway revival of Gilbert and Sullivan's *Pirates of Penzance*. This show would restore solvency to Noone's leaking coffers, and keep the former teen idol busy for many years to come—first in New York, then on tours all over the world.

Later on, at 60, completely sober and still productive, Peter Noone received another huge career boost in 2007, when he acted as a mentor for an episode of *American Idol*. In the occasional e-mail, Pete's tongue remains as wicked as ever. What's more, I'll be forever grateful that I was part of "Herman's" world for those several months in 1982.)

chapter seventeen: The Last Chorus

Many of the songs you'll write won't require any adjustments at all to the last chorus section. In those compositions, it's *repeat chorus as-is and out*. If that were the case with the two tunes we presently have under construction, their first drafts would have been completed by now, and we could be toasting our mutual genius over frothy pints of Sierra Nevada draft.

However, often the last chorus will offer you the opportunity to take a parting shot, insert the perfect exit line, a capper that puts the final patina on each little architectural wonder, and/or the bow that ties up those still-dangling loose ends. To accomplish that, the lyric of our last chorus might actually demand to be altered slightly—or completely. In some cases, even the chords and melody may be ready to wander a bit from their well-worn path on this last victory lap.

Sometimes it seems redundant and/or anti-climactic to repeat the entire chorus on its third pass. It begins to feel as if it's too laden with details—details that were certainly of significant importance earlier in the song but, now that our audience has heard this stuff a couple of times, we can't help wondering if we should foist this same information on the listener again. We're in danger of morphing into boring Uncle Otto, with his wildcattin' stories from the '60s. They were riveting the first time, and delightful in their reprise, but now we could recite those tales from memory, verbatim, and so we tune out when he starts to drone on.

We certainly don't want to have *that* effect on our listeners. We want to leave our audience with a strong desire to hear the song again. So, in order to avoid overkill, we may feel called upon to truncate our last chorus, removing phrases we don't actually need to state again, cutting the fat, getting down to the lean, essential meat of the composition, and then wavin' bye-bye—*before* we've worn out our welcome.

A truncated last chorus also has the effect of shortening the overall length of the piece, giving us a better chance at getting on the radio—should we be so fortunate as to beat all those well-stacked odds and score a cut that in turn becomes a single. We've discussed the likelihood of that major miracle earlier, but somebody's gotta write the hits; it might as well be us—at least every now and then. ("Now" would be preferable, and—for me, anyway—"then" is looking too much like "way back when.")

Other times, our compositions seem to cry out for extra stuff—an extended, final chorus-section (a "tag" if you will), which we hope will finish off our mini-movie and offer our listeners even greater satisfaction. A stretched-out ending chorus can make the song a more enduring piece, because the new information (both musically and lyrically) introduced here can help to hold the audience's attention, as well as keepin' 'em comin' back for more.

Good song-craft requires that you consider all these possibilities as the finish line of your potential masterpiece comes into view. Just like the existential question, "to bridge or not to bridge," altering the final chorus is a judgment-call, one with which you'll be faced in probably every other song you write.

So don't be lazy and pack up your axe and head for the door before the job's completely finished. Take the time to look at the structure from a few angles, before you declare "Mission Accomplished" and place that "For Sale" sign in the front yard.

≈ ≈ ≈

I have a uniquely personal experience with the altered last chorus—a testimonial success-story, if you will. If you'll indulge me, I'd be more than willing to share. (Thank you, I knew you would.)

When Tim James and I completed the two verses of *My List*, both of them were designed to set up our wordy, detailed "list" chorus. We were then faced with the inevitable question as to whether our song-in-progress called for a bridge.

We agreed that it definitely was a good idea to insert a musical interlude after the busy language of the repeated second chorus; we soon realized, though, that a bridge *and* a final chorus would add too much length to the song. Next, we discerned that repeating the same chorus a third time, despite its detail, might end up sounding redundant and anti-climactic. Truncating the existing chorus also sounded wimpy and unresolved.

"What to do?" the songwriters pondered. We then bit the bullet, and decided to take a shot at writing a whole new, completely different lyric for the last chorus.

It was a daunting task to come up with imagery that lived up to, or even surpassed the language of the first and second choruses, but persistent brainstorming revealed potential ideas, and our last chorus began to take shape.

The phrase that begins the final chorus section, *Raise a little hell, laugh till it hurts*[xxxii], provoked some discussion as to whether this was acceptable language for the conservative country-music genre. But my shrewd collaborator, Tim, mitigated the possible offense of these phrases by suggesting that we follow them with *Put an extra five in the plate at church*[xxxiii]. In addition to soothing the sting of the hell-raising, these subsequent phrases also offered an inventive, yet perfectly natural pair of rhyme sounds in the words *hurts* and *church*.

Meanwhile, I'd contend that the lyric *Raise a little hell* was the decisive line that inclined the persistently rebellious Toby Keith to believe the song might be a good one for him. Brothers and Sisters in Song: *you gotta take chances*! Make a statement, kids, or you're just another songwriter strugglin' to be heard over the constant din of this noisy world.

After Tim and I had finished that alternative third chorus, the ending still sounded a little flat. So I resorted to an old trick—the *modulation*. Moving the key upward is a technique that's frequently been effective in re-energizing the final choruses of big ballads. More often than not, a key-change sounds contrived, manipulative and cornier than Nebraska under a harvest moon. But since, as I mentioned earlier, the musical mode of the *My List* verse and chorus are almost identical, a modulation offered the same kind of modal relief a bridge might have given us. At the same time, it drew attention and gave additional impact to the new lyric of the final chorus.

Writing this extra chorus required some heavy lifting, but that extra labor Tim and I put in added longevity to the copyright. After all, Toby's record held the number-one spot on the country singles chart for five straight weeks, fending off some very stiff competition—from Kenny Chesney's *Young* and Rascal Flatt's sophisticated, breakthrough ballad, *I'm Movin' On,* among others.

Makin' Stuff Up

Of course, we hard-workin' song-scribes can't take all the credit for our lengthy stay in the top chart-position; the Toby Keith brand is a powerful one at country radio. But Chesney and Flatts are formidable hit machines as well, so holding that number-one position against their two superb singles was a major victory.

Tim and I also owe a tremendous amount of gratitude to Scott Borchetta and his promotion staff at DreamWorks for their tenacity on our song's behalf. (Hopefully, those thoughtful and pricey Christmas presents in '02 were adequate demonstration of my appreciation for the promo and marketing staff's efforts.)

≈   ≈   ≈

A great example of a final chorus perfectly altered with a simple tag is in the late Tom Jans' oft-recorded tour de force, *Lovin' Arms*. The original hit was the understated, gut-wrenching version by Dobie Gray. But the song received its greatest exposure with Elvis Presley's dramatic rendition.

In *Lovin' Arms*, the singer imagines what his life might have been had he not been compelled to wander away from the girl who he now realizes would surely have been the true love of his life. Each verse-section begins by striving to make a connection between our vagabond vocalist and his left-behind lover, with the word, "If…"

If you could see me now; If I could hold you now; If I could touch you now[xxxiv]. If only, he pines, the woman could be made aware of his forsaken fate—as he's become a lonesome drifter, exposed day and night to the elements, wandering the highways in search of shelter—she'd surely invite him back, and he'd be *lyin' in her lovin' arms again*.

Then, to make this reverie a bit more urgent, a bit more tactile, Jans puts in that perfect parting shot in his ending tag: *I can almost feel your lovin' arms again*.

It's not your warm, fuzzy Hollywood ending. In fact, this final, more-vivid imagining makes the listener ache even more for the desolate isolation of the song's central character.

When it comes to true beauty and genuine emotion, this song hits the nail on the head with every note and every word. Each statement is clear, simple and economical. It's the equivalent of one of those gritty '70s movies—realistic, raw and unflinching, yet poetic and sparse. That's why *Lovin' Arms* has risen to the status of a standard. To me, though, it's that tag that ultimately brings home the true heart of the song.

Makin' Stuff Up

≈   ≈   ≈

Lennon and McCartney's *Help* offers a fascinating study in inventive song-structure, as well as a tag at the end of its final chorus that functions very effectively. The song opens with an introductory section of music and lyrics that never repeats again in the song. One could say that *Help* begins with the bridge. (The Liverpool lads would've been hard-pressed to call this bridge a middle-eight, unless they made the enigmatic claim that they started the song in the middle. Anyway, we'll be discussing some different, untraditional, structural concepts in a later chapter.)

The Beatles' addition of the vocal fanfare at the end of the song (*Help me, help me, oooo...*[xxxv]) not only reiterates the singers' plaintive cry for assistance, but also puts a conclusive, theatrical ending to the record, offering an extra—quite memorable, I might add—hook to the piece.

One might make the claim that this tacked-on section is really more of an arrangement concept than a substantive part of the song's composition. As it really emphasizes the song's emotional impact, though, I think it makes a major contribution to the artistic value of the copyright, and gives the listener another great reason to want to hear the song time and time again. You've just gotta give credit to those youthful Brits for their song-craft.

≈   ≈   ≈

A typical way to amend or augment a last chorus is to insert an extra tag-line over fresh interim chord-changes between the meat of the chorus and the icon-phrase that concludes it. This is the technique we decide to try out with our ballad, *Everything and Nothing*.

We have good reason for trying this. Our bridge indicated that our singer is prepared to express his devotion with affection, tears and a pledge to give his woman anything her heart desires—*if* she'll only promise to stick around. A final chorus, presented all the way through as it's already-written, ultimately seems to fall a little bit short when it follows that emotionally charged bridge-section. We need to come up with a little bit of musical interlude to give more power to the very last utterance of the icon-phrase, *She's everything, and I'm nothing without her*.

Makin' Stuff Up

We take advantage of this opportunity to add a lyric-line over this musical interlude, to re-emphasize the guy's admission of complete dependency. However, in this effort, what we run into is not just a story-telling challenge, it's also a bit of a rhyme-scheme quandary. This new line has to say the perfect words—but it has to include the right *sounds*, too. We want our last line to leave the listener's mind and heart fulfilled, while giving ultimate satisfaction to those eager ears. As a reminder, here's our bridge, going into our third and final chorus:

> *I'm gonna take her in my arms, and let my tears flow*
> *Whatever she wants, I'll give her, if she'll promise not to go*
>
> *She's everything to me*
> *And I'm nothing, if I'm not crazy for the girl*
> *She's everything I need*
> *And there's nothing I'd refuse her in the whole wide world*
> *She's everything, and I'm nothing without her*

To me, the existing last chorus begins to pale in the middle of the last line, right before the final phrase of the song, *and I'm nothing without her*. That's where my intuition tells me we should insert some new musical and lyrical information.

While we've played with the opposite meanings of *everything* and *nothing* quite a bit, we haven't utilized their kissing cousins, *anything* or *something*. So here's the first thing we try:

> *She's everything, ain't it something...*

The brief phrase, *ain't it something*, is leading to the new statement we'll be making over our next new "tag" segment of music. What that statement is, we don't know yet. We *do* know, however, that this changed lyric sounds absolutely fantastic in this spot, already having the effect of refreshing the ear.

So now we're searching for a new lyric to write over a two-bar passage. To fill this new section musically, we gracefully insert the 6-minor to the 2-*suss* resolved to the 2-seven. This interpolated lyrical phrase must, for the last time, and with more poignancy than ever, set up our icon-phrase, *She's everything, and I'm nothing without her*.

In scatting over these changes, we discern that our rhyme could fall on a syllable that picks up the sound of the word *her*. However, we soon agree that this would have the counter-productive effect of making this inserted tag sound a little too pat and predictable. It would probably be more satisfying to the ear, we decide, if the rhyme was a cousin sound to *something*. These choices are few, though—and even fewer of them have any real potential.

What we finally stumble upon, after missing the mark at least a couple o' dozen times, is a rather wordy summation statement, with the rhyming word (*comin'*) placed in the middle of the phrase. Somehow, though, it sounds natural and conversational and (if I do say so myself) sets up the final icon-phrase perfectly. I love it:

She's everything, ain't it somethin'
I'll do anything, to keep her comin' home to me because
She's everything, and I'm nothing without her

We've successfully refreshed *Everything and Nothing*'s last chorus by inserting an extra phrase of music and lyric to re-invigorate what might have been a predictable, ho-hum ending. Our forlorn love-ballad now has a solid first draft. It's Miller time!

≈   ≈   ≈

But wait! … We still have another last-chorus to address—and, as it turns out, it's gonna be an uphill climb ...

The concept of *Goin' Down Swingin'* is a solid one. If offers a whole bunch of opportunities to use language, character and story in very playful ways. At the conclusion of our bridge, it seems that we've done quite a bit of toying with the various meanings of the three words that comprise our title. So now we find ourselves hard-pressed to think of how to make this title work in a new way, this one last time.

Dang! Have we actually painted ourselves into a corner with our infernal cleverness? The only way we can find out is to plow ahead by continuing to brainstorm, and discussing whatever remaining various ways we could goose our chorus for its sprint to the finish.

In our first chorus, *goin' down swingin'* implies that the jealous boyfriend might be determined to conquer his competition with his fists. *But no. Surprise!* It seems that Billy unexpectedly makes a wiser choice in verse two, and the chorus to follow has him trying to *swing* his way back into Sally's heart with some surprisingly adept dance-floor moves.

Makin' Stuff Up

Then our bridge has him *goin' down*—quite literally—by taking a serious tumble on that very same hardwood. We left our lover's triangle at the hospital.

The question that's yet to be resolved is this: Which one of these two suitors is about to win out with the girl? After acting as ambulance driver, our cavalier singer is comforting Sally, while Billy is presumably suffering some kind of medical procedure. The vocalist may be holding the girl's hand, but Billy's hurt, so her sympathetic heart could just as easily be lured in the direction of the injured ex-boyfriend.

We decide to have our singer be victorious for two reasons. First, most recording artists love to come off as the winner in the songs they choose to sing. Secondly, Billy winning his girl back would completely scuttle our chances of using the refrain of our song again.

What we eventually come up with is a final chorus with some altered lines in some rather interesting places and some strategically placed tag-phrases between the refrain lines of the out-tro section.

Goin' down swingin', in its conclusive incarnation, has Billy—with broken leg and bruised ego—driving down Interstate 35 toward his San Antonio home, singing along with the tunes on his cranked-up FM station to soothe his aching heart. The last thing we reveal is that Sally has accepted a date with our singer.

With this approach, we definitely run the risk of making this song more than a little convoluted—*or,* this just might be the ticket. I'm honestly not completely sure at this juncture. Last chorus:

Sally left Billy back in San Antone
He was past tense, 'least that was what she was thinkin'
Now Billy's in a cast drivin' home alone
Headin' straight south in his '05 Lincoln
If Billy's goin' down, Billy's goin' down swingin'
(Singin' 'long with the radio)
If Billy's goin' down, Billy's goin' down swingin'
(Guess who's got a date with Sally-o)

Okay, I think we've earned those beers now. First round's on me!

chapter eighteen: Fudge & Scar Tissue

In the early fall of 1982, I found myself eyeball to eyeball with the ominous specter of a very bleak Christmas. My young wife (the second) was nearly ready to explode with our son, and about to take maternity-leave from her job as the assistant to a hotshot Beverly Hills talent-agent. With an album in the can, I was hanging in limbo—with no income—waiting for lawyers to get around to dotting *i*'s and crossing *t*'s on my record contract, so that I could collect my long-awaited artist-advance.

Every rent check, every tank of gas, every bag of groceries, every utility bill brought the balance of our bank account that much closer to zero. Not one to shirk the responsibilities of providing for my family, I began seeking any opportunity I could find to make a buck. First, I subjected myself to day labor. On one such day, I unloaded an entire boxcar packed with burlap feedbags—by myself; on another, I helped clear out the backstage area at the Hollywood High School theater. Both of those tasks rewarded me with a $20 bill at the end of eight hours of sweaty, filthy, backbreaking toil.

It didn't take long before I began to think that there must be employment more suited to my talents, something that perhaps even offered more substantial remuneration. This particular thought had only just dawned on me when a gig with those very qualifications presented itself. As a courier for Music Express, it was my responsibility to drive the width and breadth of the Los Angeles basin toting presumably priceless documents, master recordings, advertising swag, you name it. If it had to get there from here, I was the guy who *schlepped* it.

Wearing a blue, pin-striped, short-sleeved shirt, with my iron-on name patch attached to its left breast pocket, I'd arrive dutifully at various management offices, record company headquarters, recording studios, wherever the dispatcher dispatched me … with my trusty clipboard in hand, ready to take precious cargo from one location to another. I knew most of the highways and byways of the greater L.A. area, and I kept my trusty *Thomas Guide* on hand when sent on a mission into unfamiliar or potentially hostile territory.

One particular delivery included tapes for a mastering engineer, Greg Folgenetti. I'd first met Folgenetti years before at Elektra Records' West Coast office, where he was working in the tape-copy room. In that small, dark alcove on La Cienega Boulevard, Greg had played me the master-mix of Queen's operatic, career-launching masterpiece, *Bohemian Rhapsody*—long before it was released.

I arrived at Artisan Sound on Ivar Street, in the wilds of the Hollywood jungle, and handed Greg the tape-box. As he signed for the delivery, he mumbled, "If I didn't know better, I'd say you look exactly like Randy Bishop."

"That's probably because I *am* Randy Bishop," I told him. Although that should have explained the uncanny resemblance, Folgenetti refused to believe my claim.

I was just getting into the rhythm of my daily routine, reporting for duty at the Burbank Music Express office at some un-Godly early-morning hour, and spending the remainder of my shift shuttling from one end of Megalopolis to the other, when a fantastic songwriting opportunity came along.

Legendary drummer/songwriter Carmine Appice and I had worked together on a couple of projects—both with mutual friend, Rick Derringer. The Danny Spanos EP had yielded a Southern California radio staple, a passionate rocker entitled *Hot Cherie* (I wrote the song's lyrics). Doctors Of The Universe was an odd, cobbled-together studio band that tongue-in-cheekily endeavored to exploit the New-Wave trend of the early-'80s. I had performed a good portion of the DOU album's vocals, and co-written several of the songs.

Anyway, Vanilla Fudge was preparing to record a reunion album— with original members Appice, Mark Stein and Tim Bogert. Having enjoyed early success as a combo recognized for its theatrically psychedelicized covers of Motown and Beatles songs, the Fudge had missed out on all those lucrative publishing royalties. Singer/keyboardist Stein was determined this time out to write the songs on their new project. Although an extremely capable composer of melody and chord-patterns, Stein found himself unable to come up with satisfactory lyrics. So Appice graciously recommended *yours truly* to fulfill that task.

There I was, traversing the concrete and blacktop of Southern California, a portable cassette player on my passenger seat alongside that official Music Express clipboard and essential *Thomas Guide*, listening over and over to the *la-la-las* and *dee-dee-dees* of that celebrated Mark Stein tenor, vibrato-rasp. As each lyrical inspiration popped into my head, I'd repeat it over and over, hoping the next stoplight would last long enough for me to scrawl those passages on the dog-eared, yellow legal-pad I had propped on my knees.

> When you're scouring your imagination for words, there's nothing better than engaging in a fairly mindless motor activity to set your subconscious mind free. I don't know how many times I've been at the wheel of a car, and a great lyric line and/or melody has come blasting out of nowhere. The challenge is remembering it. That's why I highly recommend that every songwriter always carry a hand-held recorder of some kind to store those random inspirations. You never know when genius will strike

Somehow, between picking up posters and delivering mastered discs, and without rear-ending a single bumper, I managed to scribble eight full lyrics for the album, *Mystery* (released on ATCO Records in 1984). I'm as proud of those compositions as I am of any I've ever written. Meanwhile, even though the project didn't meet with massive commercial success, it still feels great to be able to count Vanilla Fudge as one of the many illustrious artists who've chosen to bless my songs with their considerable talent.

≈ ≈ ≈

My brief career as a courier came to its end on a blustery, early-December day in the northwestern San Fernando Valley. The chilly north wind was relentless, and the temperature had plunged into the 40s—particularly frigid for Southern California. I dropped off a delivery to a company in Tarzana, and was keeping my eyes peeled for a pay phone to call in for my next assignment.

I stopped at a funky, little, off-brand gas station and was almost knocked down by a stiff gust as I stepped out of the car. Wearing the old, black-leather jacket I'd owned since high school, collar up, and a baseball cap, I walked around the building holding my clipboard in my right hand like a shield.

Makin' Stuff Up

A courier has to take advantage of every opportunity for bladder relief. As I pushed open the door and stepped into the foul-smelling, bacteria-ridden men's lavatory, a swift and powerful blast of wind rushed at my back, and I was startled by a sudden, deafening crash. In a split second, I was struck by a cascading avalanche of rock-hard, heavy material.

As I stood there with my knees trembling, surrounded by fragments shattered glass, I looked up to see the source of this brutal maelstrom. There, over the door, I noticed that the chain holding the transom had broken, causing the window to swing down and explode into a thousand pieces. I felt a throbbing pain and looked down. A good-sized, triangular shard of glass had pierced the only exposed skin on my body—the back of my left hand. I pulled the three-inch-long, glass dagger out of my flesh, and a geyser of blood spurted six inches into the air.

There were no paper towels to cap the gusher. Clutching my punctured left hand with my right, and fueled by shock and adrenaline, I staggered unsteadily around the building to find help. The attendant tossed me a slightly used garage towel, and I wrapped the rag around the spouting puncture, putting pressure on it in an attempt to slow my loss of blood. He pointed me in the direction of the nearest hospital.

Somehow, holding my bleeding left paw above my shoulder, I drove myself, one-handed, to the emergency room to get stitched up. Washing up later, I looked in a mirror. There, on the very tip of my nose, several layers of skin were missing.

A chill of realization ran down my spine: *Had I not been wearing a baseball cap and a leather jacket*, I thought to myself, *my face, my head, and my upper torso might have been mangled by falling glass.*

I was very fortunate not to have lost my nose, or possibly even my life! I had somehow been protected by *unseen* angels. Obviously, I was not destined to meet my demise alone, with a blast of late-autumn wind, in a germ-infested facility, on a brisk day, in the remote West San Fernando Valley. My life's mission, evidently, had not yet been completed.

By the following morning, the back of my hand had swelled up to more than twice its normal size. In 72 hours, it had turned into an impressionist painting in earth-tones, and was filled with a solidifying mass of scar tissue. The injury required months of physical therapy to regain any flexibility in my fingers, during which time I was completely unable to play guitar or piano.

Makin' Stuff Up

I contacted a personal injury lawyer to try to get some restitution from the gas station. I was, after all, a recording artist with an album coming out, which would likely require touring. This accident prevented me from playing my instruments. Before our trial date, the station's parent corporation filed bankruptcy. By settling out of court, we were able to win a modest settlement.

And here's the ultimate irony of this story: One fine morning on the job for Music Express, I was dispatched to pick up some documents at the headquarters of Columbia/Epic Records in Santa Monica. Holding the manila envelope in my hand, I was surprised and amused to observe its intended destination: the law office of Loeb and Loeb Attorneys in Century City, attention, John T. Frankenheimer, Esq.

The package I dutifully toted from Santa Monica to that Century City high-rise was my own fully executed artist contract, sent from my own record company to my own lawyer—at long last, finally ready for my signature. Of the hundreds of couriers cruising the honeycomb of greater Los Angeles on that particular day, I was the one who was summoned to execute this, of all tasks.

chapter nineteen: The Feedback (we *all* need)

As a breed, we songwriters fall into the same general personality types as do law enforcement officers, biology teachers, carpenters ... even real-estate agents. Some of us are introverts, while others are more outgoing. Our native, individual temperaments can't help but affect the process of our work.

Exceptionally introverted writers tend to thrive on the privacy of the composition procedure itself, but often find it difficult—even somewhat painful—to expose the end-result to the world. An exceedingly shy, pensive tunesmith usually feels more at ease pondering a work-in-progress over and over, sometimes for weeks (or even months) on end, remaining unsure about one detail or another, and never really achieving certainty that a song is actually finished.

At the other extreme, an overly extroverted writer will often be so eager to share his latest song with whomever will listen, that he's wont to rush out of a writing appointment and give a debut performance without giving the piece its proper reflection. *Give the world a break, and sleep on it, Pal. You're bound to wake up tomorrow morning with some new and necessary refinements.*

I've always tacked toward the more subdued side of the stream; for years, I was very uneasy about playing my new songs for people. *What if they don't love it as much as I do?* I feared. Even worse, *What if they don't get it at all?* Somehow, as my song-craft matured, and I became more confident and more aware of my role as a writer, I gradually learned to seek out, accept and utilize the input of professionals, as well as selected laypeople—family, friends, acquaintances ... even perfect strangers—all for the purpose of improving my writing.

The "role as a writer" to which I refer is that of "communicator." All writing—fiction or non-, artistic or journalistic, for the screen or for the page, or in these words-attached-to-notes we call 'songs'—has communication as its central goal. The better our work communicates, the more likely it is that it will reach a substantial audience. How in the world are we ever going to know if we're succeeding, unless we're brave enough to expose the fruits of our labor to somebody?

Whether you're the timid, reclusive type, or you've won the trophy for "Most Gregarious Songwriter of the Year" for 10 years running, getting feedback is absolutely essential to the writing process—and even more essential to your ultimate success as a songwriter.

When I say feedback is essential, I'm *not* saying you should accept every critique—constructive or otherwise—as gospel. Comments you receive do not necessarily amount to marching orders. I'm not advising you to run right out and immediately address every single suggestion by every single person who hears every single one of your songs. Doing that would have you tearing your hair out trying to please everyone else, while you willingly abandon your own instincts and standards, and muzzle the voice of your own personal creative muse.

I am, however, saying that you should take feedback with a grain of granola, like when your mom tells you how much she loves (or even how much she loathes) your latest tune. (As I'm sure you've discovered by now, most moms are incapable of giving objective feedback.)

When you play your fresh-off-the-press inspiration for that certain someone, you must train yourself to watch them listening with discerning eyes, and then absorb their input with open, yet guarded, ears. If you're sitting there expecting some predetermined, specific reaction, you're bound to either fool yourself into believing you're getting the very response you desire, or you're liable to be deeply disappointed with whatever reflection (or lack thereof) you *do* receive—other than that specific desired one. Either way, the input you receive will not be of much use to you—because of your own inflexible notions.

Feedback is there for you to use; it's also there for you *not* to use. Listen to those comments intuitively, and as objectively as you possibly can, without getting defensive. Meanwhile, never forget that, as a communicator, if something in your song consistently misses the mark, failing to have its intended effect, you may just need to return to the drawing board for some re-drafting. Here's the most important thing to remember:

ONLY ACCEPT AND APPLY THE FEEDBACK THAT RINGS TRUE TO YOU.

Makin' Stuff Up

Here's what I mean. Whether we admit it or not, during the writing process, we *all* have apprehensions, lingering doubts, about *this* word or *that* melodic passage. Suppose I'm in love with a certain line in the first channel of my latest masterwork-in-progress. The language is fresh, playful and packed with spell-binding alliteration. Meanwhile, secretly, I'm worried that it sounds a little precious or (heaven forbid!) that most folks won't immediately comprehend its nuanced meaning.

In a pop song, it can be fatal to cling to a lyric that, for one reason or another, stops the audience from keeping up with the story. If a question mark appears in the mind of a listener—*What? What did he mean by that?*—then at least the next few lines disappear into the ozone, until that listener figures his/her way out of that momentary confusion. By that point, they'll probably never catch up, and the emotional impact of the entire song is lost. As writers, we have the advantage of knowing what we're *trying* to say, but sometimes we don't pick the best way to unravel our story for those who may be hearing it for the first time.

Also, remember that our audience can't see our punctuation or spelling—unless, for some reason, they happen to be reading along with a lyric sheet as they listen. Sometimes an apostrophe, a strategically placed comma, or a word that sounds exactly like, or similar to, several other words might be a stumbling block in a listener's ability to clearly absorb our lyric. Always try to avoid any language that could possibly be misinterpreted due to unseen punctuation or spelling, or confused by regionally accented enunciation.

We almost always harbor a sneaking suspicion or two about our early drafts. When you get a comment that reaffirms one of your secret misgivings, you know for sure you've unearthed an issue that should be re-addressed in a re-write.

On occasion, you'll get a criticism that comes out of left field, taking you completely by surprise—and not necessarily in a good way. Maybe the passage that doesn't work for this individual is your absolute, slam-dunk, favorite phrase in the entire song. This is when you have to rely on your own gut. If you truly believe in the line, keep it—but only after you get a second, possibly even a third opinion on the song. If everybody gets confused, or has a negative response, toss it. Make it better.

There's a rather awful slogan writers often use that applies here. *"Don't be afraid to kill your babies."* (Sounds like some horrific Greek tragedy, doesn't it.)

Makin' Stuff Up

Remember, you're a communicator. Failing to communicate simply because of your own stubborn insistence on doing it one particular way can be very self-destructive.

Warning: When you play the tune in question for trusted listener number two or three, it wouldn't be a good idea to draw attention to the specific, contended passage *before* they hear the entire song. Let *them* bring it up; if they don't mention it, ask them later (without prejudice) whether they had any particular feelings or strong opinions about that particular phrase—one way or the other.

Something might stick in Person A's craw, while the very same thing slips right by B. When you point that particular part out after the fact, Mr. B or Ms. C might think it over and reveal an intensely held opinion—or exhibit a complete lack of concern. Then, once again, if communication is the issue, "Don't be afraid to kill your babies."

I find it especially valuable to keep tabs on body-language while another person is listening to my song. This doesn't come naturally; I have a tendency to want to close my eyes and furrow my brow, hoping for a positive response. However, by observing my listener, it becomes obvious—even before I hear a single word of feedback—as to whether my song is pleasing, confusing ... or wafting right past him or her.

I began learning to watch body-language by playing my new songs for my wife. A person whose central mission in life is to be liked, Stacey would never want to appear unappreciative by articulating something specifically critical. I taught myself not to rely on the words she used in response to the song, but to pay closer attention to *how* she listened to it. As many of our most accessible and patient listeners are our close friends and relatives, reading body-language can be far more useful than those blindly supportive compliments (or prejudiced negative notices) we're bound to receive.

Not exactly getting the positive reaction he expected from the publisher, the young songwriter defends his work: "But everybody loves this song!"

"Really?" queries the puzzled publisher. "Who exactly is everybody?"

"Well," the writer stammers, "my mom, my sister, my Aunt Matilda ..."

"Everybody," interrupts the bemused publisher.

"Yeah, man! Everybody!" The songwriter rests his case.

(Your mom may love the sound of your voice, and may be completely blind to all of your various shortcomings. *Please excuse me for making the assumption that you're in any way flawed, but* ... Was she ironing your dad's shirt, with an eye on *As The World Turns*, when you rushed into the kitchen to foist your new one on her? Maybe her mind was on the upcoming church bazaar, and two-thirds of your presentation went in one ear and out the other. If your song had been *that* great, doncha think she might've stopped her chores and turned away from her soap for three consecutive minutes to pay your latest potential hit her complete attention?)

That's why it's of critical importance for you to have access to at least one reliable person who's willing and able to give you honest, thoughtful, comprehensive feedback. For me, that person has been my business partner at Writer Zone Music, Co-owner and Creative Director Steve Bloch.

Steve is a true rarity: He's a guy with the capacity to listen to a song once, and have intelligent things to say about it. Because of that highly honed skill, he's frequently invited to be a panelist at songwriting conferences around the country. Lucky me! I shared an office with him for five years. In those sporadic moments when he wasn't totally enmeshed with another writer giving his astute feedback, I'd take advantage of Steve's golden ears and expertise.

A talent agent from Los Angeles, Steve Bloch followed the early-'90s gold rush to Nashville, repping a handful of songs by two or three California-based tunesmiths. He likes to tell the story of his first Music Row pitch meeting and the message the A&R person from Columbia Records left on his machine, enthusiastically placing one of his submissions "on hold."

"This is easy," he congratulated himself. "I'm gonna get rich in this town." A true lover of songs and songwriters, and smitten with the fever of Garth Brooks-era possibility, Bloch began to commute from Tinseltown to Music City on a regular basis. Soon thereafter, he decided to establish residence in Tennessee and hang up a shingle as a Music Row publisher, under the banner, Southern Cow Music.

Every music-biz pro has a dozen or more war stories depicting those inevitable near misses, almosts, and sure-shots that somehow, suddenly went hopelessly errant. Bloch, however, is perhaps the most snake-bitten publisher I've ever met. His battlefield tales are classic.

Makin' Stuff Up

Like fictional TV secret agent Maxwell Smart used to say, "Missed it by *that* much!" Those words could be the subtitle of much of Bloch's publishing career so far, but that hasn't stopped this large, kind, convivial man from establishing his presence in the songwriting and music publishing world as a reliable, perceptive critic of songs. No one I've ever met is more dedicated to the process and/or has more talent for helping a songwriter make his or her song a better one.

The Steve Blochs of the world are few. However, if you're truly serious about becoming a great songwriter, you'll seek out somebody to listen to your material—someone you can genuinely trust, who cares about helping you be the best writer you can be, and who's not afraid to give your songs some tough love.

I don't know how many times I've played a new song for a publisher to a complimentary, even laudatory response such as: "That's incredible, Rand! Keep writing those kind of songs!" (*an actual quote from one such publisher*). Then, after the tune sits there for months collecting dust, I inquire as to why the demo hasn't had a single pitch.

It turns out that the guy didn't really like the song in the first place. Perhaps he had some unexpressed, now long-forgotten issues with the lyric or structure. Maybe he didn't like the singer we hired, or the tempo, or the snare drum sound, or … *WHATEVER*! I'll never know. All he gave me was a stroke of the ego, not a smidgeon of input to help me provide him with a product he felt confidence in representing.

We songwriters don't need to be patronized, stroked or BS'ed. We appreciate help in making our songs great (don't we?). That requires honest, objective feedback—and *YES, WE CAN TAKE IT*!

≈   ≈   ≈

So now you've cornered a few folks and played them our crude worktapes. The responses have been mostly positive, although you've detected a few momentary mind-wanderings and eye-glazings. One publisher, whom you've been actively courting, gave you the "That's incredible. Keep writing songs like that…" response, followed by a patronizing smile and a dearth of constructive specifics.

One particularly intriguing question comes from somebody who's always in your corner, rooting for you to write that first smash—your spouse, your boyfriend, girlfriend or life-partner. You've just listened together to our pleading ballad, *Everything and Nothing*. You detect a little tear in the corner of your audience-of-one's eye. *Aha*, you're thinking, *this song is really connecting gangbusters*, until you hear this despondent query:

"Why do they have to break up?"

Now, you're well aware that this remark could be motivated by self-interest. Every song you write, of course, is subject to extra scrutiny from your significant-other. This is a love song, after all, and the fact that you've put a relationship in jeopardy in a song automatically casts a potential shadow on yours. So you try to clarify: First, you explain that the song's theme was your co-writer's idea, not yours. And then...

"Well, they don't have to break up," you explain. "Or, they haven't yet. That's what the singer's trying to avoid."

"But ... he loves her so much. Why can't they just be happy?"

Hmmmm, you're thinking. *That's a very interesting question. Why didn't Rand and I think of that?*

Meanwhile, *Goin' Down Swingin'* has been met with some foot-tapping ... and more than a few perplexed smiles. Everybody said the song was "cool," but, for the most part, the responses were somewhat reserved. After the first chorus, it seemed as though the plot of the story kind of lost its impact, or maybe meandered off the trail somewhere along the way.

When we play our songs for other people, we tend to listen with entirely different ears. Sometimes intros and turnarounds drag on forever. Suddenly a line that seemed so effective on paper becomes unsure when exposed to the air of a trial-run. Sections of the song I was absolutely certain were essential to the telling of the story fall into question—perhaps now appearing unnecessary or extraneous.

When, with the perspective of the passage of time, I look back at the hundreds of songs I was once so confident about—the ones that eventually failed to receive the positive, enthusiastic acceptance and support I expected them to get—I usually discern one or both of the following reasons: First, the song isn't emotionally true; it's too contrived, germinated in my head instead of coming from my heart. Second, at some point, the composition usually becomes too complicated or convoluted, either musically or lyrically—usually both.

When you're wrestling with a song, trying to tell a story, your efforts can often lead you down side-roads and into tangled underbrush. While the view along this pathway may be fascinating and make perfect sense in the moment, the snapshots you bring home often fail to capture its transitory wonder.

MORE TIMES THAN NOT, IN SONGWRITING, SIMPLE IS BETTER.

It's a true test of our skill and discipline to keep ourselves "on point," using precise, concise, yet fresh language to weave our tales.

≈   ≈   ≈

My scheduled appointment with the always-candid Mr. Bloch yields some very helpful input. Some comments are predictable, others totally surprising.

After checking messages and answering some email, Steve sits down with a cup of coffee and swings my studio-door closed, focused and ready to absorb our two new songs.

I'm always reluctant to give a listener lyric sheets—particularly a music-biz professional. The temptation to read ahead is difficult for anybody to resist, especially someone who hears a dozen new songs every single day. You want your story to unravel at its own pace, letting its musical atmosphere and lyrical detail weave together in real time, as if the song was receiving its debut performance on the radio.

However, knowing that Steve will likely want to refer to the lyrics after my presentation with his comments, I hand him the pages. And he, being the sensitive and experienced listener that he is, pushes them aside and urges me to start. I begin with *Everything and Nothing*.

By the end of the initial quatrain, it's clear that Steve is impressed by the first four lines of the song. His body-language says it all. *He's hooked*, I say to myself, feeling a rush of overconfidence. *Now it's time to reel the big fellah in.*

At the song's end, he says, "That's beautiful, Rand. I only have one comment."

I'm expecting to hear some small, specific suggestion, possibly about changing a couple of words here or there, or switching the sequence of a line or two.

"Well," he continues, "it's more of a question than a comment, really. Why does she have to leave him?"

"She doesn't," I explain. "That's what he's trying to stop her from doing."

"Yeah, I know that. I get it," my astute friend says. "But why couldn't this song be a completely positive love-song?" (I, of course, have no idea yet that you've garnered a similar response to the same song.)

At first, I'm not just disappointed by Bloch's suggestion, I'm instinctively resistant to it. In no other creative medium besides songwriting could this happen.

If you wrote a mystery novel, it would be highly unlikely that your publisher would read it and say: "This is hilarious. I think it would work better as a satire."

If you were pitching a pilot for a domestic sit-com, a network exec would never offer this response: "This has great potential as an hour-long crime-drama."

Yet, here I am, the songwriter—after having carefully co-crafted a heartfelt plea directly from the heart, depicting a man desperately trying to keep his relationship from falling apart—hearing a suggestion that I fundamentally change the entire concept of my song to that of a man testifying his everlasting devotion for an equally dedicated lover.

Meanwhile, this input isn't coming from my adoring mother, my self-interested spouse or some rube without a clue. This is being delivered by someone with years of experience, someone who has earned my respect … and someone who, as my business partner, has a real interest in my success.

Hmmmm, I think to myself. *Why didn't we think of that?*

Well, the answer to that self-query is an easy one. As I mentioned from the get-go, back when you and I first started toying with this particular concept, the hardest song in the world to write is the devotional love-ballad. When you endeavor to construct one of those, it seems like all the good materials—words and melodies—have been used a thousand times before. You want this kind of song to be direct and sincere, but whatever you write tends to sound clichéd and hackneyed.

"I mean," emphasizes Bloch, "what woman wouldn't wanna hear those words coming from a big ol' strappin' guy?"

She's everything, and I'm nothin' without her, I'm thinking. That's strong testimony, to be sure.

Then, being the shrewd song guru that he is, Bloch picks up the lyric sheet and proceeds to point out the very few places in the existing song that would need changing to accomplish this task. In addition, he remarks that the musical mode seems to work equally well, should I choose to take this new approach.

Yeah, yeah, yeah, I'm thinking. *I wasn't born yesterday. I know it would require only a few simple tweaks.* "But what would we be left with?" I ask.

"I think you'd have a much more pitchable song," says Bloch. "A lot more singers would want to sing it."

(Our company is, after all, bottom-line, in the business of manufacturing product for the marketplace, and Steve is the head of my sales team. I *do* want to provide him with merchandise in which he has confidence. On the other hand, I don't want to extract the essence, the true heart out of any song, just for the purpose of making it more "commercial.")

Disheartened and confused, I swallow my pride and tell Steve that I'll certainly seriously consider his feedback.

≈   ≈   ≈

As I launch into our happy-go-lucky number, *Goin' Down Swingin'*, Bloch's body language immediately tells another story altogether. Up until now, I've been so sure that this song is that rare up-tempo piece that hits pretty close to the center of the bulls-eye. With colorful, clearly defined characters, a detailed plot, some very playful language and a great groove, I'm thinking that this song could actually be a license to print U.S. currency.

My friend, Steve, however, immediately finds several self-imposed impediments that might prevent us from crankin' up the cash machine just yet. After complimenting the song's opening line, and remarking about how much he likes the phrasing that leads into the chorus, he begins his constructive criticism:

"Here's what I'm wondering."

Uh, oh, I'm thinking. *Here it comes.* And so it does ...

"Who do you root for in this song?"

Steve goes on to point out that all the characters are likable, but nobody is either noble or contemptible. You can't really fault Billy for being a jealous guy and for wanting to win his girl back, and he never really does anything to make himself undeserving of her affections.

Our singer, after all, seems to be just another cruiser at a bar—not exactly heroic. Then there's Sally, the girl who skedaddled outta River

City, still wearing the ring that probably cost Billy three months of his hard-won salary.

"Yeah, but …" I argue, "the singer drives Billy to the emergency room. That makes him a genuinely nice guy."

"Okay," Bloch responds. "But by doing that, you also sacrificed Sally's opportunity to finally cut the cord with Billy. Billy's too nice. You've gotta make him more of an A-hole." Steve goes on to show how many places the second verse becomes contradictory and where the characters are inconsistent. By now, my head is spinning. The song I thought was so close to being a slam-dunk has clanged off the rim and ricocheted back to half-court. *BRICK*!

[Note to self: *I've always been concerned that Billy asking Sally to dance in the second verse lets the air outta the balloon.* Any feedback that reinforces that intuition should get extra attention.]

I take a deep breath to gather myself. I see great potential in this song, and I really want it to work. So, the writer in me re-awakens, and I begin brainstorming on a few "what-ifs."

"You've gotta make Billy more aggressive, more threatening," Bloch re-emphasizes. "Then we can cheer for the singer, and we'll have a much better idea why Sally left the thug in the first place."

"What if," I suggest. "I'm just thinking out loud here, but … What if Sally's the one who pulls Billy onto the dance floor—you know, to stop him from pummeling our singer?"

Steve trusts that I'll figure out a way to make this work. He doesn't have time to get into every plot-twist. But he agrees that this *might* be a workable idea.

We move on, to the specifics of the bridge, discussing whether or not our singer should act as ambulance-driver. (Steve's strongly opposed to keeping that idea, although disposing of that part of the plot would make me a *baby-killer*.) Then there's the ending of the song: he insists it has to show how truly unhappy Billy is about his humiliation—after taking an injurious spill on the dance floor, and losing his trophy girlfriend to a perfect stranger in one fell (pun intended) swoop.

"If Billy's singing along with the radio, make sure we know he's singing somethin' sad. Maybe Hank Williams."

That's Steve's final suggestion.

These are actual examples of constructive feedback, the kind of criticism that can help a writer make his or her song a better one. Some writers seek it. Some don't. Some would be receptive to it. Some wouldn't.

This is how I see it, my brothers and sisters in song: We're *not* artists; we are craftspeople. We're in the business of custom-tooling functional, usable pieces for mass consumption. While we desire to make each work original in its own way, we do want that work to be solidly constructed, ergonomic and to perform with efficiency.

For instance, if we were designing and building a chair, we'd want that chair to carry our own creative imprint, but we'd also want our creation to be recognizable *as* a chair. More than that, if we desire to do much commerce with our handiwork, we'd be well-served to make that chair one that folks are actually gonna want to place their posterior on—time and time again, for extended hours, and for many years to come.

Okay, my friend. I've listened to and accepted most all of Mr. Bloch's feedback. Now we've got our work cut out for us:

Substantial re-writing is called for—and we're just the writers to do it. I'm excited about getting back at it.

So let's reconvene and get these songs right.

chapter twenty: The Next *Eye of The Tiger*

"Tommy, Rand," exclaimed the brick-solid man with the black, shag haircut. "Dis song is gonna be da next *Eye o' da Tigah*." After some enthusiastic handshaking, the man with the compliments exited the studio control-room, grabbed the wall-phone just outside the door, and hastily dialed an outside number.

A minute later, just before he slammed the receiver onto its cringing cradle, we heard the same, perturbed, South Philly inflection shouting— for the entire building to hear: "*Git me a real prodoossah in heah! Dese assholes don' know what theah doin'!*"

Tommy Faragher and I had met Sylvester Stallone less than two weeks before that February afternoon in 1983. Tommy, a tall, boyish, immensely talented singer, keyboardist and songwriter, with a tousle of brown curls, had emerged from his fraternal Faragher Brothers band intent on pursuing a solo career. To the furthering of that end, Tommy and I had spent the past several months in daily sessions, writing and demoing songs for him to sing—and, ostensibly, for me to produce.

One particular Faragher/Bishop co-write was somewhat atypical of the soulful, romantic, pop/R&B style Tommy generally championed. *(We Dance) So Close To The Fire* was more representative of the hard pop/rock of the era. That song's lyric described a couple living on the edge of self-destruction—a subject on which I had some first-hand authority.

Our demo of *So Close* had mysteriously found its way to Stallone, who, at that point in time, was intensely engaged in directing his own script of *Staying Alive*, the highly anticipated follow-up to the sleeper/blockbuster that had snuck up like a phantom cyclone and whipped the closing years of the previous decade into disco madness— that pointy-collared, stack-heeled flick called *Saturday Night Fever*.

Essentially a low-budget "B" movie, *SNF* was primarily responsible for lifting youthful John Travolta from TV sit-com star to big-screen-idol. Of more interest to the songwriting team of Faragher and Bishop, however, was the *SNF* soundtrack album, which had sold about a zillion copies worldwide. Getting a song in the sequel was tantamount to hitting the powerball. So when music supervisor Robin Garb called, Tommy and I had no reservations whatsoever about skipping the two blocks east down Melrose Avenue, from Pasha Studio to the gates of Paramount Pictures, for our first audience with writer/director Stallone.

He's not a tiny man, as some have claimed, but at all of maybe five-foot nine—in those Italian, high-heeled boots—he didn't look like the heavyweight contender he appeared to be in those *Rocky* movies, either. As Tommy and I entered the cozy, cluttered editing room, Stallone cheerfully greeted us with the most obvious information of the day:

"Hi, I'm Sly." His vise-grip on my knuckles indicated that, even when he was *behind* the camera, my new pal kept himself in Rambo-shape.

On a Moviola editing machine, Sly proceeded to screen a few minutes of a rough-cut scene from the film-in-progress. It amounted to an elaborate dance-number, in which a finely sculpted Travolta, clad in nothing but headband and loincloth, spun and leaped through what looked to be a shady underworld; he was surrounded by various other perfectly toned, young dancers, all of whom were writhing and moaning in the cloud of smoke hovering just above the surface of a vast stage.

This scene, we were to learn, was the opening extravaganza of Stallone's fictitious Broadway musical-from-hell, *Satan's Alley* (based on the epic 14th century poem, *Dante's Inferno*).

Then, director Stallone guided us to a second Moviola, for a repeat screening of that exact same *Satan's Alley* clip. Much to the songwriters' surprise and delight, the music accompanying this repeat performance was … our demo of *So Close To the Fire*.

Stallone pointed to the screen, remarking, "See! Now it looks like da guy kin akshooly dance."

In the director's eye, our music enhanced Travolta's dance-moves, making the actor appear more convincing as the consummate Broadway gypsy his character (the vain, self-possessed Tony Manero) had become since he'd emerged victorious from that *SNF* disco championship, five years before. Sly then went on to unashamedly testify his personal affection for our song, promising, in no uncertain terms, that he intended to use it in the film—although he couldn't guarantee it would end up in this pivotal scene.

The well-known singer/songwriter contracted to custom-craft the music for the first clip we'd viewed had been tendered a cool $150,000 for his handiwork. Music supervisor Garb gave Tommy and me *our* assignment. We were requested to produce two separate versions of *So Close*: One completely restructured arrangement would ostensibly provide the musical backing for the seven-and-a-half minute *Satan's Alley* dance sequence—a major scoring job. The second was to be a three-minute version, for possible inclusion on the RSO Records soundtrack album. All this, Garb iterated, we would be expected to accomplish without a contract—*or* a budget. We'd be working totally on spec.

We soon learned to be on constant high-alert for Stallone's spontaneous arrivals at the studio. More than a half-dozen Southern California recording facilities were cranking out custom recordings for the film, and the director spent a good part of every day traversing the streets of the L.A. basin, shuffling from facility to facility to check on progress and offer his sage feedback.

The scuttlebutt among the various *Staying Alive* music production teams verified that we were all having the same experience. Sly would arrive and disrupt the proceedings by commandeering the producer's chair. Then, inevitably, he'd get distracted and abruptly depart. In his wake, everything he'd just participated in had to be completely re-recorded.

Over the previous several days, our illustrious *auteur* had been intently focused on his idea of overdubbing tubular bells onto the *So Close* track. To this purpose, Tommy and I had spent untold hours trying out every sampled and synthesized chime we could find—to no avail. Every attempt ended up sounding all wrong, usually sour and out-of-tune. Thus, Sly had come to the conclusion that the producer—*that would be me, Mom*—was somehow incompetent.

After the day of his *Eye o' da Tigah* compliment (the one that had segued into an inexplicably schizoid telephone-tirade), Stallone began showing up with a new sidekick in tow. Ray Kennedy's only claim to fame was his co-writing credit on a few songs by The Babies. But Kennedy, a swashbuckling (and far-too-perfect-looking) specimen of Irish/American manhood, certainly had Stallone believing he was some kind of musical *wunderkind*. After a playback of our work in progress, a brief, private confab between Sly and Ray would be followed by a

Kennedy pep-talk, accompanied by some affirmative Stallone head-bobbing. Then the odd couple would make a dramatic exit—presumably on their way to repeat this routine at the next recording facility on their itinerary.

After a few days of visits from the dynamic duo, Tommy and I were informed that the *Satan's Alley* footage had been re-edited. Since we were recording on two-inch, 24-track, analog tape, in order to preserve the sonic integrity of our production, we had only one alternative: to completely re-record the lengthy, complex film-version of *So Close* to the new cuts.

Music supervisor Robin Garb informed us that a Betamax tape of the latest edit would arrive momentarily—Paramount being only just a stone's throw east, across Gower Street on Melrose. So we logically booked studio-players for the re-tracking session. Cartage arrived, and the Pasha hallways were jammed with bulky anvil cases, all packed with drums, percussion instruments, guitars and amplifiers. However, the newly edited tape never arrived from Paramount.

For three days, we hovered in limbo, with the Musicians Union clock ticking away. Unable to reach Robin for an explanation, I felt a sense of panic set in, as my head filled with every possible worst-case scenario. Finally, I received that long-awaited return call. When I answered, Garb acted surprised that we'd been so concerned. Then I heard some familiar chord-changes in the background on his end of the line. No doubt about it, the song leaking into his phone was *So Close To the Fire*.

I asked Garb where he was calling from.

"The Record Plant," he replied.

With my heart pounding as frantically as the drum solo from *In-A-Gadda-Da-Vida*, I started up my car and Grand Prixed across Hollywood to the Plant. When Tommy and I walked into the tracking room, Mike Porcaro was re-doing his bass part on a new track of *So Close To the Fire*. My palpitating heart nearly stopped when, through the glass, in the control room, I saw tan, golden-haired Ray Kennedy, smiling smugly from the producer's chair.

A minute later, down the hall, in one of the hot-tub rooms, I sat stunned, getting the official party-line from Robin Garb. Sly, the music supervisor explained, had decided that our song would be better served by Kennedy's production.

"In the long run," Garb patronized, "this will be a good thing. Now your song will definitely make the movie and the album."

Makin' Stuff Up

Feeling humiliated, furious and absolutely crushed by this brutal encounter with major Hollywood-movie politics, I rushed home, packed a bag, grabbed my dog and motored north to clear my head. After driving for 12 straight hours, I arrived at my parents' getaway condominium on the Oregon coast—still fuming and deeply wounded. There, thumb-tacked to the condo's front door, a note awaited me, comprised of only four direct, concise words:

Randy, Call Spencer immediately.

My conversation with Spencer Proffer at Pasha was bittersweet. Evidently, Ray Kennedy had completely botched his production, and Sylvester Stallone was literally begging me to come back and build a track around the new vocal Tommy Faragher had sung in my absence. To make matters more urgent, the director needed a rough-mix of the completed, restructured, seven-and-a-half minute film version for a rapidly approaching screening—in 72 hours' time.

Well, what songwriter/producer doesn't relish being needed—especially by an Oscar-winning director? I put my dog in a kennel, caught a pricey, last-minute flight back to L.A. ... and then spent three consecutive, sleepless nights in Pasha Studio, polishing Kennedy's offal. The screening turned out to be a big success. At long last, Stallone confirmed that *So Close To the Fire* was locked in as the underscore for the *Satan's Alley* dance-sequence.

Tommy Faragher and I signed our contracts with Paramount Pictures and the Robert Stigwood Organization (RSO) for the movie and its soundtrack LP. Attending the film mixing session, I received some nice compliments on my production from ubiquitous movie-mixer, Joel Moss.

It was a very sweet victory. Two virtual nobodies had won a featured spot on the most coveted soundtrack of the year. Unfortunately—for me at least—that pride and elation would be short-lived.

chapter twenty-one: The Rewrite

With some writers you'll meet along your pathway to Hitsville, the very first thing they blurt out amounts to absolute brilliance. You'll be left breathless, hard-pressed to keep up with those first inspirations. In fact, when collaborating with one of these rare intuitive geniuses, you'd be well advised to keep a recorder running at all times—lest something very special be easily lost, forgotten, dissipating forever into the ethers.

Often, however, with this type of writer, that first gush is about all you're gonna get. They're sprinters—elegant, graceful and fleet of mind—who find themselves completely spent after the first hundred meters. These guys and gals are often not very interested in rewriting— nor are they very good at it. As a result, they're likely to be impressive in the sheer volume of their output, but extremely inconsistent in the quality of each offering.

I tend to be the turtle, not the hare. With every new song, I'm prepared to run a marathon. Regardless of the number of writing appointments required to really finish off a composition to my complete satisfaction, I'm ready to report for duty. Once I've committed to a song concept, I'll turn over every rock and chase down every varmint in the county to bring it to justice. It's rare for me to emerge from an initial sit- down with a complete first draft I could confidently play for anyone, let alone a copyright I'd be willing to call fully baked and ready to be named as one of this evening's specials.

I love re-writing. There, I've said it. It's not because I'm habitually ambivalent or perennially indecisive. Over the years, I've developed a passion for the process of honing my work. The blank page is an intimidating, potentially enervating specter. Getting started on a new song requires overcoming those old fears, the devil whispering in my ear, making me wonder if I can do it again, this one more time. A draft of lyrics makes my heart flutter with anticipation. I'm pretty sure I'm gonna discover ways to make those words sharper, clearer and craftier.

I can't wait! Let's get down to it!

≈   ≈   ≈

It's been a week, maybe longer, since we came up with our desperate love-ballad, *Everything and Nothing*. We both report that our test runs on the tune have indicated that the song might be more effective if we readdress its basic concept, changing it from a plea for reconciliation to a straight-ahead declaration of a man's devotion to his lady love.

Wow! With the amount of thought we put into each line, completely going back to the song's fundamental premise seems like a daunting task. With that very thought in mind, we listen back to our work-tape:

They were bright and clear and blue as the sky
My heart was no match for her laughing eyes
Since that steamy June Sunday in Riverside Park
When I first held her hand, she's held onto my heart

I worked double shifts to buy her that ring
Proposed in the fall, planned a wedding next spring
Been out slavin' away, savin' up for our life
Guess that wasn't enough, 'cause now she's sayin' good-bye
And (Yeah) I realize…

She's everything to me
And I'm nothing, if I'm not crazy for the girl
She's everything I need
And there's nothing I'd refuse her in the whole wide world
She's everything, and I'm nothing without her

Now I look around at how she's fixed up this place
That bunch o' wild flowers in a thrift store vase
And that cat she rescued, (that's) always hissin' at me
I'd even miss him, too, if she should pick up and leave
Gotta make her believe…

Makin' Stuff Up

Repeat chorus

I'm gonna take her in my arms, and let my tears flow
Whatever she wants, I'll give her, if she'll promise not to go

> *She's everything to me*
> *And I'm nothing, if I'm not crazy for the girl*
> *She's everything I need*
> *And there's nothing I'd refuse her in the whole wide world*
> *She's everything, ain't it somethin'*
> *I'll do anything, to keep her comin' home to me because*
> *She's everything, and I'm nothing without her*

Although this particular tune isn't your typical one-to-one "I love you, and I'll love you forever" sonnet, we're relieved to discover that it could fairly easily be distilled down to a declaration of pure love, by simply eliminating the discontent of the *ingénue*. Since we've crafted a ton of back-story and detail into this relationship, in essence, the preponderance of heavy labor has already been accomplished. Due to our mutual efforts, this piece has long-since evolved beyond love-song cliché.

Since we've decided to take our unanimous feedback to heart by removing the song's jeopardy—the woman poised to walk out the door—let's take a hard look at what specifically would have to be changed.

First things first. We need to address that flaw in the lyric we identified long before we exposed this song to outside scrutiny. As we remind ourselves constantly, it's highly inadvisable to use a strategic noun or verb more than once in a song (with the possible exception of a summation bridge that repeats language and information introduced earlier, serving to turbo-charge those words and add emotional impact to the song's story, message or theme).

Sometimes, in our haste and enthusiasm, we let a repeated word slip by unnoticed. In the first verse of this song, we've doubled up on the word *heart*—an obvious "no-no." Let's scuttle one of those tickers now, before we address the big picture. As we're using *heart* as the rhyming-word of the last full line of the verse, we'd be better off not tossing that one overboard. If we can avoid it, we don't want to have to re-work two complete lines to create a new rhyme—especially when this pair of phrases completes our verse section so nicely. Doing that, we agree, would be throwing out the rubber ducky with the bathwater.

So it's the second line of verse one that we decide needs the organ transplant:

My heart was no match for her laughing eyes

The laughing eyes are great; we'd also be smart to keep those pretty little blinkers, because they explain what was *bright* and *clear* and *blue*. So the question becomes, how do we employ those eyes another way? More brainstorming, more contemplating and a few errant attempts later (each of which fails to come close to matching the grace of the line we're attempting to tweak), we finally stumble on an idea that actually helps set up our new concept of a testimonial of devotion:

I saw my every tomorrow in her laughing eyes

Wow! That's powerful stuff. The singer is revealing that, from the get-go, he knew this was the only girl for him, while simultaneously further describing those inviting peepers. While this new line is three syllables longer than the original, requiring the singer to anticipate the phrasing, we concur that adding three eighth-notes (as a pickup) is not too serious a side-effect to endure following such a successful transplant procedure.

After a high-five, we endeavor to identify the next spot that begs for our attention. It's as obvious as the lobes hanging from my golden ears: At the end of the four-line double-verse section comes:

Guess that wasn't enough, 'cause now she's sayin' good-bye
And I realize...

Nobody's digging this dark cloud hanging over our singer. He's been bustin' tail to provide for a future with the lady of his dreams. How about we make all those interminable days of clockin' in at the plant pay off for our working class hero:

Just knowin' she's there, makes it all worthwhile
Yeah, I realize...
She's everything to me, etc.

Makin' Stuff Up

The chorus—*thank the song-gods*—is rock-solid, perfectly sound, as-is. So now we discuss the final line of verse two, which ends in *if she should pick up and leave*. We finally decide there's no reason why this guy wouldn't ponder what his life would be like if the girl inexplicably took a hike—so our entire second stanza can remain unchanged.

Yippee! This re-writing is a spongy slice of devil's food cake.

So far, what seemed to have every potential of being a major re-building project, has turned out to be no more than a minor renovation. The fact is, we did a whole lot of good work on the characters and imagery a week ago, when we battled through our first draft.

Since the only difference in the story is the relative contentment of the *yin* half of this *yin/yang* circle, the picture only needs a nip here and a tuck there, in order to shift its focus from a man trying to save his relationship to the same guy celebrating and declaring his dedication to nurturing and sustaining it.

Next we address the bridge. I, of course, still have certain personal qualms about having a guy cry in a song—especially when that simpering fellow is the singer. Male performers usually want to appear to be in-charge, to be strong and self-reliant. By having the singer emit some salty teardrops, I suspect it's likely that the candidates to whom we can pitch the song might be somewhat limited.

Then I'm reminded that our audience is predominantly female. Many of those ladies could presumably be moved by a man letting down his guard to reveal his vulnerability. If he's willing to shed a few to show the woman how he feels about her, I guess it makes him a better man, a bigger man—not to mention a more secure man. Okay, once again, we keep the crying.

That last line of the bridge, however, calls out for our attention. We've already allowed a line referring to the girl leaving to remain in verse two; I don't think we need to dwell on our singer's abandonment issues. Let's find a new and improved way to conclude our bridge. This is our solution:

Whatever it takes, I'll do it, I've just got to let her know…
She's everything to me, etc…

Whatever it takes, he'll *do* it. That's how much he loves the girl and, even though men tend toward hiding or denying their feelings, this bruiser is lettin' 'em all out. What woman (with any connection to sanity) wouldn't be attracted to a guy like this?

Finally, we address the tag in the last chorus. Once again, our previous concept required a line here that referred to the lady staying or leaving:

I'll do anything, to keep her comin' home to me because...

I still love the way this line sings, and how the sound-alike word, "comin'" appears in the middle of the phrase instead of at its end. But, wait a minute! It's our singer who's out there pullin' double shifts. *He's* the one doing the "comin' home," not our comely, blue-eyed, wild-flower-pickin' cat-lovin' chickadee. This is where we go here:

I'll do anything, to keep comin' home to my girl, 'cause
She's everything, and I'm nothing without her

That seems to solve those issues *and*, Ladies and Germs, this line offers a bonus, by adding an additional cousin-rhyme in its repetition of the word "girl."

This was quite possibly one of the easiest re-writes in songwriting history. All prevailing issues—and *more*—have been addressed. If our audience indeed wants a pure devotional love-song, that's what we've accomplished:

EVERYTHING AND NOTHING

They were bright and clear and blue as the sky
Saw my every tomorrow in her laughing eyes
Since that steamy June Sunday in Riverside Park
When I first held her hand, she's held onto my heart

I worked double shifts to buy her that ring
Proposed in the fall, planned a wedding in the spring
Been out slavin' away, savin' up for our life
Just knowin' she's there, makes it all worthwhile
Cause I realize...

Makin' Stuff Up

She's everything to me
And I'm nothing, if I'm not crazy for the girl
She's everything I need
And there's nothing I'd refuse her in the whole wide world
She's everything, and I'm nothing without her

Now I look around at how she's fixed up this place
That bunch o' wild flowers in a thrift store vase
And that cat she rescued, (that's) always hissin' at me
I'd even miss him, too, if she should pick up and leave
God, I hope she believes…

Repeat chorus

I'm gonna take her in my arms, and let my tears flow
Whatever it takes, I'll do it, I've just got to let her know

She's everything to me
And I'm nothing, if I'm not crazy for the girl
She's everything I need
And there's nothing I'd refuse her in the whole wide world
She's everything, ain't it somethin'
I'll do anything to keep comin' home to my girl, cause…
She's everything, and I'm nothing without her

What we have here is a love song with vivid imagery and fully realized characters—not just a vapid ditty about a couple of saps fawning and drooling over each other.

Excellent work, my friend! Now we can return to our trusted comrades-in-critique with a finished piece we're pretty sure is vastly improved, while retaining all of the substance and appeal of our first draft.

≈   ≈   ≈

Our next re-write looks like it's gonna be substantially more labor-intensive. *Goin' Down Swingin'*, the peppy boy-meets-girl-in-a-bar tale I was once so confident about, has revealed itself to be somewhat of a mind-boggling puzzle. Our little melodrama has left our listeners without a hero to cheer for, and no villain to hiss. As a result, although the music gets 'em tapping, and certain lines evoke an amused response, the characters and plot fail to reach out and engage their audience—at least, that's our experience so far. Remember, though, the creative process's the one thing we, as writers, have any control over. So let's give it the old college try, dig in and figure out this Rubik's Cube of a song.

Once again, we lend our ears to our work-tape, recorded at the end of last week's writing session:

Her legs stretched from Dallas to Houston and back
I ordered two longnecks and sat down to chat
I said, "I've never seen you 'round Waco before"
She said, "I'm new in town, Honey. Name's Sally, what's yours?"

Then I saw the rock she was wearin' on her left hand
And over Sally's shoulder stood a very tall, strong, and angry man,
yeah...

Sally left Billy back in San Antone
He was past tense, 'least that was what she was thinkin'
But Billy is a boy with a jealous bone
If Billy's goin' down, Billy's goin' down swingin'

Just when I thought I'd have some hell to pay
He asked her to dance, I didn't stand in his way
His sneer told me that he'd just soon I was dead
They were cuttin' up the hardwood, like Ginger and Fred

My eyes scanned the room for the nearest exit sign
Was thinkin' I got lucky once, I'd better beat it while my life is still mine

Sally left Billy back in San Antone
He was past tense, 'least that was what she was thinkin'
But out there on the floor, the boy's right at home
If Billy's goin' down, Billy's goin' down swingin'

A piece of ice on the dancin' floor
That boy's not dancin' anymore
I gave 'em a ride to the emergency room
Now I'm holdin' Sally's hand sayin' he'll be good as new

Makin' Stuff Up

Sally left Billy back in San Antone
He was past tense, 'least that was what she was thinkin'
Now Billy's in a cast drivin' home alone
Headin' straight south in his '05 Lincoln
If Billy's goin' down, Billy's goin' down swingin'
Singin' along with the radio
If Billy's goin' down, Billy's goin' down swingin'
Guess who's got a date with Sally-o

Ain't a lick wrong with our first verse and chorus. The situation's clear, the imagery strong, and the three main characters have been introduced—our long-gammed *femme fatale*, the cruisin' cowboy narrator *and* his menacing nemesis. The alluring Sally left anger-challenged Billy—so perhaps we're safe to presume the dude's got some (as yet unrevealed) very negative qualities.

Our second verse will need to point out some of these character flaws. Otherwise, that engagement ring on her left hand makes the girl out to be a diamond-thief, while simultaneously casting the guy who should be the scoundrel (Billy) as the ironic victim of the story.

Although I still quite like how the meaning of our icon-phrase (*Billy's goin' down swingin'*) morphs from *fightin'* to *dancin'*, we decide that Billy Boy needs to get more aggressive with our singer. And we can save the second meaning by having Sally save her new suitor from inevitable conflict, by pulling her caveman ex- onto the dance floor. That would get Billy scootin' his boots (*swingin'*, as 'twere), and makes Sally somewhat of a heroine for creatively keeping the peace.

We also surmise that any singer who might consider singing this tune is probably not gonna feel real comfortable coming off as a coward, slinking off into the Waco night to avoid fisticuffs. So we give him a chance to show that he's willing to stand up for himself.

A rewritten verse two:

Billy's beady brown eyes were seein' red
And his sneer told me that he'd just soon I was dead
I doubled up my fists and said, "Let's take it outside"
Just then, Sally took his hand, sayin' "Billy, not tonight!"

'N' they were cuttin' up the hardwood, boy that pair could dance
Billy still wearin' that smirk that told me I had no chance

Note that we kept two phrases from our first draft. Writing a song can often be like assembling a puzzle. When you're stalled or trapped, desperately searching for a rhyme, seemingly at a loss as to where to go next, it's not a bad idea to consider re-ordering the lines or phrases to create fresh opportunities. The passage, *his sneer told me that he'd just soon I was dead*, is fraught with overt meaning, with its crystal-clear, visual, and nuanced subtext. It helps paint a picture of Billy's snarling aggressiveness, while simultaneously reinforcing his role as Archenemy Number-One. We retain that line, 'cause it's a goodie.

Excellent re-writing of our second verse. We've clearly established who the bad guy is. We've given our singer a chance to demonstrate that he's no shrinking violet, and the girl's shown a certain altruistic willingness to maintain a level of serenity.

We'd left that one alternative line-three in our second chorus as a space-filler, knowing that we'd probably re-address that one later on:

But out there on the floor, the boy's right at home

A few mornings ago, I woke up with an improved line resounding in my obsessive brain:

But Billy brought some real slick moves from home

This line's not only more visual, it's more singable. The re-write is craftier, too, as it places the name, Billy, in the exact same spot it inhabited in the same spot of chorus one—*But Billy was a boy with a jealous bone*. (Remember, when altering lines in second and third choruses, it's a good idea to try to keep as much language from the original chorus as you possibly can. Paying attention to details like this will make for a hookier, more sing-alongable end result.)

Now it's time to tackle the bridge. Here, it seems, we arrive at one of those occasional situations where spelling, punctuation, enunciation or sound-alike words have the potential for confusing the listener. Don't forget: the vast majority of folks aren't reading along on a lyric sheet; an unseen comma or apostrophe, or a word pronounced similarly to a very different word can result in some unfortunate misinterpretations.

"You know," you reveal, with a grin that broadcasts an approaching naughty punch-line, "when I played our work-tape for a couple of my friends, they kind of misunderstood the first line of the bridge—and not in a good way."

Makin' Stuff Up

The bridge, as it stands, opens thusly:

> *A piece of ice on the dancin' floor*
> *That boy's not dancin' anymore*

"Ah, yes," I mumble in amusement, suddenly recognizing the problem, "I can see where there might be a tad bit of confusion."

The word "ice," especially when pronounced in Southern dialect, tends to sound more than a little like another three-letter word—slang one might use in referring to the *derriere* of one of those two-steppin' kids. And since we've preceded the word "ice" with "a piece of," we've certainly set ourselves up for a potentially awkward lyrical misinterpretation. As responsible purveyors of good, wholesome family entertainment, we know this is an issue we'd better address.

The "piece of ice" in question had been a very useful device. We used it to turn dancing Billy into sprawling, injured Billy, which gave a fresh and very literal meaning to our title phrase, *goin' down swingin'*. It's very easy to imagine how, in this bar environment, an errant ice-cube might find its way to the dance floor and underneath Billy's boot. It's a shame that we have to sacrifice this perfect image but, in the interest of making our plot move ahead with lucidity, that's exactly what we'll have to do. *Don't be afraid to kill your babies.*

Besides, there must be other things that could trip the guy up. A spilled Coke would work ... but this is a bar. Folks drink alcohol in bars. (Not to mention the fact that Coke is dark-colored, making it far less insidious than that slippery, clear, little cube of ice.) Here's what we end up with:

> *A Bud bottle rolled 'cross the dancin' floor*
> *That boy's not dancin' anymore*

This completely believable scenario evokes a rather slapstick image of Billy taking the kind of awkward, slo-mo, extremity-waving tumble that might easily result in the cocky lad ending up in that cast we want to see him wearing in our final chorus to come.

Now we can address Steve Bloch's concerns about our singer being the ambulance driver, shuttling the wounded and humiliated—in more ways than one—Billy (along with the concerned and compassionate Sally) to the hospital. Although I still feel this selfless act gives our central character a bit of true nobility, I can see how it tends to confuse the relationships. If Sally's so anxious to break it off with Billy, why would she tag along to make sure he's all right?

This is the time and place where our girl can make her definitive statement that the relationship is *OVER*. It evidently wasn't enough that she moved to another town to get away from her good-ol'-boy beau. That radical action didn't quite get the message across. Following him to the hospital would definitely give mixed signals. We're gonna let somebody else take Billy for treatment. Meanwhile, our singer, being the big-hearted palooka that he is, stays behind to assuage any residual guilt (or sympathy) Sally might be harboring for her ex- ...

> *They carted him off to the emergency room*
> *While I held Sally's hand, sayin' "He'll be good as new"*

We're in the home-stretch now, with one last chorus and an out-tro to go.

Steve Bloch advised me to make it clear that, as our boy, Billy, motors home to San Antone, he's not happy about the vacant passenger-seat to his right. "If he's crooning along with the radio," he suggested, "at least have the song be something sad. Hank Williams, maybe." (If it's Hank, we'd have to assume that the tune wafting through the speakers was *I'm So Lonesome I Could Cry* or *Your Cheatin' Heart*, not *Honky Tonkin'* or *Jambalaya*.)

It's also quite common to equate traveling south with *goin' down*, as in "goin' down south," so we endeavor to keep that concept in there. Finally, I've been feeling some moral qualms about Miss Sally makin' off with that pricey engagement ring.

With those thoughts in mind, we tweak our final chorus lyric and explanatory tag lines. Here is our (immensely improved) song:

Her legs stretched from Dallas to Houston and back
I ordered two longnecks and sat down to chat
I said, "I've never seen you 'round Waco before"
She said, "I'm new in town, Honey. Name's Sally, what's yours?"

Then I saw the rock she was wearin' on her left hand
And over Sally's shoulder stood a very tall, strong, and angry man,
yeah...

Makin' Stuff Up

Sally left Billy back in San Antone
He was past tense, 'least that was what she was thinkin'
But Billy is a boy with a jealous bone
If Billy's goin' down, Billy's goin' down swingin'

Billy's beady brown eyes were seein' red
And his sneer told me that he'd just soon I was dead
I doubled up my fists and said, "Let's take it outside"
Just then, Sally took his hand, sayin' "Billy, not tonight!"

Soon they were cuttin' up the hardwood, boy that pair could dance
Billy still wearin' that smirk that told me I had no chance

Sally left Billy back in San Antone
He was past tense, 'least that was what she was thinkin'
But Billy brought some real slick moves from home
If Billy's goin' down, Billy's goin' down swingin'

> *A Bud bottle rolled 'cross the dancin' floor*
> *That boy's not dancin' anymore*
> *They carted him off to the emergency room*
> *While I held Sally's hand, sayin' "He'll be good as new"*

Sally left Billy back in San Antone
He was past tense, least that was what she was thinkin'
Now Billy's in a cast, drivin' south alone
Cryin' alligator tears in his '05 Lincoln
Billy's goin' down, goin' down swingin'
(Singin' 'long with Hank on the radio)
Billy's goin' down, goin' down swingin'
(He took his ring back from Sally-o)
Billy's goin' down, goin' down swingin'
(Now I'm scootin' 'cross the dance floor)
Billy's goin' down, goin' down swingin'
(With the girl I didn't even have to fight for)

After another round of taste-testing on our rewrites, we *should* be just about ready to stick a fork in our two new musical tomes and think about demoin' 'em up.

chapter twenty-two: Still Staying Alive

My heart was pounding in my throat as I stood in the foyer of Pasha Studios, unable to believe my own eyes. I re-read the packet of documents that had arrived only minutes before—via courier, in a manila envelope, and addressed to my attention.

"Dear Mr. Bishop," the cover letter from the legal department of Paramount Pictures began, followed by this terse text: "Please initial the enclosed replacement pages from your production contract with RSO Records and return ASAP."

It had been less than two weeks since I'd placed my signature on the original production agreements. The royalty rate, being ridiculously low, was nothing to brag about. After the other artists on the soundtrack LP had taken their chunk, there was barely a forkful of pie left for co-writer/vocalist Tommy Faragher and me, the songwriter/producer. Even so, Faragher and I had felt privileged to officially join that impressive roster and scoop up those remaining crumbs.

We, in fact, had run a treacherous gauntlet to get our song, *(We Dance) So Close To the Fire*, into the most coveted film and soundtrack album of the year, *Staying Alive*—the long-awaited sequel to *Saturday Night Fever*. Since signing that contract, I'd flown back to Oregon to retrieve my stranded car and my anxious dog from the kennel in Newport. The relaxing return cruise southward on Interstate 5 had given me plenty of time to relish the accomplishment. Having heroically pulled off a minor miracle for screenwriter/director Sly Stallone, I felt I had the right to feel pretty dang good about myself.

Now, slack-jawed and stunned, my first thought was that the package I held in my hand was someone's idea of an elaborate, cruel joke; however, my second perusal confirmed that, as illogical as it seemed, this was indeed the real deal. The changed language the Paramount attorneys were expecting me to approve was absolutely inexplicable— and certainly unacceptable to me. I needed some reasonable explanation for this injustice, this travesty, this LIE … spelled out in brusque black and white, demanding my endorsement.

I rubbed my eyes and read it a third time:

Credit for the track, *(We Dance) So Close To the Fire*, performed by Tommy Faragher on the RSO soundtrack LP for the Paramount film, *Staying Alive*, shall read as follows: Produced by Stewart Levine and Randy Bishop.

I picked up the phone and dialed Joel Sill, head of music supervision at Paramount. "Joel," I labored to explain, as I tried to steady my trembling disconcertion, "Stewart Levine did not produce *So Close To the Fire*. I did."

Sill's response to the truth of my statement was as brief as it was disrespectful. "Randy," he said, "I don't want to hear any of your (*insert profanity here*) whining." He then went on to inform me that, should I refuse to approve Levine's production credit, *So Close To the Fire* would be removed from the soon-to-be-released RSO soundtrack LP.

In a panic, I called my lawyer, John T. Frankenheimer, at Loeb and Loeb. "There's nothing you can do, Randy," John said. "They've got you by the shorthairs. If you don't initial those pages, they can take the song off the album."

Flashback to 1977 …

I had just been signed as a staff writer with Irving-Almo Music. My champion there was Almo president Chuck Kaye, a true gentleman and a major player in the world of music publishing. Chuck's half-brother, Joel Sill, one of Almo's professional managers, had (for some unexplained reason) not been supportive of adding me to the company's prestigious writing-staff. Evidently, Joel had carried around a belly-full of resentment for his older, rival half-sibling since they'd grown up together in the household of music-biz legend Lester Sill (Joel's father, Chuck's stepfather).

When I arrived on the Irving-Almo scene, Joel decided to exercise some latent fraternal demons … by taking it out on the starry-eyed, young songwriter his half-bro had decided to put under contract. Unaware of this metastasizing family drama, I was delighted to be in such illustrious company, listed alongside such luminary master-popsters as Paul Williams, Will Jennings and Tom Jans, and I was busy applying myself daily to the task of justifying Chuck's faith in my song-craft.

On one such day, I was shuffling down the Almo hallway, when Joel spontaneously summoned me into his office.

"I just wanted to let you know," he began, his intense, squinted gaze glaring from behind his desk, "I was opposed to signing you."

Naively thinking that maybe Joel was merely daring me to be great, hoping to provide this up-and-comer with additional incentive to prove his initial judgment wrong, I mustered up a feeble smile. But he then proceeded to get down to the real point of this carpet-call.

"I will do anything and everything I can," he continued, "to make sure that you do not succeed at this company."

Indeed, my one year with Irving-Almo ended up not exactly being the most productive *annum* of my career. Was that Joel Sill's fault? Maybe he had something to do with it, but I think my lack of success there was more about the songs I wrote during those 12 months. (Trying so hard to pen material for the commercial market, I lost touch with my own intuition, and turned in some pretty vacuous stuff.)

However, one thing seems certain: Five years later, Joel Sill was still intent on sticking it to Randy Bishop. After the seven-and-a-half minute version of *So Close To the Fire* Tommy and I had bled for had been mixed into the film—and a week before that manila envelope of misery arrived at Pasha—Sill had given me a call.

"Randy," my old nemesis announced, with a tone that dripped condescension from every syllable, "we're planning to mix the *Staying Alive* album digitally. (*This was 1983, by the way, when digital audio was just becoming mainstream.*) I know you've never mixed in digital, so I'm bringing in my buddy, Stewart Levine, to help you out."

My heart, still tender from my recent hired/fired/hired-again jerk-around from director Sylvester Stallone, was immediately filled with trepidation over this vote of non-confidence. Under these tenuous circumstances, however, I decided it was best to pretend gratitude. I swallowed my first response, and thanked Joel for his "generous" offer of Levine's assistance.

Production vet Levine was known for his work with the Jazz Crusaders and BB King, among others. The tall, convivial producer requested that we send over the two-inch, multi-track masters to Ocean Way Studios for the mix. Tommy Faragher and I gave Levine a respectful couple of hours to get familiar with the tracks. Then we showed up, for the purpose of contributing our requisite two cents to the process—only to discover that the previously affable Levine was intent on barring us from the control-room.

Like two expectant fathers from an earlier decade, Tommy and I waited in the Ocean Way lounge, drinking bad coffee, channel-surfing and shootin' the breeze, waiting for permission to view the offspring we'd struggled so mightily to conceive and birth over that previous month. We mulled over those intruding, daily visits from dilettante "music producer" Stallone, the persistantly uncertain status of our song, and our on-again/off-again creative participation in the *Staying Alive* soundtrack. Now, once again, Faragher and Bishop had been cast overboard into shifting waters, while powers out of our influence toyed with our destinies.

Finally, after a few hours of biding our time, sipping rancid java and ridiculing local news and syndicated game shows, the artist and I were invited into the control room to listen. Halleluiah! It sounded like Levine and his engineer were on the verge of a clean, punchy mix.

And then, a curious bit of serendipity took place. It just so happened that versatile instrumentalist Victor Feldman was playing vibes and percussion in an adjacent studio. I knew Vic—a real gentleman's gentleman, most famous for his tasteful keyboard parts on Steely Dan's records—from his vibe-work on the Nicol and Marsh album I'd produced four years before.

Cockney Londoner Feldman, wearing his trademark Ringo-style, corduroy fisherman's cap, wheeled his tubular bells into our studio. Ten minutes later, Vic had achieved organically the sound that had stolen days of our time in the struggle to duplicate the instrument's complex textures with synthesizers and samplers.

With a few tweaks, the *So Close* mix was finished. At that point, Stewart Levine again started to get all buddy-buddy with me, as if he'd been there through the trials and tribulations that had led to this unlikely triumph: our little song winning a featured spot in this prestigious film, and a place on its soundtrack album. (Of course, Levine had not crawled through the bowels of Hades with us; he'd merely sat in a dark room for four hours, offering his sage suggestions to a mixing engineer.)

So now here I was, standing in the foyer of my home studio, holding the papers that would give Levine first co-production credit—a designation he clearly had no right to claim. If it had been totally up to me, I would have told Joel Sill and Paramount where they could stick it. The dishonesty and unfairness of this virtual armed robbery sickened me. However, I couldn't risk the possibility of being responsible for Tommy

Faragher not getting his song on the album; my pride and ego were not *that* far out-of-whack. After tossing and turning on it overnight, I called Sill the next morning.

Swallowing hard, I said, "Okay, Joel. I'll initial the pages."

"Okay," he sighed. "Good."

Then I drew my line in the sand. "But ..."

"OH, WHAT IS IT *NOW*?" Sill demanded, with the stern impatience of a man of importance, with much more important things to do.

"Stewart Levine," I reminded him, "has never even been in the same room with the film version of *So Close To the Fire*." (In fact, the lengthy, custom-scoring job that incorporated our song into *Staying Alive*'s climactic scene had been completed and mixed into the movie at least a week *before* Levine even heard the song.)

"Okay. You're right," Sill reluctantly agreed to this obvious piece of information.

"So," I said, "under *NO* circumstances will I approve him receiving any on-screen production credit in the movie."

"You have my word, Randy," Sill promised. "Stewart Levine will not be credited for the film version."

The day of the *Staying Alive* premiere arrived. Tommy Faragher and I pulled up to the storied Chinese Theater in the vintage Mercedes convertible we'd borrowed from Spencer Proffer. With our ladies on our arms, we walked the red carpet into the theater and giddily took our seats for the screening. We elbowed each other every time the film score quoted a lick from our song. Then we gripped our armrests, as the *So Close* intro crescendoed, and snarling, buff, criscoed John Travolta was lowered to the raked Broadway boards in what looked like a wild animal cage from a Tarzan movie.

The extended *Satan's Alley* modern dance sequence was borderline-camp. Stallone had made it even more banal by overlaying the moaning and groaning of the tortured residents of Dante's underworld, and whispers of "Fire!" hissed in devilish voices (*a la* Arthur Brown) while Travolta leapt and spun his way through those replicated blazes.

Along with most everyone in the house that night, I quickly realized it would be highly unlikely that *Staying Alive* would ever approach the success and mass appeal of its predecessor. But my biggest disappointment came as Travolta, portraying chorus-boy-*cum*-Broadway-star Tony Manero, strutted through Times Square to the four-on-the-floor groove of the Bee Gee's title song. The Faragher and Bishop spouses whooped and whistled proudly when, there across the infamous Chinese Theater screen scrolled the words:

(We Dance) So Close To the Fire
Written by Randy Bishop and Tommy Faragher
Performed by Tommy Faragher

Despite the continued enthusiasm of our ladies, though, the next line following those credits placed a cold stone in the pit of my stomach:

Produced by Stewart Levine and Randy Bishop

Paralyzed by resentment and anger, I allowed this unjustified production credit to steal the joy from what should have been a moment of triumph. In fact, the aftertaste of this bitter pill lingered in my mouth for many years to come. My name was up there on the screen—*TWICE*, in fact. No one else on earth, with the possible exception of Joel Sill, cared a lick that another producer's name appeared before mine, or whether or not that other producer had actually earned his designation.

> If I've learned anything since that devastating Chinese Theater movie-premiere night, it's this: We songwriters—indeed, all creative souls—owe it to ourselves to savor every success, to celebrate every bit of recognition, and receive every single honor with gratitude and humility ... as if it were an unexpected gift. Show business offers no guarantees. Success can never be taken for granted. For our work to come to any kind of fruition requires a convergence of many simultaneous factors; thus, actual achievements can often be few and far between. If those rare victories are not appreciated in real time, they will soon slip away, taking the opportunity for experiencing those elusive warm-fuzzies with them.

In January, 1984, when the Grammy Nominations were announced, Tommy Faragher and I were named in a list that included the Brothers Gibb and Sly Stallone's younger, more-musical brother, Frank. Although the songwriters from the sleeper-hit of that year, *Footloose*, took home the statuettes, I still gaze with amused pride at the engraved invitation I received from the Recording Academy, which reads:

"Randy Bishop, Songwriter, has been nominated in the Twenty-Sixth Annual Grammy Awards for: *Staying Alive.*"

An appropriately ironic accolade for a journeyman songwriter, I'd say. The fact that, at that juncture, I'd survived for the better part of 15 years as a professional tunesmith was an accomplishment in and of itself. That I continue to be privileged to apply my craft nearly 25 years later is no less than miraculous.

The ultra-talented Bee Gees, of course, had re-invented themselves in the international public eye at least three times over, in order to achieve the apex of their success during the disco era of the late-'70s. The gifted, prolific trio from Down Under was certainly more than deserving of this Grammy recognition (or any other honor they might receive, for that matter).

Frank Stallone, a man who doesn't lack for talent, might have had a bit of a leg-up with his older sibling, the screenwriter/director (*Ya think?*). Brother Stallone had the only non-Bee Gee hit from the movie, with the top-five rocker, *Far From Over*. Tommy Faragher and I were lucky enough to have been in the right place with the right song. And we had, against all odds, with bull-headed fortitude, endured the brutal Hollywood movie-studio fire-walk to be included on that exclusive, enviable list.

About a year later, after finishing my obligatory schmooze at a tony Tinsel Town charity event, I was standing at the curb waiting for the valet to return with my car. As I chuckled to myself over some clever punch-line from Jay Leno's just completed stand-up routine, a stretch limo pulled up, nearly clipping the toes of my shoes.

I took a long, quick stride back, as the chauffer swung open the rear door. Out stepped a pair of stunning, leggy models, barely-dressed to the nines. Then, who should emerge from the Caddie but … Frank Stallone. He did the Hugh Hefner bit, dwarfed as he stepped between his dates, linking arms with the two gorgeous Amazons. Heads high, the striking threesome began to strut toward the entrance gate of the outdoor venue.

"Hey, Frank," I called out. He turned his head, obviously enjoying the recognition, especially at this particularly conspicuous moment in time. "Looks like you're doin' okay."

As he and his escorts continued their six-legged walk, on the way to make a dramatic, stylishly late entrance, Sly Stallone's little brother tossed the following remark over his shoulder:

"You just gotta write a few more hits, Rand. Just a few more hits."

chapter twenty-three: Alternative Structures

So far, we've stuck to the shape utilized most commonly in contemporary song-craft: verse-chorus-verse-chorus-bridge-chorus (ABABCB). As I'm sure you know, though, there are a number of alternatives to the standard ABABCB operating procedure. (The earliest standards in the pop lexicon, for instance, were written using a very different template.) Any decent book on tunesmithing should devote at least a few pages to some of these other options. So, here we go.

Early pop songs

Flashing way, way back through those *Waynes' World* wiggly fingers to the earliest American pop songs—classics composed in the 1920s, '30s,'40s ... and even into the early-'50s—we discover that songwriters constructed most of their tunes by following this basic design:

First came a single verse, most often sung in free time (recitative). This section functioned to introduce a series of choruses, each of which had a slightly altered (more likely, a completely different) lyric, sung on the same chorus melody. A bridge-section was inserted at some strategic point (usually after the second chorus), to be followed by a final chorus (usually a repeat of the first), and often including a tag or coda section. This structure could be classified as ABBCB+ (the '+' being the tag).

Over the years, the introductory verse-sections from even the most recognizable titles were commonly omitted from recordings and performances (*Get to the hook, Frankie!*). So these jewels have nearly all been cast aside, and thus our recollection of the great pop classics from those decades seldom includes their verses. Those songs are now almost always rendered as *chorus-chorus-bridge-chorus-tag/coda*, and out: BBCB+.

Since we tend not to recall that there ever *were* actual verses to most of those great songs, you and I are now tempted to refer to what were originally intended to be choruses as verses—because they now function structurally more in a verse-like capacity. As confusing as it might seem, most of us contemporary songwriters would probably now categorize these structures as *verse-verse-bridge-verse-tag* and out (or AABA+), even though technically they are BBCB+, the "A" section having gone the way of the extinct Caribbean monk seal.

Evergreen standards like *Somewhere Over the Rainbow*, *As Time Goes By* and *What'll I Do* all originally kicked off with verses, which only those of extremely advanced age and excellent long-term memory (or die-hard historians of the classic pop repertoire) would even recognize.

In sprightly numbers like *You're The Top* and *It's Delightful*, the inimitable Cole Porter-penned verses, confessing (with false modesty) the writer's inadequacy to express the emotions he was actually fixin' to express—quite brilliantly, of course—in his upcoming choruses. He spoke to the love-object of the evening from the point of view of a befuddled wordsmith (*At words poetic / I'm so pathetic*[xxxvi]), while occasionally coining such ingenious tongue-in-cheek phraseology as *Tin Pan-tithesis*[xxxvii].

Those old verses made for some delightfully creative and playful language. However, like the *Dead Sea Scrolls*, they sadly gather dust, ignored and seldom appreciated.

Chorus-first songs

And so these great-American, chorus-laden classics were our nation's soundtrack until the mid-1950s. It was then that a genre of music (branded by Cleveland disc jockey Alan Freed with the tag "Rock and Roll") unexpectedly hijacked the AM airwaves. This new phenomenon brought with it a plethora of popular songs that were basically all-chorus, all-of-the-time.

Lieber and Stoller's *Hound Dog* is a perfect example of the simple all-chorus type of structure. It begins with the chorus (*what else?*), which is followed by something some might call a verse—but it's really just an alternative chorus with the exact same chord-changes and melody. Both sections end with the identical line, *You ain't never caught a rabbit, and you ain't no friend of mine*[xxxviii].

Makin' Stuff Up

Through the years, many hit songs have commenced with the chorus. *Louie, Louie* comes to mind. In Richard Berry's harrowing tale of what a guy is willing to do to reacquaint himself with his lady love, the singer starts off by regaling his titular pal, with the refrain *me gotta go*. The first verse that follows begins to explain why this departure is so critical. There's *a fine little woman* waiting for our lonely crooner.

Even though the verses to *Louie, Louie* are sung over the same 1-4-5 chord-changes (which also make up the foundation of the chorus), they accompany a completely different melody and phrasing. Unlike *Hound Dog*, Berry's epic rocker is actually a *chorus-verse-chorus-verse-chorus*, etc. structure—BABABABB.

Starting a song with the chorus can be a big temptation. This technique offers the distinct advantage of grabbing your audience from the get-go with the song's hookiest stuff. However, there are challenges built into this concept: For one thing, a chorus can only successfully begin a song if it can stand alone and doesn't require a set-up. In most contemporary pop songs, the chorus relies on information supplied by a previous verse. That more common kind of chorus only really pays off if its listeners know some important things about the concept of the song, its characters and their situation.

For example, it wouldn't have worked all that well for Bob Dylan to begin his classic folk standard with *The answer, my friend, is blowin' in the wind*[xxxix]… Maybe Alex Trebek might have written it that way, but not Bobby Zimmerman. In order to fulfill its role as *the answer,* my friend, Dylan's chorus required that he pose the infamous list of *how manys* that make up each of the song's verses.

A chorus—or at least the icon-phrase within the chorus—often functions very much like the punch-line to a well-constructed joke. You wouldn't tell a humorous anecdote backwards, expecting to get the same laugh. By revealing the zinger before the set-up, you'd be taking the zing right out of it. By the same token, you wouldn't want to sacrifice the impact of a chorus that naturally soars off the ideally angled verse-ramp that launches it.

But what if you *have* written a very catchy chorus, one that functions quite well on its own, thus making it logical to open your new song with it?

Okay, you're thinking, *this chorus makes for an extremely hooky beginning,* and so you commit yourself to trying a chorus-first structure. You soon realize that you're also gonna need some super-special verses, in order for them to be noticed after and between these stunning, impactful choruses. Now you labor over those words and that melody, taking great care to make your stanzas either extra-clever or particularly poignant—whichever the song calls for.

Then, after penning two verse-sections of which you're justifiably proud, you play the tune through. Here's the next thing you're likely to discover: at the end of your precisely crafted second verse, the chorus that sounded so fresh and delightful the first and second times around … now seems stale and over-used when it begins its third jog around the track. It's a structural thing. You're in serious danger of losing momentum—and of giving your listeners a case of chorus-fatigue.

Where do I go from here? you ponder. One idea is to follow the second verse with an extremely truncated chorus—probably one that goes right to your icon-phrase—then on to an instrumental section, or a bridge.

With your song starting on its chorus, it takes some extra thought to make it compelling from beginning to end. That's one very good reason why we tend to return to the old, reliable ABABCB structure over and over again: it nearly always works without too much extra calculation. However, with a modicum of savvy and a willingness to experiment, you can usually find a way to make a chorus-first song work, too.

Chorusless songs

Another very common alternative song form is *the verse-verse-bridge-verse,* AABA shape. These chorusless songs can often be tidy and graceful, but require consummate skill to provide them with adequate hookiness for your listener to hang onto.

An elegant example of this template is Hugh Prestwood's absolutely flawless *The Song Remembers When.* The songwriter's simple "yesterday" verses hover over three basic chords, adhering to six and seven-syllable phrases written with vibrant imagery, within a rich, melodic mode that builds steadily to each stanza's climax, and ultimately to the painful truth of the song's icon-phrase.

With precise timing, after two, vividly drawn verse-refrain sections, Prestwood frees the musical confines from those three chords with his bridge—offering the late-arriving 6-minor and the 2-chord in their first appearances. Meanwhile, the bridge-lyric waxes philosophical about lessons learned from past heartbreak.

Makin' Stuff Up

The final verse then has our singer moving on with her life, while reminding herself, *even if the whole world has forgotten, the song remembers when*[xl]. All it takes is a single repeat of that final refrain, and Prestwood has accomplished a seamless and perfect song.

Lennon and McCartney often utilized the AABA template, as exemplified by one of their earliest smash hits, *I Saw Her Standing There*. If there's a more impeccably composed pop ditty, I don't know what it is. From its *Some Enchanted Evening* concept (with the singer captivated by that comely stranger across a crowded room) to its detailed description of the stages of falling helplessly in love-at-first-sight with her, this song hits its every single note directly on its shiny little head.

Could there be a more intriguing or a more descriptive opening phrase than *She was just seventeen*[xli]...? Are we not immediately dying to know more about this girl, and learn why these lads have chosen to write a song about her and render it with such exuberance? The simplicity and universality of the lyric, added to the passion of the performance, amounts to a virtual replication of the experience itself.

The early Beatles' songs sang of young love with such desperate authenticity that every teen and pre-teen on the planet could easily relate. That's the main reason why the Fab Four captured the hearts of the world: They connected to their core audience—big time!

Never forget that we are communicators. We may desire to be perceived as mysterious and artsy, with our work provoking in-depth analysis of its nuances and obscurities, and garnering respect from tastemakers and critics. In the long run, though, our songs need to say something that resonates with our listeners, something that strikes an organic, authentic bond with them.

There have been many trends and styles throughout the history of visual art: from realism to expressionism; from the romantics to the impressionists, da-daists and modernists. However, there's one common factor in the best of these works that has sustained public interest, sometimes for centuries—they all make people *feel* something. Our songs, like those great pieces of art, exist for one reason only: to provoke and inspire an emotional response.

What could be more fundamental to the visceral experience of life than to feel your heart go boom as you cross a room on your way to hold a girl's hand for the first time? Two young Liverpudlians named John and Paul understood that and applied that understanding to their song-craft. (The "quiet one," George, was no slouch either.) Meanwhile, all of our lives have been incrementally enriched because those creative fellahs shared those youthful passions with us—in song.

I Saw Her Standing There (a basic, straight-forward, and seemingly banal boy-meets-girl story) transcends the insipid, ho-hum predictability of the thousands of songs that cover similar thematic territory. There have been millions of paintings of pretty girls, but there's only one *Mona Lisa*. Simple and direct, yet a masterpiece all the same.

I feel compelled to mention another absolutely flawless *tour de force* that was composed in the AABA structure. I'm often asked the question, "What is your favorite love song?" I've named a few in this book— mostly rip-your-heart-out sad ones like *Just Once*, *Yesterday*, *What'll I Do* and *I Can't Make You Love Me*. As I'm sure you recall, I've also strongly suggested (and more than "just once") that positive, devotional love songs are tough to write without falling into the vapidity of tiresome, worn-out, Hallmark clichés.

My response to the "favorite love song" query is usually met with bemused shock. In my opinion, James Brown distilled his devotional testimony of true and lasting love to its purest and most potent essence in his funk masterwork, *I Feel Good*. Yeah, go ahead and laugh; then, when you're finished with your chortling, think about it.

I Feel Good contains not a wasted syllable, not a single note that doesn't bear powerful witness to the absolute ecstasy of finding and holding onto that one and only love of a lifetime. In its sheer directness, emotional truth and absolute commitment, *I Feel Good* could possibly be the greatest love song ever written.

Seemingly random structures

Some songs seem to have no shape or structure at all. Yet, for whatever reason, they meander their paths through their various, sometimes indefinable sections, in a way that makes absolute sense to our ears.

In 2001, David Ball, one of contemporary country music's best and most distinctive voices, had a career-revival with a song entitled *Riding with Private Malone*. I remember running into my friend, Thom Shepherd, one afternoon at the Hillsboro Village post office (37212, "the hip zip"). I was happy that day to boast that Toby Keith's recording of *My List* was in the can, and that it was scheduled as the third single from his current DreamWorks CD, *Pull My Chain*.

Makin' Stuff Up

"I've got a single coming out, too," Thom grinned proudly.

A perennially upbeat young fellow, with an irresistible Opie Taylor-like charm, Shepherd seemed overly optimistic about the chances of his independent release, by an artist who hadn't seen the top-five in nearly ten years. Sure enough, *Private Malone*, a record with a nostalgic '70s flavor, of a song that seemed to have little or no evident, innate structure, climbed all the way to Number Two, and remained a country-radio stalwart for many months.

The success of this recording has everything to do with the song's powerful concept, great storytelling by co-writers Shepherd and Wood Newton ... and an excellent performance by a distinquished song stylist, David Ball.

I'm Not In Love is one of the most textural and exquisite productions in the history of pop music. In 1975, seemingly overnight, the single—by a floundering UK group called 10CC—was suddenly blasting from every radio speaker on the planet. Blending the art-rock sensibilities of band members Kevin Godley and Lol Creme with the pop song-craft of Graham Gouldman and Eric Stewart, *I'm Not In Love* resulted in a mishmash of beauteous, yet seemingly unrelated song-segments that amount to Picasso-esque pop impressionism.

Graham Gouldman began his impressive career as a teenaged, second-generation tunesmith. By his 21st birthday, he had been credited with no less than five million-selling hits, including *For Your Love* and *Heart Full of Soul* by the Yardbirds, *Bus Stop* and *Look Through Any Window* by the Hollies and *No Milk Today* by Hermit's Hermits. He then went on to a Stateside stint, writing bubblegum songs for such groups as Ohio Express, before returning to the UK to join with Godley, Creme and Stewart to complete the foursome that eventually became known as 10CC.

(I habitually quote the first verse of Gouldman's Hollies smash, *Bus Stop*, as perhaps the finest example of concise lyric-writing in the last half-century. In a series of two- and four-word phrases, each painting its own clearly defined picture, this gifted song-scribe (then a pimply faced adolescent) wove the boy-meets-girl-while-waiting-in-the-rain-for-public-transportation tale. In the 28 well-chosen syllables that make up verse one, we see clearly how a shared umbrella began a shared life. Talk about Haiku! *Bus Stop* is a masterfully composed lyric, one that's definitely worth studying.)

Makin' Stuff Up

Back to *I'm Not In Love*, the epic pop-classic Gouldman penned with 10CC bandmate, Eric Stewart. The composition begins with what could liberally be called a chorus, as it's certainly the song's most memorable section and both commences and closes with the composition's plaintive icon-phrase.

Melodically, the second section is the mirror-image of the first, but it saves the hook for its final line. These first two puzzle-pieces thus function very much like choruses from a traditional standard (*sans* verse) from the '30s or '40s.

What makes these segments unique is that they are intentionally incomplete, with both ending with a dangling statement: *I'm not in love, just because...*[xlii] This has the dramatic effect of articulating the emotional ambivalence of the singer. Although he's adamantly denying that he has fallen for the girl, the actions he describes demonstrate a very different reality altogether.

The song then drifts into a 45-second, dreamlike, musical pastiche, interwoven with spoken word—specifically, a seductive, female voice whispering, *Be quiet. Big boys don't cry*[xliii]. You couldn't exactly call this piece a bridge, yet it acts bridge-like, in that it breaks away from the mode established by the choruses that precede it. Then the song returns to a third "chorus" that, like the second, saves the hook for its final line.

The song is now a full three minutes and twenty seconds long. By common standards of contemporary song structure, it would now have said everything it had to say and well into its fade. Yet, even as long in the tooth as this one has grown, it dares to introduce yet another section—a piece equally as hooky as its chorus. We might call this tardy part the bridge; it begins with the ironic statement, *Ooooh, you'll wait a long time for me*[xliv].

One final chorus completes the composition—lyrically identical to the first, except that it repeats the title line at its end for emphasis, this time without the incomplete, dangling *just because*. By now, this medley of disparate song-segments has surpassed 4:30, but that doesn't stop the art-rockers from indulging in a mosaic of sound and falsetto *Ba-ba-ba-ba's* for another 90 seconds, thus making this single recording linger on for more than six minutes in total.

Even with its odd shape and exceptional length, though, *I'm Not In Love* was an international smash and, for that year at least, 10CC was deservedly recognized worldwide as the hippest creative force in pop music.

Makin' Stuff Up

Another debut single had comparable commercial impact to *I'm Not In Love*, was nearly its equal in length and used an even more peculiar configuration: Queen's operatic rock opus, *Bohemian Rhapsody*. Beginning with a minute-long, introductory choral prelude of sorts, the song, despite its macabre lyrical theme, then settles into two minutes of a rather traditional sounding ballad, as the condemned singer/murderer confesses his crime and bids a regretful farewell to his mother. Then, after a guitar solo interrupts in middle of the second verse of this song-within-a-song, the rambling behemoth unpredictably takes on new guises at each twist and turn as it powers its way to its conclusion.

There's no way to map this song's structure alphabetically, or with any terminology that could normally be used to describe a pop tune. Its shape is absolutely inexplicable. Yet, because of the sheer magnificence of its composition, the obvious genius of the artists and the *tour de force* of Roy Thomas Baker's production, this oddly constructed work became a career-launching single for one of rock's greatest bands.

The prolific songwriting team of composer Burt Bacharach and lyricist Hal David were responsible for some of the most recognizable copyrights to emerge over the last 50-some years. *Walk On By*; *Make It Easy On Yourself*; *Raindrops Keep Fallin' On My Head*; *A House Is Not a Home*; *Wishin' and Hopin'*; *What the World Needs Now*; *Close To You*; *What's New, Pussycat?*; *The Look of Love*. My Lord in Heaven! These are only a few of the chart-topping songs these guys made up together since their earliest success—with *Beach Blanket Bingo*, no less.

Over their lengthy collaborative partnership, Bacharach and David explored nearly every possible song-structure known to modern music. *What the World Needs Now* is a chorus-first song, bridgeless, with an unforgettable tag full of memorable refrains at its end. *Walk On By* offers a unique two-line verse that segues gracefully into its chorus and refrain, repeating the shape again before its instrumental break and a bridge-like chorus with background vocals repeating the two-syllable phrase, *Don't stop*.

It's amazing, when you study this duo's body of work, how hooky every single section of every single song is. You almost can't differentiate among their verses, their choruses and their bridges. They're just songs, very singable songs, unforgettable songs, poignant and playful, with incredible melodies and imaginative language. Meanwhile, every one of these tunes has been recorded, time and time again, by many of the biggest stars of the last several generations of pop music.

One of the oddest compositions in the Bacharach/David catalogue was custom-penned as the theme-song for a major feature film. It begins by asking the provocative musical question, *what's it all about? Alfie* is as thoughtful, as delicate and as dynamic as a ballad could ever be. When you take a closer look at its construction, though, it doesn't seem to make much sense at all.

At first listen, *Alfie* sounds like a simple *verse-verse-bridge-verse-tag* structure. On closer examination, though, there are such subtle nuances within each section (and between them), along with such curious dissonances in its melody, that it's wild to think the song not only became a standard, but has sustained its popularity for over 40 years. It's a tribute to the eternal, universal questions posed by Hal David's lyric that Bacharach's adventuresome musical safari doesn't abandon us along the way. *Alfie* is the work of a very mature partnership between two master songwriters.

When listening to these four examples of structural rule-breaking, I'm awed by the inspiration and craft of the writers. I could name many more bizarrely constructed hit songs: Patrick Simmons' *Black Water* (recorded by his band, the Doobie Brothers) and Paul McCartney's *Hands Across the Water/Admiral Halsey* are two more examples. I'd also be remiss if I failed to mention that strange epic-journey, *American Pie*, by Don McLean.

However, in most cases, I'd offer this piece professional advise: *DON'T TRY THIS AT HOME, boys and girls*. You're better off working within more familiar, traditional templates while developing your song-craft. Then, after you've written a few hundred soundly structured songs, and you're beginning to grow bored, feeling like you're re-trekking over all-too-familiar territory, it might just be the right time to wander off into the wilderness. However, don't be surprised if you get completely lost and can't find your way home again—while losing your audience at the same time.

Anyway, consider yourself warned!

chapter twenty-four: A Song About Nothing

By the summer of 1983, I was approaching my mid-30s and transitioning from singer/songwriter to full-time songwriter/producer. The last of my major-label albums, *Dangerous Infatuation*, had been issued to a less than spectacular response—partially due to the nearly simultaneous release of Pasha labelmates Quiet Riot's debut disc, *Metal Health*, which garnered saturation airplay and multi-platinum sales.

While QR was screaming new hope into the careers of hard-rock hair-bands all over the world, their phenomenal success eclipsed my swan-song LP with the darkness of a nuclear winter.

I had first partnered with Spencer Proffer when he produced my A&M singles in 1976. Over the six years that followed, in addition to recording my own project, I'd worked on and off with the gregarious, multi-talented, entrepreneurial dynamo in several utility capacities—background vocalist, songwriter and co-producer. Now, as headman at his own Pasha/Epic Records, Spencer brought me in to write songs for a film-soundtrack project: an *Animal House* spin-off called *Up the Creek*.

Proffer pulled off a major coup for his Pasha imprint, enlisting the Beach Boys, Cheap Trick, Heart and Mott The Hoople's Ian Hunter to gather at his studio for the purpose of recording custom-sides for the film under his production.

As every single Beach Boy had his own personal manager *and* attorney, inking the band for the album and soundtrack was a smidge more challenging than negotiating the Camp David Accords—with Proffer stoically playing the Jimmy Carter role, and a dozen Begins and Sadats to bring to the table and somehow mollify. Against all odds, just like our ex-president from Georgia, Spencer miraculously pulled off the deal.

A year before, impressed with my songwriting and "associate production" work with Peter Noone, Beach Boy Bruce Johnston had taken it upon himself to suggest to his rather weary bandmates that they could make use of some fresh creative blood—specifically me, a lad with songwriting, vocal, rhythm guitar *and* production skills. I recall that first, brief visit with Johnston and his ensemble as if it was a bizarre, Technicolor dream borne of a treacherously high fever.

I arrived at Rumbo Recorders—Dennis "The Captain" Dragon's North Hollywood facility—in the middle of a potentially momentous session. The psychotic genius himself, Brian Wilson, had emerged from self-imposed exile, and was—for the first time in years—producing a Beach Boys song. He and his engineer were closing in on the finished mix of a brand-new Wilson original. Brian sat hulked over the console, making miniscule moves with the faders, while a dozen doting hangers-on lined the control room, all crossing fingers and toes in hopes that the great musical wizard was at long last returning to form.

The playback of *Sweetie* revealed a simplistic, ice-cream-chord ditty that had a distinct resemblance to The Zodiacs' classic chestnut, *Stay*. After shyly acknowledging the applause of his devoted audience, Wilson then launched into an intense confab with the mixing engineer as to how the *Sweetie* master-tape might be delivered to the record company with the greatest possible security.

Evidently, Brian was deeply concerned that this historic recording might fall into enemy hands. So he came to the only reasonable conclusion: he himself would personally courier the mix to label headquarters, and make sure it was locked away in a vault. Tucking the tape-box under his arm, Wilson rose from the producer's chair and turned to the kibitzers in the room.

Standing in full view of one and all, at well over six feet, Wilson's massive belly, matted, greasy hair and unclipped, filthy fingernails made him look like a giant, over-inflated Howard Hughes—on a *bad* day. He then proceeded to go around the room, looking deeply into each person's eyes, one at a time, repeating the same statement and follow-up question, in a strange, Yosemite-Sam lisp, his face contorted as if he'd suffered a paralizing stroke.

"I love Ssshhweetie," Wilson slurred out of one side of his mouth, "... do you love Ssshhweetie?"

He even broached the identical query to his German shepherd, who responded with some favorable, enthusiastic tail-wags and an affectionate lick on Wilson's face.

As it turned out, original member Mike Love had another candidate in mind for the guitarist/singer role, and Love pulled seniority on

Johnston. Actually relieved I would not be asked to fly into this cuckoo's nest, I had thanked Bruce for considering me for the job.

Now, a year later, an equally bizarre adventure awaited me—around the bend, and up a fateful creek.

Being bright and savvy in the ways of building value in a song catalogue—and being my publisher after all—Spencer Proffer offered several Randy Bishop demos for the Beach Boys to consider for their *Up the Creek* contribution.

Emily, I was an extremely personal piece, a song I'd written for my first daughter as a promise that I would always be there for her—despite my contentious divorce from her mother. In making their song selection for the soundtrack, the B Boys had other ideas. The band loved *Emily, I*'s blithe spirit and lilting melody—but they requested a complete lyric rewrite. In fact, they asked that the new lyric be (I'm quoting here) "about nothing."

It's not at all difficult to understand why a very specific and intimate daddy-daughter message might not be a perfect fit for the Beach Boys, *nor* a great candidate for the soundtrack of a sophomoric, frat-party-on-the-rapids romp. I'll also bet there's not a songwriter on earth who wouldn't at least be tempted to take a stab at fulfilling the needs of one of rock's most celebrated combos—even though it might mean the deconstruction of an important communiqué from parent to child.

I was *more* than tempted. I jettisoned those original words without so much as a second thought, replacing the original title with the innocuous phrase, *Chasin' the Sky*.

A Beach Boys cut? Are you kidding me? That's an achievement of a lifetime for ANY tunesmith!

The Beach Boys *Up The Creek* recording sessions amounted to a *Loony Tunes* marathon from the get-go. Brian Wilson was still easing back into the fold, emerging gradually from mental illness and drug dependency. Now a great deal more slender and hygienically presentable, Brian was on the short leash of Dr. Eugene Landy's infamous 24-hour intervention therapy. Wherever Brian went, his psychotherapist went, too. Wherever Landy went, a posse of good-lookin' young men were never far away. In fact, Landy's ever-present entourage spent most of its time in the Pasha tape-copy room, chopping and snorting lines of white powder.

Landy's boisterous contingent, added to the already extremely eccentric band members—especially a crazed, disheveled Dennis

Wilson, who stumbled in off of Melrose Avenue barefoot for the occasional drop-by—transformed the Pasha building into a veritable asylum of babbling insanity.

After Spencer made the rather dubious decision to bring in the Quiet Riot rhythm section to cut the basic track, *Chasin' the Sky*'s lilt had been beaten to a pulp. The producer then flew to Caribou Ranch in Colorado to record a rather tepid Carl Wilson vocal performance. Finally, a group of singers (Brian Wilson, Al Jardine, Bruce Johnston and me) gathered around a vintage AKG C-24 microphone to sweeten the tune with that inimitable Beach Boys vocal-blend.

By this time, I'd sung on at least a hundred background sessions. I was more than aware that studio-singing requires concentration and stamina, as the group strives to blend, match vibratos, breathe, phrase, crescendo and decrescendo as one harmonious unit. However, as we jammed out our parts on take after take, my fellow vocalists seemed to have little interest in discussing or refining the arrangement.

Someone would mess up. Engineer Duane Baron would stop the tape and roll back. Then Jardine recalled an important detail he suddenly felt compelled to share with Johnston.

"My prize mare is about to foal, Bruce," Al interjected. "Why don't you fly out to Phoenix next week to see the new offspring."

Another flawed take would be followed by a Johnston-to-Jardine *non sequitur*: "Oh, Alan, I talked to my Mercedes dealer the other day, and he said he can make you a great deal on that model you're interested in."

In the meantime, Brian seemed completely distracted by the minutia of this unfamiliar studio, as he stared with rapt curiosity at the pendular C-24.

"That'sh a pretty microphone," Brian lisped out of one side of his mouth in a cartoonish falsetto. "I like that microphone. What kind of microphone ish that?"

Roll tape. Another take. Stop tape. Playback. Brian continued his examination of the cylindrical, gold-plated mic, taking a complete and sudden reversal from his previous assessment.

"I don't like that microphone. Let'sh change the microphone."

Then Mike Love, who seemed to be in attendance only to get Brian's goat, started parading back and forth across the tracking room, his shirt hiked up above his purposefully protruding, air-inflated belly. "I'm on the Landy plan," he chanted. "I'm on the Landy plan."

Makin' Stuff Up

They were like a group of Downs Syndrome kids on a field trip to the recording studio. But somehow, when that very strange day's work was done, *Chasin' the Sky* was beginning to sound just like the Beach Boys.

My daily traversals across town from Hollywood to Westwood to retrieve my daughter, Emily, from day care were special to me. It provided a time for Daddy and daughter to bond in the cocoon of my VW bug. Em was always a smart, clever child with a subtle, wry sense of humor.

"Em, is that house green, or is it *green*?" I'd quiz her.

"Well, Daddy," she'd respond with mock seriousness. "It might be green. *Or…* it *might* be *green*." Then, we'd laugh together over the silliness of our word play, as we crawled along the congested arteries of West Los Angeles.

My daughter and I always stopped to pick up a snack on the way, and we began making up games inspired by various food-items. Cheetos, for example, would magically come to life as misshapen, alien creatures. Em would pretend that one such snacky monster was trying to escape. Capturing it, a sadistic glint would come into her eyes, and she'd open wide and chomp down on the poor, defenseless thing, ferociously biting off its bulbous, orange head.

We received some strange and curious looks from drivers in adjacent cars, as I screamed bloody murder on behalf of those many decapitated Cheeto beasts. Both Daddy and daughter found great delight in this macabre play.

On one particular, sunny, Southern-Cal afternoon, I'd brought along a cassette of the final mix of *Chasin' the Sky*. For whatever inexplicable reason, Em had found surf music irresistible since she was a toddler— especially the early Beach Boys stuff. So I was eagerly anticipating sharing the finished track with her.

"Wanna hear the Beach Boys sing one of Daddy's songs?" I asked. Of course she did. So I obligingly inserted the tape into the player and cranked up the volume. As the tune began, I glanced over at my naturally platinum-blonde child, not quite six, strapped into the passenger bucket, holding an open bag of Cheetos in her lap. The smile of approval I expected to greet me was not forthcoming. She just gazed straight ahead—with no expression.

About the middle of the first chorus, Emily reached out to the cassette player. Without so much as a sidelong glance, she just turned the knob and switched it off. Recognizing the song with its new lyric—now "about nothing"—my daughter didn't care to hear the rest. I had stolen something important from my own child to achieve something monumental in my career. There was no way I could explain to her how that exchange made sense to me. So, we drove on—in silence.

Recently, I mentioned that heartbreaking memory to Emily, now 30, married, and still living in L.A., working as the executive assistant to the head curator of the Museum of Contemporary Art. She had no recollection of the event—or of the song. All these years I'd been carrying around a heavy load of guilt, while my daughter had left the temporary trauma of that afternoon behind long, long ago.

chapter twenty-five: The Demo

O kay. Finally! We've survived the writing process from A to Z, absorbed the feedback and done the rewrites. Everybody seems to be on the same page, agreeing that we've got ourselves a couple of potential smashes here. What do we do now? What the heck good are they unless the rest of the world can hear 'em? (Remember, songs are about communication—on whatever scale possible.)

Yeah, we might-could insert these two gems into the set list at our next writer's night at the Commodore Lounge. However, our ultimate desire is for Mr. and/or Ms. Chart-topper to hear 'em, then cut 'em and make 'em into big ol' hits! We could hardly be expected to schlep around town with our acoustics and play these tunes live for everybody from receptionists to bus drivers, in hopes that some star would overhear one from the next room and jump at the chance.

WE NEED DEMOS! No, we're not just talkin' piano/vocals or guitar/vocals here (although that's a start, and would most definitely be better than nothin'). Stripped down presentations don't cut it anymore, kids. Producers and A&R folks these days wanna hear somethin' that sounds pretty close to a finished record. Both of these songs deserve a full-on production—basically a replication of a real, master recording.

The most direct and obvious way to accomplish this is to book a session at one of the hundreds of Music City project studios currently in the business of crankin' out them demonstration-recordings.

As my dear friend, studio keyboard genius Gordon Mote, puts it, "Hey, let's record it, so we can listen to it later!"

A basic-tracking demo session in Nashville has the potential of being the most joyful experience one could ever have—while keeping one's britches on. Musicians, by nature, are a fun bunch; when they're working, they're using the highly developed talents given to them by a kind and benevolent Creator. So, for the most part, players are grateful for each and every opportunity they get to express themselves through their instruments of choice.

Even if, on any odd day, one of the band isn't feeling so chipper, he or she had better be able to fake it, because the Music City talent-pool is so deep, there's always a genuinely pleasant (and available) picker ready to step in, grin, and do just as good a job—maybe even better. Nashville cats and kittens can't afford to be grouchy or uncooperative. It's not enough to be blessed with scads of innate ability, have great sounding gear, and show up on time. They've gotta be nice, too. This necessity makes for a studio atmosphere that is invariably *good, good, goooood ... good vibrations*.

By the way, "niceness" isn't necessarily a universal attribute shared by all studio musicians. On one album project in Los Angeles—a town well-known for quite a different kind of attitude—I approached the electric guitar player on the date with the suggestion/request that he dial a tad of the distortion from his amplifier settings.

I was the recording artist, so this guitar hero was contributing his talent to *my* record. He, the exceptionally self-satisfied axeman for a genuine superstar's back-up ensemble, was being compensated for his labor at triple-scale—somewhere in the neighborhood of $300 per hour. Despite all that, this was Mr. Cocky's response to my very reasonable and tactful request:

"You hired me. This is my sound. This is what you get."

Even the *crème de la crème* of Nashville's top echelon would never cop that sort of attitude. There are a hundred, equally talented, and much more cooperative guys who covet those master dates. For demo sessions, Music Row players make slightly more than 50 bucks an hour. For that relatively modest reward, they consider themselves members of a service industry, a well-trained wait-staff, poised and ready to bring you whatever delicious morsel you might have a hunger for. If you know what you're after, and are capable of expressing your preferences to these guys and gals, they're invariably willing to provide you with exactly what you ask for—satisfaction guaranteed.

And herein lies the crux. Your demo session can be a fun-filled and productive one, or it can be a stressful ordeal that fails to meet your lofty expectations. This pretty much depends on you. You need to be confident, respectful, decisive ... *AND, YOU NEED TO KNOW HOW TO SPEAK THE LANGUAGE.*

It helps to have some decent songs, too. You'll always get more sincere enthusiasm from the band if they're diggin' the music. These gifted folks spend a great deal of their lives "polishing turds," trying to make third-rate, derivative drivel sound like something competitive. They take notice when they get to play four or five well-composed originals, and they respond by putting a little more of themselves into it. Good tunes make for an infectiously good session.

However, even assuming you've brought in some real gems on this date, you also have to enter the control room completely prepared to speak your mind in a way that communicates clearly and makes sense. In essence, you're the coach, and the band is your team; your songs represent the playbook. Invariably, you're gonna hafta offer a few pointers along the way. If you don't speak up and offer some guidelines, as brilliant as thcsc pickcrs arc, you'll likely be disappointed with the results.

Here is my strong advice: Any chance you get, hang out at recording sessions, keep your eyes and ears open, shut up and *PAY ATTENTION*. Then, take notes and ask questions (politely, humbly and at unobtrusive times). It's critical to have some familiarity with the terminology of number-charts, the sound and role of each instrument in the band and the fundamentals of recording and mixing—including effects (reverb, compression, delay, chorus, etc.), equalization (or "e.q.," boosting or lowering specific frequencies) and panning (placing instruments and voices in the stereo field). If you're able to speak intelligently to the musicians and the engineer, it will go a long way in inspiring their devotion to your music.

I'm not advising you to pretend you know as much or more than the players or the technicians. Attempting to do that would likely make you look like a jackass. Just learn, at the very least, how to express yourself, using at least the bare minimum of legitimate musical and recording-studio vernacular. Then, when you find yourself unable to find the right words, admit it. Don't let yourself get all flustered when the guys fail to get your drift. Put on an endearing smile and confess that you're at a loss.

It always helps if you have comparable songs to which to refer: "You know, like the bridge in *Every Breath You Take*." Your guitarist will probably not only recall that bit of music verbatim, but will have a pre-set on his rack that, with the push of a button, can reproduce its precise color.

Makin' Stuff Up

Suppose you're cutting the first tune of your session. You're in the isolation booth, singing the guide vocal. The engineer has instructed you how to adjust your headphone mix with the "more-me" box. The band does a trial run and, in the phones, your song sounds *all wrong*. It's nothing like you imagined.

Which of the following tacts sounds better to you?

"That's just not right, guys. It's like a million times too slow, and that place in the second verse when I say, 'stop looking at me like that'? You gotta stop, and ..."

OR:

"Okay. We need to pick up the tempo a few BPMs. And, at the third beat of the seventh bar of the second verse, right after the 4-change, we need to hit a stop on the 5, for two beats."

Well, it's obvious. That first bit of coaching is unclear, unmotivating and doesn't speak in language that's helpful to the players. This kind of feedback is unproductive, and only serves to confuse a band whose only goal should be to please you.

The second example of verbal communication is specific, articulate and gives the band exact instructions as to how they can make you, the boss, happy. That again, after all, is what they're there for.

(If you're unwilling or incapable of learning how to express yourself in "studio speak," you'd be well-advised to find someone to produce your demo sessions who has that capability down pat. Then, during the recording process, only communicate your suggestions, concerns and issues through your producer, not directly to the musicians. Only then will you realize that ultimate, joyful studio experience, while achieving the results you desire.)

After all, a demo-session is not, by any stretch of the imagination, an inexpensive proposition. Nashville studio demos are costing, on average, between $600 and $1,500 per song—on the union books, with professional demo singers and mixers. Nevertheless, there's nothing more fulfilling than to have that little song you and your co-writer made up in six or eight hours come to life through the shared musical and technical wizardry of a team of legitimate pros. It's an experience every dedicated songwriter deserves to have—on a regular basis.

However, precisely because of the costs involved and the simple impracticality of doing a full studio-demo for every single song you write (and because every song doesn't actually call for a live band treatment), I'll pass on this next piece of advice:

PURCHASE, AND LEARN TO OPERATE, SOME KIND OF HOME STUDIO.

Okay, you're thinking, *I don't know a thing about recording*; and/or *I don't have the money;* and/or *I don't want to spend my life reading manuals, learning technology, patching cables*, etc.

And I say, "Get over it!"

The last thing I want to hear from any person pursuing a creative life is what they *don't* want to do. Do you want to be a successful songwriter? I presume you have some interest in that particular goal, or you wouldn't be reading this book. So listen up!

The technology available today for home recording is affordable, relatively simple to operate, and enables any and every one of us to come indecipherably close to state-of-the-art recording. There's no reason in the world why, with a bit of gumption and a small investment in cash and time, any writer with half a brain can't learn to make very competitive home demos—not for *every* song, but for a good number of them.

Of course, I've always had the desire to be Paul McCartney or Stevie Wonder, and play and sing all or most of the parts on my recordings. It's my nature. But even if you're not an accomplished musician or vocalist (or at least an adequate one, like me), a home studio of some kind enables you to take a great deal of control over your creative destiny (as well as cutting your demo-expenses to a fraction of that $600 to $1500).

I'll never forget the way my heart palpitated when I first attended a demonstration of one of the first digital workstations, the Fairlight. It had to have been the late-'80s. This miraculous keyboard featured a virtual arsenal of sampled and synthesized sounds—from drums, basses and percussion, to human voices and orchestral instruments. But what made this innovation that much more amazing were the eight tracks of 16-bit digital audio, easily synchronized to the keyboard, for recording real time performances along with your midi-sequenced tracks.

Each audio track required its own hard drive, every one about the size of a medium-sized kitchen-drawer, and every drive ran its own internal fan that made a horrendous noise. In order to take advantage of this combo-workstation/recording-studio, you had to run long, heavy-duty cables to isolate that stack of hard drives in a soundproof space. And all of this, ladies and gentlemen, boys and girls, you could purchase … for around $150,000.

Now, in this new millennium, you can have pretty much everything the Fairlight once offered for—*are you ready?*—less than three grand.

"Three grand?" you protest. "That's a lotta scratch!"

At $600 per tune, the most inexpensive five-song demo session will cost ya 3,000 bucks. If you could do even half of your demos every year in a home environment, this system would pay for itself over and over and over. Not only that, you'd have the advantage of producin' up a whole lot more tunes.

Out of sheer practicality, you (and/or your publisher) have to be pretty discreet as to which songs deserve the studio treatment. Nevertheless, you've probably got a sleeper or two (or twelve) that you're dyin' to demo. Yet, due to the cost factor, you haven't pulled the trigger on those songs. Maybe hiding within that batch is your ticket to the Top Five. How's anybody ever gonna hear that gem—if you never make the demo?

I started to get "Midi-savvy" in the mid-'80s, purchasing a few basic, multi-timbral samplers and synths, a midi interface and a Macintosh Plus, in order to construct basic tracks and arrangements. When I left my staff production/A&R position at Pasha Records in '88, I no longer had free access to a multi-track studio. At first, I invested in a used, cassette-based, four-track Fostex. That served me quite well until I took the leap to a Tascam eight-track. Then, in the mid-'90s, I bought a Roland eight-track, digital, hard-disc recorder, along with an inexpensive tube pre-amp and a decent condenser mic. Today, I run Pro-Tools and have a good selection of microphones, a state-of-the-art pre-amp/compressor-limiter and dozens of virtual instruments.

Here's the deal—from my experience. At every step of the way, from the most rudimentary, cassette-based recordings to the master-quality productions I'm capable of recording today, having a home studio has enabled me to maintain more creative control of my output.

The demo of *My List*, recorded in my attic-studio on a Roland VS 880 hard-disc recorder, didn't cost a cent out of pocket. When Tim James and I wrote the song, I didn't have a publishing deal. Neither did Tim. If I'd had to wait for a publisher to give me permission to demo that song, it might have been forgotten by now. Instead, because I invested in a basic home recording facility, and took the initiative to cobble together the best little home demo I could, *My List* had the opportunity to become a major copyright—a song that, to date, has grossed over two million dollars for its two writers and several publishers.

There are a plethora of choices out there. Yes, it's absolutely overwhelming, I'll admit. Start by networking amongst your songwriting pals. Do research on the Internet. Read reviews. Find a retail outlet in your neck o' the woods with a friendly, knowledgeable, helpful staff. There's somebody on every block of every city and town who has a little recording studio. Introduce yourself and pick brains. Bite the bullet. Take the plunge. You can do it—and somebody somewhere will be more than willing to help.

$$\approx \qquad \approx \qquad \approx$$

As we all know, demos are absolutely critical to our songs having any chance of success. However, even though demos are, to one degree or another, replications of the records we hope might someday be made from our songs, as a rule, a demo is assigned a slightly different mission than a recording made by an artist.

First of all, it is absolutely essential that the demo-singer enunciates every syllable of every word clearly, and that the mix doesn't leave a single lyrical nuance indiscernible upon first-listen. There's nothing more distracting to the appreciation of a song than for a potential customer to be forced to ask, "What was that line?" In the process of inquiring about the missed or misunderstood phrase, at least another falls through the cracks. Now the thread of the story is lost, and this pitch is probably a lost cause.

However, you don't want the singer to sound like he or she is reading from the page. You still want the vocal to sound relaxed and hip, with all the emotional impact called for by your song. So don't go overboard with your insistence on clear enunciation; just make sure folks are gonna understand the words the first time through.

It's common for studio musicians (especially electric guitarists) to offer to overdub multiple parts. Every layer usually sounds as cool or cooler than the pass before, so you always hate to leave any of those parts out of the mix.

However, please remember this: you're not producing a demo to feature any particular musician or exhibit the hippest new sound. You're selling the melody, lyric, emotion, dynamics and/or groove of your song. Mixing requires making choices. A 16-bit, 44.1 sample-rate, stereo WAV file (the digital format stored on CDs) can only capture and contain so much of the sonic spectrum, and the human ear can only absorb so much aural info at any given time. Anything that distracts from the song itself, no matter how cool it may be on its own, should be de-emphasized in the final mix—or removed altogether.

While you want your demo to sound like a big ol' hit song, blastin' out of a car stereo every 90 minutes on every high-wattage Clear Channel station, you also don't want to scare anybody off with the brilliant perfection of the vocal performance and the production. A lot of records fail to match up to the song demos. And a lot of those cuts don't end up getting released—many times because the artist or the label staff ultimately feels insecure about them. You want a great vocal on your demo, but you don't want it to outshine every singer you're about to pitch the song to. After all, "Demo" is short for "demonstration recording"—not "artist master."

I'm not advising you to sing out of tune, or to intentionally insert overt mistakes. Give your customers a great template that suggests a smash copyright—but don't be afraid to leave a raw edge here and there.

You want the artist to be thinking, "That's a great song—but *I* can sing it better than that guy."

You want the producer to be thinking, "That's a surefire hit—but *I* can make a better record on it."

Recording demos can be a heck-of-a-lotta fun. On other days, or in various parts of the process, crafting those suckers can make for tiresome, tedious work. Regardless of the experience of making them, though, demos are absolute necessities. They are the product-samples you and your sales staff will use as you attempt to create commerce with your wares.

The better your demos represent your line of goods, the better opportunity your unique designs will have of getting the greatest exposure. The more exposure your songs get, the better chance any one of them has of finding its way into the recording studio again—next time, hopefully with a major recording artist, or the next burgeoning superstar. Only then will that song have any chance of getting on the radio, of becoming a heavily programmed video and selling a few million copies and downloads.

Makin' Stuff Up

It all begins with writing a great song, but a great demo can make a whole lotta difference. Learning the skills of demoing your songs is of nearly equal importance to your developing the craft of writing them. So apply yourself to the task of refining your demo production, invest the time and energy to learn the vernacular of the recording studio, and put some cash together to finance your own mini-production facility. These efforts will surely pay off in the end. Bottom line, you'll be a more secure and confident songwriter—and, ultimately, a much more successful one as well.

chapter twenty-six: Not So Common Ground

"**R**andy, we've got a little problem." Those were the words Spencer Proffer chose to kick off our impromptu confab with Rhythm Corps' manager.

Proffer's introductory statement was directed toward me. However, as I sat there in a chair in the center of Spencer's office, I had already detected a certain uneasiness in the demeanor of the other Randy in the room—the guy sinking into the floral upholstery of the sofa placed tastefully against a wall decorated with platinum discs and celebrity photos.

Randy Sosin, an almost-always relaxed, outgoing and pleasant young fellow, seemed unusually reserved and pensive. With Proffer's prompting, Sosin proceeded to reveal the reason for his unusually somber mood.

"The four members of Rhythm Corps share equal credit for *every* song," Sosin explained. "That's how they've always done it."

"I know," I responded. "That's one of the many things I really admire about those guys."

Rhythm Corps' primary songwriters, singer Michael Persh and bassist/background vocalist Davey Holmbo, were magnanimous in their willingness to give creative parity to drummer Richie Lovsin and guitarist Greg Apro. Then again, these four, talented young rockers from Detroit were truly an all-for-one and one-for-all outfit. That quality had been one of many reasons I'd been so irresistibly attracted to their group in the first place.

However, it seemed the band members had been proofreading the proposed liner-notes and credits for the soon-to-be-released album we had just completed. According to the deeply concerned Sosin, Lovsin and Apro had expressed alarm to see a fifth writer's name added to *Father's Footsteps*—cut one, side one of the LP. The writer making this title a quintuple co-write, thus breaking the policy to which Sosin had only just referred, was none other than *yours truly*, Randy Bishop.

Then Sosin made no bones about his final point. "If you're not willing to remove your name from that song," he stated, looking directly at me and clearing his throat for emphasis, "the band will insist on going back to the original lyric, and remix the song for the album."

I have to admit it, I wasn't the best A&R guy in the history of the Los Angeles music scene. I tackled my creative duties with dedicated exuberance. However, I tended to avoid the requisite late-night bar-hopping and insidious back-slapping with that rat pack of ambitious, too-cool-for-school music snobs who prowled the clubs representing the other labels.

It was 1987, and I'd been working with Spencer Proffer on and off for 11 years. After my own album for Pasha Records stiffed three years before, I'd made the logical transition from songwriter/recording artist to songwriter/staff-producer and A&R rep.

I received a modest monthly advance for my publishing deal. But my A&R position at Pasha was rewarded only with a box of business cards and an alcove storage room, which served as my "office." My occasional production compensation dribbled in on a project-by-project basis. The upside was, in this capacity I had every opportunity to make a real name for myself on the hardscrabble, dog-eat-dog streets of the Hollywood music scene.

This is what one record company executive actually said to me: "You know, Randy, you'd go a lot further in this business if you smoked pot and did blow."

A well-practiced aficionado of alcohol, I had eschewed drugs some years before—they seemed to come between me and my humanity. It seemed odd indeed to be part of an industry that labeled illegal and socially unacceptable behaviors as virtues.

Anyway, I was in my late 30s. I still enjoyed being in the recording studio, carving away at whatever production I was working on at the time. But the after-hours club routine had lost its sparkle years before, so I wasn't completely in the loop when it came to which bands my A&R fraternity bros were buzzing about at any given time.

I don't remember the exact reason why I went to see Rhythm Corps, or even which Hollywood Boulevard club they were playing that night. I do recall standing on a balcony above the stage, and the band charging headlong into their opening number—the aforementioned *Father's*

Footsteps—with tremendous ferocity. Apro's six strings rang out like a veritable orchestra of guitars, and Lovsin, bushy blond curls and easy on the eyes, pounded the skins of his drums with solid power. Holmbo's choppy eighth-notes motored the bottom end, and he chimed in on his harmony parts with no-holds-barred commitment.

With all this, it was the passion and presence of Persh that absolutely captivated me. The slight, sinewy lead singer, with his fine, dishwater-blond hair, prowled the stage like a graceful, jungle primate, effortlessly stretching his raw, elastic vocal instrument from a whisper to a scream. There was no question as to the young man's devotion to his message. And what a divine message it was: Peace. Brotherhood. Equality. Justice.

Towards the middle of the set, Persh strapped on an Ovation acoustic 12-string and pounded out the opening C to F changes of a mid-tempo piece. When he cried out into the Hollywood night to exhort the musical question *Can we meet on common ground?*[xlv] I had a profound feeling in my *solar plexus* that this song could be a career-breaking hit.

I felt like I'd been waiting my entire life to find this band. They encompassed every quality I identified as essential to the very greatest rock-ensembles: a totally identifiable palate of sound, a uniquely beautiful aesthetic sense, a strong visual presence and a passionate commitment to a strongly held point of view.

It was a piece of cake winning the enthusiasm and support of the label. With my boss, Spencer's endorsement, I signed Rhythm Corps to Pasha/CBS Records and took them into the studio to produce their debut major-label album.

The better I got to know these four dyed-in-the-wool musicians, the more impressed I was with them, and the more they won my respect. Like a very functional family, the boys—*and* their ladies—all lived together in one cozy, Hollywood, storybook cottage. There they wrote and rehearsed every day, and shared every dime they made. Rhythm Corps was like some tiny utopian nation unto itself, setting an ideal example for the world with their cooperative lifestyle and singularity of purpose.

As I was welcomed into their culture, I felt like friendly Uncle Rand, from just across the border. I relished going to the studio every day to help these Motor City rockers hone the muscle and grace of a dozen of their songs into a cohesive album.

Every one of the Corps' compositions rocked, and had a poetic sensibility that made its words rich, nuanced and intriguing—yet still accessible and hooky. One particular song, however, to me, seemed to fall slightly short lyrically. It was the one with which they opened every show, and the one we logically envisioned placing in the first slot on our album-in-progress.

Father's Footsteps was a great song-concept—a statement about breaking away from the repeated mistakes of prior generations. But its verses lacked focus, failing to live up to the care, craft and inspiration demonstrated by the rest of the album's material. For weeks, I goaded Michael and Davey to do some re-writing, and they kept promising they'd get around to it. Finally, it came time to cut Michael's *Footsteps* lead-vocal, and the lads were still stalled in procrastination mode.

I had no intention of foisting myself into the writing process, but I felt I had something substantial to offer. Through the years, I'd had considerable experience collaborating with artists. Besides, my strong work ethic told me we had to move on. So I appointed myself "Song Doctor" and took matters into my own hands.

I collared Michael, and we sat down together on the piano-bench in Pasha Studio A. About 90 minutes later, we'd scribbled out two verses that we both acknowledged were vastly improved. On the spot, Michael wholeheartedly agreed that I should be given a co-writing credit on the song. Then, as always, standing in front of a vintage AKG C12, Persh sang his butt off. When Davey came in to do his harmony parts, it seemed unanimous—the newly rewritten verses were vastly improved over the originals.

That was where we left it—until a few weeks later, when Spencer called me into his office for this extemporaneous discussion with the manager/messenger, carrying with him the rest of the band's discontent.

When I reminded Sosin that Persh had offered to include me on the copyright, he replied, "Michael now feels that what you did was part of your role as producer."

"Oh," I responded. "And how do you think Mutt Lange would feel if Def Leppard said the same thing to him?"

"You're not Mutt Lange."

Although Sosin's remark was obvious to one and all, it was a completely unnecessary, disrespectful and hurtful comment, directed toward the person who had discovered and championed this manager's band, plucking them off the streets of Hollywood, which had resulted in a substantial, multi-album commitment from the nation's biggest and most powerful record promotion and distribution machine.

I was incredulous in my disbelief, wounded to the core, completely blindsided by this sudden turn. Here was a group of guys that had, up until that moment, demonstrated only the highest level of integrity in everything they ever did—in their art, *and* in their lives. Clearly, they were unable to see how petty they were acting in regard to this issue.

My subsequent decision to leave Pasha wasn't only because my publisher, Spencer, a close collaborator for more than a decade, sat there in silence, refusing to take my side, while this due-credit was snatched away from me. What I'd come to realize over the previous year was that I had strayed far away from the creative love of my life. If I had to fight for a 20% share of one single song—if *that* was my total output over those last six months—then I wasn't taking full responsibility for the gifts my Creator had given me. I needed to get back to what I was born to do, the craft that inspired and nurtured me: writing songs.

Indeed, songwriting has been, for the most part, at the center of everything my life has been about ever since then.

≈   ≈   ≈

Shortly after putting the Rhythm Corps project to bed, I got a call from a young gent named Bob Skoro. The newly appointed head of west coast A&R for Mercury/Polygram Records was a fan of the Corps' earlier independent releases, and he expressed a desire to hear the album I'd produced—and meet me face-to-face at the same time.

A handsome, confident fellow, about 10 years my junior, Bob Skoro earned his degree in architecture. Admittedly, he had no background or legitimate training in music. In the early-'80s, as a summer intern at Chappell Music in New York, Bob identified what he believed to be a particularly outstanding, fledgling hair-band, performing in a New Jersey club. He introduced said band, Cinderella, to the honchos at Chappell, who signed 'em up. Soon thereafter, the group ascended to multi-platinum status. Thus, Skoro, the architect, became Skoro, the music publisher, with a golden reputation for spotting talent. By 1988, he was running the L.A. office of a major record label.

As Bob guided me into this temporary office on Sunset Boulevard, he pointed to an eight-by-ten glossy, casually Scotch-taped to the cinder-block wall.

With absolutely sincerity, he inquired, "What do you think o' these guys?"

A more comprehensive gander at the photo revealed five figures, wearing bandana headbands, torn jeans and T-shirts, and sporting smeared eye-liner, multiple tattoos, piercings and purposefully disheveled hair. With smoke curling from the cigarettes that drooped from the corners of their snarling mouths, the fivesome looked as though they'd just crawled out of the graffitied dumpster against which they posed.

Not recognizing this particular pack of miscreants, I responded, "I don't know, Bob. How's the music?"

"Well, that's just it," Skoro explained. "They can't really write … or sing … or really play their instruments. But if they could, they'd be huge. Don't you think?"

(As it turned out, this ensemble of ne'er-do-wells was a band called L.A. Guns. Skoro went on to sign the act and, under the architect's creative supervision, the resulting *Cocked 'n' Loaded* LP sold more than a million copies.)

In August of 1988, *Common Ground*, the very song I had identified as Rhythm Corps' career-breaker, was the most played song nationwide on Album Oriented Radio, and its inventive video was running in heavy MTV rotation. Rhythm Corps, however, never quite equaled the platinum sales success of L.A. Guns.

chapter twenty-seven: The Artist

There's probably a pretty good chance that, at least so far, I haven't addressed you directly. What I mean by that is this: maybe your songwriting process is something altogether different from the model I've described. That's because the actual reason you express yourself in song isn't to persuade a major star to take your tune into the studio and make it into a big ol' hit.

"Well, that would be great, of course," you're saying. You wouldn't exactly refuse to cash the royalty checks. But really, to be perfectly honest, that's not the predominant thought in your head every time a song idea from somewhere in your sparkling subconscious grabs your conscious attention and demands that you realize it in sound and fury.

In fact, the star you're writing for is reflected in the mirror. You *are* "the artist," and your songs are meant for *you* to perform. Maybe you go it solo; maybe you've partnered in a duo, trio or band. But it's you, in one configuration or another, who's intended to be the actual vehicle responsible for pluckin' and warblin' the compositions over which you toil day after day.

I started writing songs out of what I thought was pure necessity. The enormous, worldwide, primarily self-composed successes of The Beatles and Bob Dylan created somewhat of a stigma for young, aspiring pop musicians of the era. Rock 'n' roll bands and solo artists in the mid-'60s seemingly *had* to be songwriters. If you didn't have original songs, you weren't cool, and the specter of uncoolness was absolutely unacceptable for a high-schooler with rock-star ambitions. (Thousands of star-struck wannabes must have been inspired by similar pressures, because nearly overnight, every other folkie and rocker suddenly fancied him- or herself a songwriter.)

Surprisingly enough, what resulted was a renaissance decade that gave the world some of the most inspired songs of the pop epoch—along with its share of derivative disposables and genuine stinkers. Many of the

Makin' Stuff Up

'60s classics were penned by writers who'd never been told they *couldn't* write a song. Many of these were fledgling tunesmiths, with little or no instruction in the do's and don'ts of pop song-craft. Intuition reigned; rules were broken left and right; and fresh, dazzlingly radiant statements were made in the popular songs of the day.

Being your typical oldest child—and an overly confident, headstrong teen—I knew it *all* back then. It's unlikely—had I been fortunate enough to encounter some empathetic, wizened soul willing to mentor me with the kind of advice I'm about to impart to you—that I'd have been capable of absorbing, let alone applying much of it. However, I'm gonna give you much more credit than I could ever give my own former self. And having ripened into a bit of a professorial old coot, I'll be using the next few pages to spout some of the insight I've gained while partaking of this bizness of music—as a creative participant.

Over my lengthy, journeyman career, I've actively contributed to literally dozens of talent-development projects, many of which resulted in young artists of divergent styles and wide-ranging appeal signing to labels, and ultimately releasing recordings for commercial exploitation. In several of those instances, I was the performer myself. A number of times, I acted as the producer. Sometimes I was both. In most cases, I helped shape and/or co-write some or all of the material.

What follows is an overview of the actual lay-o'-the-land that you, as a singer/songwriter with ambitions of grand-scale success, should be aware of.

Talent and career development is a process. Often the process begins with the self-expression of writing. In the long run, though, having a career involves much more than just making up a dozen songs, then recording and releasing a CD. There are decisions to be made at every step—some conscious, some not—each of which is potentially critical to the relative pace, effectiveness and success of your journey. Beyond those choices (over which you actually have a good deal of control), there are many more elusive factors in play: serendipity, fate and destiny (or luck, as some folks are wont to call it). You'll need a lot of that stuff on your side as well if you're ever gonna reach your goal—*if* your goal is to reach millions of music-fans.

By being aware of certain realities, taking some stock of the artists who've come before and how they achieved their success (or missed the mark), you can actually nudge your own developing career in such a way that it's more likely to bump into the fates that hold the keys to the treasure and fulfillment you desire.

≈   ≈   ≈

While I find it ostentatious to refer to any work promulgated by the industry of pop music as "art," I do recognize and acknowledge that some singers, musicians and songwriters have created music that rises to a level one might recognize *as* art—or that at least qualifies as "artistic." So for the purpose of clarity, and to use a common, contemporary label, I'll succumb to applying the term "artist" or "recording artist," even though a more precise idiom (like … "music craftsperson") might be more apropos.

> *IN THE CREATIVE WORLD OF MUSIC, THERE ARE "ARTISTS" … AND THERE ARE "PERFORMERS."*

Talent notwithstanding, "artists" and "performers" are two very different breeds. Artists aspire to careers; performers aspire to hits. Artists seek to express a unique statement and reveal a *persona* consistent with that point of view; performers merely endeavor to entertain—by showing off their various talents, and displaying their most appealing physical features.

When we look back over the last five decades and the ever-evolving phenomenon of pop music, which stars do you think shine brightest? Are they the most beautiful? Are they the most talented? Or are they, in fact, merely the most provocative and/or the most intriguing?

Along with the icon acts of the '60s, Dylan and The Fab Four, that decade introduced us to such groundbreaking ensembles as The Beach Boys, The Four Seasons, The Rascals, Grateful Dead and The Doors. (And let's not forget Jimi, Janis, Smokey, Diana, Merle and Loretta.)

The '70s gave us David Bowie, Marvin Gaye, Jackson Browne, Otis Redding, Cat Stevens, Aretha Franklin, Elton John, Linda Ronstadt, Stevie Wonder, Carole King, Billy Joel, Joni Mitchell, Al Green, James Taylor, Earth, Wind and Fire, Donna Summer, Tom Petty & The Heartbreakers and The Eagles. This era, too, gave birth to arguably the best work of the Rolling Stones, The Who, Led Zeppelin, Bee Gees and Pink Floyd, as well as fostering the rise of Aerosmith, Blondie, The Police and Talking Heads.

Makin' Stuff Up

It's probably unlikely that any of the abovementioned dudes and dudettes would've been gracing the covers of celebrity or fashion magazines on their looks alone. There were plenty of other musicians and singers treading the talent pool who could out-play and/or out-sing any one of them (with the possible exceptions of Jimi, Stevie and Aretha, that is). However, each of these legendary acts captured the world's imagination with an undeniably unique style and attitude—as reflected in the music they recorded, and the individual and/or group *personas* they put forward.

Every one of those notables from the '60s and '70s is certainly deserving of the appellation "recording artist"—as *I* define the term.

While a number of equally talented—often, much more physically attractive—entertainers might have cranked out their own handful of hits during those same decades, most of those acts somehow never quite sustained the mass interest and devotion to their music engendered by the aforementioned iconic artists. Sometimes it's a mystery as to why the public embraces one figure or group for decades, while another might be forgotten—or even virtually ignored. However, most times it's fairly obvious to one and all as to which ones are the originals, the groundbreakers, the *true* artists. They are the souls who speak directly to the music lovers of the world—while cleverly defining and refreshing their brand, time and time again, for the dual purposes of re-igniting their own creative spark and re-kindling the fascination of a fickle public.

Since the dawn of the video age in the early-'80s, the industry trend has swung even more toward giving the prettiest, the sexiest, the youngest and the best dancers the chance at having a recording career. Still, Tom Petty—in my opinion a rather homely dude (*Sorry, Tom*)—pulled off a strong resurgence in the MTV era, while U2, certainly not a band of dreamboats, also emerged and rose to long-term prominence. A veritable freak of nature, Michael Jackson, became the most successful music and video artist in history. And a woman with marginal vocal talent and average songwriting ability, who would probably never be considered a classic beauty, ascended to queenly status.

Madonna is the perfect prototype of an artist who fully understands what it takes to seize stardom and maintain its *élan*, decade after decade. Love her or despise her, every aspiring artist has a great deal to learn from the way the girl from Michigan has so deftly handled her music and her image.

Makin' Stuff Up

Like Bowie—a songwriter, musician, singer and producer with far superior gifts—Madonna has always projected her own peculiarly provocative point of view, while cultivating an ever-shifting public *persona*. Since she's also always surrounded herself with musicians at the very vanguard of her dance/pop genre, this celebrity songstress/hoofer has been able to defy the years, holding center stage into her 50's—a rarely accomplished feat for a white, female recording-artist. While it seems amazing that someone with such limited natural resources could pull off such a coup, it's a tribute to her creative vision, her tenacity and her self-marketing ability that little Ms. Ciccone has done just that.

Bruce Springsteen is another ideal example of true artistry. Since his earliest recordings in the mid-'70s, "The Boss" has kept his enormous, worshipful fan-base eagerly looking forward to hearing what he has in store next, while they've remained faithful to his impressive body of work. Springsteen, now closing in on 60, is still going strong.

A number of substantial artist careers have been established since those I've named—including (but not excluded to) Sheryl Crow, Eminem, REM, John Mellencamp, Beck, Mariah Carey, Pearl Jam, Red Hot Chili Peppers, Randy Travis, George Strait … and the most influential band of the new millennium, Coldplay.

In the '90s, country emerged as another legitimate mainstream pop format, with artists like Garth Brooks, Tim McGraw, Brooks & Dunn, Alan Jackson, Faith Hill, the Dixie Chicks and Kenny Chesney. Not all country stars write their own material; however, like Linda Ronstadt and Aretha Franklin, these artists all project a distinct *persona* and are associated with a repertoire of songs that connects strongly to their legions of fans.

Hip-hop has produced some dynasties, with Jay Z and Sean (Puff *whatever*) Combs. How is it that Snoop Dog, a man of very questionable physical appeal and innate talent, has sustained his viability for so long? Because, my friends, Snoop is an artist, with a unique point of view: he knows his audience, keeps them fascinated and delivers the musical goods, time after time.

≈   ≈   ≈

The digital age has brought about swift and incredible (not to mention intimidating) changes in the way music reaches people and the ways people choose to enjoy it. Downloading has rendered the record-album nearly a relic of the past. No longer do a majority of music enthusiasts run right out and buy an artist's latest compilation solely based on fan loyalty. Consumers now tend to appreciate their favorite music personalities one cut at a time.

As a result of new and ubiquitous technology, regionalism has also virtually disappeared. New recorded music arrives—via corporate-conglomerate radio, cable TV and the Internet—everywhere at the same time. So it's become a rarity for one part of the country to embrace a new sound in advance of the rest of the world.

This song-by-song, instant availability of music has been responsible for bringing down the barriers between formerly competitive cultures of music fans. In the early-'90s, a teen would have been *either* an alternative-rock fan, a goth fan, a metal fan, a country fan *or* a hip-hop fan. Devotees of those music genres hung out together, listened exclusively to that one kind of music, and sometimes even dressed like the artists they followed.

Now, however, it's not uncommon for a youthful pop aficionado to have tunes by Daughtry, Rascal Flatts, Dashboard Confessional, Miley Cyrus, Hinder, Beyoncé and Carrie Underwood coming up in regular rotation on that iPod Shuffle. In this day and age, there's little or no stigma about the music you choose to listen to. Good music is good music, regardless of whether it's country or hip-hop, power-pop or metal.

Today's marketplacc has become more "song-oriented"—as it was in the long-ago 1950s, when the 45 RPM single was the mainstay of one's pop-music collection. This trend gives new performers the opportunity to break worldwide based on one lone, massive, breakthrough hit. At the same time, though, qualifying for "artist" stature has become that much more difficult, because the public's shortening attention span doesn't tend to stick with every hitmaker's career, while megahits seemingly last forever on pop radio playlists, and get themselves attached and licensed to myriad advertisements, TV shows and feature films.

In the new millennium, the biggest hit songs can generate ludicrous amounts of income. Meanwhile, although these enormous, international copyrights are often responsible for giving an up-and-coming popster a tremendous amount of "overnight" visibility, the omnipresence of these recordings can also quickly reduce a potential creative force to one-hit wonder status, due to the fatigue caused by that sole, immensely successful (but ultimately very, very tiresome) song.

Makin' Stuff Up

Look no further than English singer/songwriter and multi-instrumentalist James Blunt, whose smash ballad, *You're Beautiful*, made him a very familiar and ever-present face on the pop landscape in 2006. Creating a follow-up to that one song has, at this writing, eluded Blunt's reach. The stigma of that one hit has possibly jeopardized what might have been a promising career as an authentic "recording artist."

There's no place where the dividing line between "artist" and "performer" becomes more evident than on the stage of the most brilliant pop star-marketing machine in history, *American Idol*. For a certain kind of singer—usually the big belter—this "reality" competition show provides a quick study in what it takes to be a pop star in the modern world. It's an on-camera boot camp for new music-biz recruits. At the same time, on a yearly basis, at least a half-dozen fresh, young personalities get the chance to establish their own personal brand through weekly exposure to millions of living rooms across North America.

The *Idol* competitors, however, rarely possess a real artist's sensibility. A few, like Kelly Clarkson and Chris Daughtry, have later revealed their own artistry or evolved publicly to artist stature. It's no fluke that, so far, Clarkson and Daughtry have sustained the most successful and lucrative recording careers out of all the many talented youngsters who've weathered the grueling *Idol* pressure-cooker. (Remember, artists seek careers; performers seek hits.)

Ultimately, most of *Idol*'s entrants are strictly performers, talented interpreters, whose very show-biz survival relies on finding and choosing the right vehicles (songs, plays, films, etc.) to feature their innate charms and gifts. While there can be a certain art to making those kinds of choices (Linda Ronstadt, Aretha Franklin, Tim McGraw and George Strait certainly have had lengthy runs as artists while never penning a single tune), creating the songs, and making the personal statements that control your own destiny, are characteristics we commonly associate with a successful, contemporary recording artist.

Online meeting-places like My Space, free video sites like YouTube and a plethora of virtual music-retail stores have opened up new and very direct ways to self-market music. Now, with these tools available, the playing field has been leveled, such that any ambitious and savvy purveyor of pop can expose his/her/their original work to the entire world.

Artists no longer have to wait for that big record-deal to reach the masses. If your music has any viability at all, and you take the initiative, you and your songs can and will find an audience.

Makin' Stuff Up

≈   ≈   ≈

So what can be learned from the iconic, pioneer acts from the last five decades of recording artistry? Please allow your author to make a few observations:

A RECORDING ARTIST IS ALWAYS PLAYING TWO SIMULTANEOUS ROLES.

First, he or she is *always* the artist. Secondly, though, and of equal importance, he or she must be aware of being a product, a brand, a commodity. Throughout the course of a career, the artist is constantly straddling an invisible line that divides these two very divergent, dual personalities. As a result, it's critically important to *your* career development that you become and remain aware of when and where you may be called upon to emphasize your energies toward one or the other—or both—of these identities.

The artist is your creative self, the side of you who puts his or her heart on display through your music, expressing your most intimate feelings, personal experiences and candid observations—with words, chords, notes and rhythms. The artist can be vulnerable, charming, funny and/or rebellious. But, above all, your artist-self must be honest, forthright, authentic and genuinely human—revealing the very essence of what you care about most. In other words:

THE ARTIST HAS TO EXPRESS HIS/HER OWN PERSONAL POINT OF VIEW.

The artist in you must feel deeply about something, take a stand and reveal those emotions with heartfelt passion. (Please note: *these earnest expressions don't necessarily have to be world-changing*. A message about appreciating life might come in the guise of a "party all night" song. A message promoting world peace might hide within a song about trying to patch up a miscommunication with a friend or a lover.)

Above all, you—as the artist—must dedicate your writing to subject-matter that genuinely resonates emotionally inside you. If *you* don't truly care deeply about what you write and sing about, how could you expect anybody else to be at all interested?

You have to respect your audience and expect them to "get it." They know intuitively when you, as the artist, are being honest—*and* they can usually discern when their emotions are being purposefully manipulated. If your listeners allow themselves to be emotionally stage-managed, it's because they *want* to believe in something, not necessarily because they believe that *you* believe in it.

However, one of the absolute worst things you can do as an artist (or a writer for that matter) is to think too much about what *might* push your audience's emotional buttons … instead of continuing to explore the stuff that gets *your* engine roaring, while at the same time trusting that your own, personal inspirations have universal truth.

If *you* care about something, your audience is likely to follow. Give them credit for that. If you spend your creative time chasing after what you think they might fall for, you may get away with it once or twice. In the long run, though, they'll surely abandon you, in favor of another artist who dares to speak directly and honestly to them.

The *persona* you cultivate by performing your songs, both live and in the recording studio, is the side of you we'll call "your product." Yes, the recordings of your songs are the actual hard commodities you're ultimately attempting to market. But don't fool yourself, it's really *you* (and/or your band) that your customers are buying.

Think about your favorite artists through the years. You went out to buy the new Sting, Sheryl Crow, Beck, Chesney or Eminem CD—not because of any individual song, but because you were a true fan of the artist. (I bought every Tom Petty and the Heartbreakers, Dire Straits and Peter Gabriel album for the same reason.) If you intend to sustain a career as an artist in this biz of music, you should always be aware that you are continually branding yourself in the eyes of your public.

Just like the former schoolteacher, Mr. Sumner (or that Mathers guy), even though you, as the artist, write songs from your own heartfelt place and from a specific and unique point of view, there are probably thousands, if not millions, of music-lovers out there who could and would strongly relate to your music—*if* they were somehow given the chance.

Ultimately, you have to know *who* your audience is. Then you need to develop the ability to see yourself through their eyes and listen to your songs through their ears, so you can help them see who you really are. Much more than talent, this awareness is the most important component in the success of any artist.

Makin' Stuff Up

THE ARTIST IDENTIFIES WHO HIS/HER AUDIENCE IS, AND THEREFORE KNOWS HOW TO CONNECT DIRECTLY WITH THEM.

I'm not advising you to pander to your audience. I'm strongly suggesting that you endeavor to have a truly intimate knowledge of exactly who those folks are: *What's their age range? Do they tend to be male or female? Are they working class, academic, or professional?* Ask yourself what it is—about *your* image, *your* attitude and *your* music— that appeals to these people. Then get out there and offer them the most sincere material you can muster up, while choosing to focus on the themes in your body of work that are most likely to be of genuine interest to them.

You shouldn't have to stoop to writing something you *think* they'll like. As you get to know them better, you should eventually become able to suss out which songs in your catalogue are most likely to connect most strongly with your core crowd. That will enable you to specifically target your product to your own demographic base.

The artist in recent memory who, to me, exemplifies this quality most dramatically is the very man to whom I owe my loudest and most sincere vote of gratitude. Toby Keith would probably be shocked and amused to hear himself compared in any way to Madonna. However, the big guy from Oklahoma has a whole lot in common with the little lady from Michigan.

Like Madonna, Toby has limited natural resources. Aside from his exceptional size (he had a brief semi-pro football career), Toby's looks aren't that impressive. He doesn't have the most sonorous vocal instrument in the world, nor is he the greatest tunesmith who ever put words and notes together.

However, before he ever recorded my song, and long before I ever met the man, I found myself occasionally pondering the dude's phenomenal success. And in observing his obvious imperfections, I became immensely impressed by Toby's ability to market his own unique *persona*, and connect so directly to his audience. The guy had an incredibly remarkable career going: cranking out number-one hit after number-one hit, headlining arenas and acting as national commercial spokesman for Ford trucks. I developed the theory that Toby must have some kind of genius for a manager.

Makin' Stuff Up

After meeting the artist and interacting with his management, I realized how very off-base my speculation was. Toby himself is the actual brains, the mad professor, the one and only architect of his immense success.

When my friend Jim Collins first came to Nashville, he'd never written a song. An "A-level" headliner on the Texas honky-tonk circuit, Jim, an excellent singer, modestly referred to himself as a "beer salesman." He only became a songwriter because a publishing offer seems to come along with every Music Row recording contract, and his publisher began pairing him up with several top Music Row tunesmiths. After two record deals failed to expand his Texas-sized performing career to the national stage, Jim stuck around Nashville and kept on writing songs, resulting in some great success—country smashes like *She Thinks My Tractor's Sexy*, *Then They Do*, and *The Good Stuff.*

In the late-'80s, back in the Lone Star State, Toby Keith would sometimes be third on a Jim Collins bill. Years later, Jim confided that Toby's early bands were far from first-rate, his songs were average at best, and his vocals were less than stellar. But even then, Collins had a powerful inkling that Keith was bound for stardom. After his sets, the big fellah would sit at his merchandise table for hours, selling audio-cassettes and T-shirts, shaking hands with the guys, hugging the ladies, grinning for snapshots and signing autographs. Keith, the product, the commodity, was getting to know his core consumers first-hand, and discerning what it was about his personality and his music that appealed directly to them.

Armed with this knowledge culled from those hundreds of nights interacting with his fan base, Toby allowed his naturally cocky, devil-may-care, roustabout nature to emerge as the essence of his stage-image. This rebelliousness also began to be reflected in the songs he wrote and performed. He was developing his own unique point of view, an attitude that certainly didn't adhere to the safe, "aw, shucks" demeanor so common in the performers who permeate the contemporary country airwaves.

This freewheelin' *persona* didn't initially endear Keith to the kingmakers of Music Row. On his first Nashville foray in pursuit of a publishing deal, Toby visited nearly every music publisher in town, toting a cassette of six original song demos. Although those half-dozen tunes received pass after pass from those industry "experts," five out of those six ended up being top-five hits for the artist. One of those rejected songs, *Should've Been a Cowboy*, eventually received more spins on country radio than any other song of the '90s—a decade that will forever be remembered as the era of Garth Brooks.

Y2K brought an unexpected disaster for Toby Keith, a setback that ultimately turned into the best break of his career. He was dropped from Mercury Records. A man with less bravado might have slunk off back home to Oklahoma in defeat—but not our Toby. He rebounded bigger and better than ever, partnered with James Stroud and DreamWorks Records, releasing a song that Mercury had previously refused to let him record.

How Do You Like Me Now? exemplifies the most fundamental nature of Toby Keith's appeal. No other artist could have pulled that tune off with the kind of charm and wit that so successfully invited his audience to share in the tale of "nay-nay-nay-nay-nay" revenge over a former high-school crush. Nearly every country music fan could relate to the never-say-die guy who, not so long ago, couldn't get himself arrested, but now was reaching the highest echelons of his profession.

Those are the kinds of songs that every performing singer/songwriter needs to write—songs that only *that* artist could deliver with absolute authenticity, songs that, in three succinct minutes, reveal the true character of the artist to the world:

Girls Just Wanna Have Fun (Cyndi Lauper), *Your Song* (Elton John), *Piano Man* (Billy Joel), *Yellow* (Coldplay), *New Years Day* (U2), *I Wanna Hold Your Hand* (The Beatles), *Fire and Rain* (James Taylor), *Sounds of Silence* (Simon and Garfunkel), *All I Wanna Do* (Sheryl Crow), *Just Like Teen Spirit* (Nirvana). ...

The list could go on and on, but it's clear how each of these career-making classics reveals so much that is totally unique about the artist giving voice to it. I'd find it impossible to imagine any other performers convincingly unveiling those ten copyrights. It requires an artist with tremendous self-awareness (and a complete knowledge and understanding of his, her or their audience) to write, record, release and perform a song as definitive and essential as those I've just mentioned.

You must have faith in your own natural, innate appeal. You must trust your own instinct when it comes to the subject-matter you care most about, the themes you choose to explore in your writing. Then, you must develop the ability to package your essence in your songs, and cultivate an image that truly connects with your public. Only then will you thrive in the marketplace—on whatever level is appropriate to your individual artistry.

≈   ≈   ≈

In my numerous lives as a recording artist, I reshaped the direction of my songwriting and remade my image many times over. In almost every incarnation, I was consciously or unconsciously trying, to one degree or another, to mimic someone else—following a trend and style that was popular at the time. As a result, while I had some natural intuition and innate talent, I seldom ever revealed my own individual musical identity. Ultimately, each of my many record-deals failed to result in the level of success to which I aspired.

One of the big dangers, from my experience, is the following all-too-common scenario: A gifted, attractive young artist walks into an A&R person's office. The artist does a little dog and pony show, performing several original tunes. It's immediately evident that there's some really strong raw material here to make some very appealing music. *And*, the guy behind the desk is thinking, *if she's moldable, we might be able to have some real success with this one.*

"So," says the A&R hotshot, "I see you as the next Jewel..." (or Alanis, or Avril, or whoever's the hottest ticket of that particular year).

"Thank you," the artist responds graciously. Meanwhile, she's thinking, *I could pull off the Jewel thing for a while. Then I'll show 'em who I really am.*

As aspiring artists, we're all anxious to get on with it. We want our shot, *and we want it NOW*! When some Somebody takes a shine to us, when an industry power-broker sees potential in our talent, our resolve to make our own personal statement to the world can be softened—in a split second.

The man with the contract and the checkbook wants you to be his puppet, so you're tempted to offer your hands, feet and posterior for him to attach the strings. This you'll do, while harboring the secret assumption that you'll be able to spread your own creative wings at some point down the line—after establishing yourself with an album or two.

Unfortunately, it almost never works that way. If you're a real artist, with your own point of view, your own style, passions and comfort zone ... if you know your own audience, and they get you ... you can't just become something else—no matter *how* talented you are. It just won't work. By falling for that one, you're setting yourself up for years of disillusionment.

Unless you can make the required adjustments, believing wholeheartedly in the new role you're being asked to portray, don't do it. Succumbing to that temptation wouldn't be fair to you … or your audience. (It wouldn't even be fair to that slavering Svengali behind the desk, who sits there so eager to plunk down a few hundred grand to mold you and sell you to a public he so obviously has no respect for.)

Be yourself. Be real. Be genuine. Unless you can do it without a single reservation, don't grab for that dangling, golden carrot. Remember, your audience loves you for who *you* are, not for the image some record company exec wants you to be. Who *you* are is what your songs and your *persona* should reflect, not some copycat ideal created in the mind of an A&R person, someone who's only trying to win industry points and hang on to his or her job past the next quarterly corporate-earnings report.

As much as you may admire another, more successful, or perhaps even more innovative artist, don't attempt to replicate what they do. It's okay to observe and appreciate their commercial and/or artistic accomplishments. But fight the urge to copy anyone else in your songwriting, or your musical or visual style. Be brave. Carve your own way based on your own true identity and point of view.

At the end of the day, regardless of what level of recognition you may ever reach, you will only find an authentic connection with your audience (and true, creative fulfillment) if you achieve it honestly and authentically. Yes, *do* listen to and consider the advice you may receive from those (like your humble author) who've "been there and done that." *Do* partner with accomplished and highly skilled collaborators, and associate with seasoned pros from the songwriting, publishing, production and recording world.

But if you consider yourself a real "artist," you should ultimately ever do only what feels right, what continues to speak truth for you in your heart of hearts. Write songs that reflect your own truth, your own vantage point, and frame those songs for your audience.

chapter twenty-eight: Turn On the Light

By 1990, at 40, I had worked my way to the periphery of the Los Angeles music scene—both figuratively *and* literally. I felt magnetically drawn to return to my native Pacific-Northwest roots. But my wife, Stacey, was working steadily in Hollywood as an actor, doing commercials, theater and occasional film and TV roles. Her career, her family and her friends were all in the greater L.A. area. So our rented house on that *cul de sac* in Granada Hills, in the furthest northwestern corner of the blistering San Fernando Valley, was as close to the Oregon border as I could get her to move.

I had just completed a totally unproductive, two-year wheel-spin in a three-way publishing partnership with Gold Mountain Entertainment and Virgin Music. I found myself broke and standing in a virtual pea-soup fog, with no compass to point the way.

Most of the successful professional songwriters of the day were producers adept at crafting poppy R&B-light for the likes of Paula Abdul and Vanessa Williams. For the life of me, I couldn't summon up a single spark of zest for that sort of prefabricated, top-40 fare. Nor did I seem to have any real talent for composing that stuff, let alone a single iota of gumption for producing it.

I spent a couple of months working on a suite of children's songs I called *Sunny Day*. The result was an album starring a fictional sister and brother—conveniently named Stacey and Randy. *I Like Bugs, Ssshhh, Mom's Got A Headache* and *Wild, Wild Party in the Loquat Tree*, among others, combined to form an operetta, describing a wondrous, exhilarating day-in-the-life of these two wide-eyed five- and six-year-olds. There was even a table-setting lesson called *The Fork Goes on the Right*. My wife (a wonderful singer, BTW) and I recorded a demo LP at home, on my four-track porta-studio.

For the most part, though, my creative muses had been leading me more and more toward expressions of a spiritual nature, and my newest batch of folkie incantations of oneness with a creative god-force of infinite intelligence didn't exactly fit into any recognizable commercial genre. Stacey and I had found our spiritual home in a tiny, storefront, Valley Village church called the Metaphysical and Self-Awareness Foundation. There, I co-created and co-produced a monthly fundraising event called the White Light Cabaret. On the first Friday of each month—for six years—the White Light provided me with a stage to perform my new songs, and a small, but extremely receptive audience to appreciate them.

I wanted more than ever to use my music to make the world a better place. One anthemic ballad, entitled *Piece of the Wall*, celebrated the fall of Communist East Germany and the re-unification of Berlin. On some far less-serious notes, I satirized the beliefs of some of my more far-out church fellows, in a piece describing an affair taking place in a parallel dimension. That number, *Hanky Panky on the Astral Plane,* turned out to be one of my most requested and popular White Light numbers.

When I finished a new song, I'd invariably play it for Stacey. She'd be moved, assuming that the emotion expressed was inspired by my love and devotion for her.

"I'm sorry, Darling. But this song is really about God," I'd clarify. While Stace admired the loftiness of my sentiments, she couldn't help but show a little bit of personal disappointment.

I did anything I could to make a few bucks: temp jobs, work-for-hire and so forth. I produced a solo album for Stephen Paul, a man with a nimble, scientific mind who, despite his steady physical disintegration due to Ryder's disease, never abandoned his dream to be a successful singer/songwriter.

Known worldwide in audio circles for his innovations in restoring and modifying vintage tube microphones, Stephen—who succumbed to liver cancer in 2003—was an authentic genius with a Mensa-level IQ. The gold-plating techniques he employed in the creations of his ultra-thin microphone membranes were even borrowed by NASA and the Pentagon. Paul's Studio City home recording facility was overflowing with his handiwork—amazing custom-tweaked microphones, each worth more than my Toyota Celica, and a collection of various other priceless pieces of audiophile gear.

Part of my compensation for producing Stephen's album included some hours in his studio, where I cut five of my newest pieces, including the chant-like invocation, *We Bless*. Soon after that, through one beloved, lifelong friend, Amanda McBroom, I would be reacquainted with another huge personality from my past.

Jac Holzman began his music-mogul career riding a motor scooter through the streets of New York City, wearing a pair of fake-leather pants. Schlepping an orange crate filled with Theo Bickel albums from one Manhattan record store to the next was certainly an inauspicious beginning for Elektra Records. And, curiously enough (but absolutely true), the cash that sustained the prestigious, hatchling label through its earliest growing pains came from a series of LPs called *The Elektra Authentic Sound Effects Albums*.

By 1967, Elektra had launched the careers of Judy Collins and The Doors, and Holzman had become a major player in the industry. After selling Elektra to Kinney Corporation for untold millions (on the heals of Harry Chapin's success in 1973), Jac sat on the board of Warner Entertainment for decades, focusing on audio innovations, and specializing in quadraphonic sound.

(Jac had signed me to my first two record deals, with my bands, Roxy and The Wackers. The gracious, unpretentious executive once visited the latter group's band house, Wackering Heights, a lodge-like abode situated on a hillside between a sheep pasture and a grove of second-growth redwoods in Eureka, California. There, the multi-millionaire cooked us dinner and hand-washed our dishes—before being spirited off to our comely publicist/bookkeeper's waterbed for a night of naughty pleasuring.)

Now, Jac and I were reunited at another remote lodge—the magnificent Tehachapi getaway home of Amanda McBroom and her jolly husband, talented actor/singer George Ball. Although Jac didn't exactly care for my recently truncated first name (from Randy to Rand), he seemed quite enamored of a song-demo I shared with him.

I had written the spiritually tinged, devotional love song, *On This Journey*, for Stacey—in honor of our third wedding anniversary. Meanwhile, Jac had surrendered to a long-sublimated urge, returning to the record business to launch a brand new imprint he named Discovery Records—targeting the virtually ignored adult-demographic. He heard some real potential in my new material, especially *On This Journey*.

Over the next couple of months, my old patron and I met regularly at his new corporate digs in Santa Monica. Although Jac's enthusiasm for *On The Journey* maintained its intensity, I was honestly skeptical about the sonic integrity of the production. It was, in fact, a demo, recorded on quarter-inch eight-track tape. The latest batch of tunes, so pristinely captured at Stephen Paul's place—especially the hypnotic *We Bless*—were far more representative of the production values and atmosphere I desired to achieve as an artist.

Bottom line, though, it seemed that all the essential elements had once again serendipitously converged. I allowed my heart to swell with a certainty that—even as I entered my fifth decade of life—I was about to experience the good fortune of cutting yet another record for a legitimate label.

In order to further define the direction I intended to pursue, I put nose to grindstone and wrote about 15 new songs, recording stereo piano/vocals live at home on a high-quality cassette machine. The album-listening experience I envisioned was an ambient, gently flowing, spiritually themed one—meditative and hypnotic. Although Jac professed to like the latest batch of tunes, he still strongly favored *On This Journey*, while persisting in his suggestion that I re-attach the "y" to my first name.

"'Randy Bishop' sounds like a star," Jac explained. "'Rand,' on the other hand, seems bland and undistinguished."

Shortening my name had not been a frivolous choice. My esoteric studies at the MSA church revealed that I'd actually been confusing the universe by sending out three separate numerological vibrations—with disparate legal, professional and casual names. *That could be a reason why*, I theorized, *I've been struggling so mightily to achieve the success I've always genuinely deserved.*

By removing a single vowel from Randy, my legal name *and* my professional name became a unified, consistent "seven"—a very powerful, highly spiritual number. This was ancient science, going back many millennia. Numerological symbology permeates the Bible and the texts of the *Kabala*. Who was I to defy law that had been woven into the cultural fabric of western civilization for eons?

I was certain that my old friend would come around. But Jac was never able to see things my way. We continued to lock horns over my name *and* my musical direction. And, just as it had 13 years before—with Clive Davis—my insistence on doing it my way cost me a recording contract.

"I'm sorry, Randy," I heard Jac say over the phone, in a low-voiced, minor chord of finality. "I'm going to have to pass."

Makin' Stuff Up

In the agony of my distress, I dropped the phone and collapsed to the floor. And there, curled up in a fetal position, I grieved over the loss of what I was certain would be my very last chance to revive my career as a recording artist.

The next music-biz inspired tears I would shed, however, would be those of pure joy and creative fulfillment.

≈   ≈   ≈

In the ongoing process of booking the White Light Cabaret, I became aware of a growing community of like-minded musicians in Southern California, all applying their talents to expressions aimed at a higher purpose. While networking with some of these performers, I heard about a Culver City couple and a project that sounded intriguing.

Entering Kate and Charlie's condo was like stepping out of a time machine into a bygone era. The place was stuffed wall-to-wall with antiques, doilies and knickknacks that looked as though they'd been passed down from a prissy maiden aunt.

Charlie Pullman, a boisterous, mustachioed South Philadelphian, had arrived in L.A. with a hunk o' cash he'd culled from his real estate endeavors and plans to invest his largess in entertainment ventures to promote greater awareness of the Earth's threatened environment. Kate Cunningham, a sturdy, green-eyed, red-haired lass from West Jersey, flashed a smile that ignited the air of the museum-like room.

The three of us comprised a very complementary trio: Kate was as charming as she was persistent. I was A&R-experienced, industry-connected and skilled in the recording studio. Charlie had oodles of gumption, the bank account and an endless supply of ideas. Pullman proposed the already fully realized concept for our initial project: an environmentally themed compilation album for the "family" market, to benefit Earth Island Institute and Save The Children.

"We're gonna call it *Put on Your Green Shoes*," Pullman proclaimed.

The couple had not yet recruited a single music act to their cause, nor did they have any real contacts at the labels. Nevertheless, we formed a 501-3C not-for-profit corporation (Songwriters and Artists For the Earth, or S.A.F.E. for short). Our first goal was to entice a pump-priming act to sign on. Accomplishing that, we agreed, would have the effect of getting the *Green Shoes* ball rolling.

Makin' Stuff Up

Cyndi Lauper turned out to be our pump-primer. Charlie's Philly buddies, Eric Bazilian and Rob Hyman, both of The Hooters, had co-written several of the songs and backed up the eclectic diva on her breakthrough *She's So Unusual* album, seven years before. Under the pseudo-moniker, Three Kats and Jammers, the Lauper/Bazilian/Hyman threesome submitted what was to become our album's inspired, playful title-track, *Put On Your Green Shoes*.

It took two years. One-by-one, however, Richie Havens, Rockapella, Olivia Newton-John, Willy Nelson, Indigo Girls, Dr. John and Kenny Loggins all pledged to lace up their green sneakers by contributing a track. We also attracted several popular children's music artists to the cause, as well as a group of non-musical celebs to render voiceover messages.

Indigo Girls selected one of the songs from the demo *Sunny Day* album Stacey and I had recorded. At their own expense, Emily and Amy produced a contagiously appealing version of *Wild, Wild Party in the Loquat Tree*—a bluegrassy tune inspired by the unusual confab of critters feasting on the prolific, yellow-fruited tree in Stephen Paul's backyard.

S.A.F.E. inked a pact with Sony Kids Records, under the auspices of miniature dynamo Linda Morgenstern, and I set out to produce the remainder of the original songs. It was a labor of love, supported by Pullman's generosity and motored forward by Cunningham's entrancing, never-say-die grit.

By far, the highlight of my *Green Shoes* experience was the New York vocal session for Richie Havens. The song was *Light of the Sun*, a world-beat, solar-power-themed number, custom-crafted for the project by Kate, Charlie and myself. Earlier that day, Rockapella had laid the Ladysmith-Mombaso-styled *Turn on the light* chant over the slinky groove of our reggae-infused basic track. As a producer, I'd never been more proud of a work in progress.

Enter the man, the legend. When Richie Havens walked into the room—tall, striking and grinning ear to ear—every eye in the studio was drawn to him. Wearing an African tunic and multiple strands of hand-carved and seed-pod bangles around his neck, he seemed to be enveloped in an aura of peace, his pendants making music, as he nearly floated into the tracking room to take his place in front of the vocal mic.

Havens proceeded to remove his native baubles, one noisy strand at a time, carefully placing them on a nearby chair. Then he slipped the headphones over his short Afro, grinned again and, in a throaty baritone-whisper, requested that the engineer roll the track. It was clear that this man was no stranger to the recording studio, and that he was completely prepared to give us a nearly flawless first take.

I sat in the producer's chair, watching through the glass, with my finger poised on the talkback button. The song's intro began, and Rockapella made their pre-recorded musical entrance. Then Havens closed his eyes and sang:

Isn't it obvious, every day
It's shining above us all, and it's here to stay[xlvi]

At that point, an unexpected wave of emotion shivered through my body. Richie's was a voice that seemed to come from the center of the earth, through his open-toed sandals, and up through his tree-like frame to emerge from his mouth like honeyed gravel. This was the same vocal-instrument that had re-introduced the world to George Harrison's *Something* and *Here Comes The Sun*. This was the same artist who had—with a single, flailing, open-tuned, acoustic guitar accompanying his passionate rasp—captured the rapt attention of 400,000 muddy hippies on Max Yasgur's field, with his gripping, free-formed rendition of *Motherless Child*.

And now, in this dark, Manhattan studio, Richie Havens was giving voice to *my* words and *my* music—a song with an evolutionary message to benefit two life-saving, world-changing organizations.

I had been privileged to hear my compositions interpreted by some of the great singers of my generation: Ann Wilson, John Farnham, Allan Clarke, Peter Noone, Mark Stein, Carl Wilson—to name some of the best. In later years, I'd be blessed to have my songs sung by Tim McGraw, Lorrie Morgan, David Ball, Dan Seals, Rhean Boyer and Toby Keith. But one of the greatest thrills of my journeyman career arrived while sitting in a control room in New York City, watching and listening to one of the most soulful and distinctive stylists in music history render his vocal performance on *Light of the Sun*.

My tears were involuntary, and they tumbled easily and humbly down my cheeks. I was finally using my music for a higher good, for a cause far greater than my own enrichment or the gratification of my own ego.

Makin' Stuff Up

My production of Richie Havens (with Rockapella) performing *Light of the Sun* was selected by Viacom networks as the music for their Earth Day public service spots on all of their cable channels every spring for a number of years to follow. Neither my co-writers, Kate and Charlie, nor I were ever (financially) compensated in any way. Nevertheless, that song and that recording remains, to this day, one of my proudest career accomplishments.

Afterword

In the fall of 2002, Toby Keith's traveling circus was scheduled for a one-night stand at Rupp Arena in Lexington, Kentucky. It had been a phenomenal year for me, one during which I'd achieved something enormous, a milestone that had eluded me over those previous decades of chasing and lunging after that dangling music-biz golden carrot. At long last, I was the composer (and co-publisher) of a major copyright.

That previous spring, the big guy from Oklahoma's recording of *My List* had climbed to number-one on the Billboard country singles chart and held that position for five consecutive weeks. This song, the one I'd co-written more than two years before in the attic-studio of a rented Nashville house, surrounded by peeling, mildewed wallpaper, would go on to become country radio's most-played single for that entire year.

After seeing success at the highest level snatched away from the very tips of my fingers more times than I could have counted on those very same fingertips, I reveled in the satisfaction that I was now credited with an accomplishment that could never, *ever* be taken away from me.

Scoring a number-one song was my gold medal, my Oscar, my Pulitzer Prize. I was equally as gratified for my family and friends—the folks who'd believed unconditionally in me and my talents for so many years—as I was for myself. All those narrowly missed opportunities, those myriad dead-ends, close calls and U-turns—now, in the rear view mirror, at this transitory highpoint along the highway of life, those struggles and frustrations were well worth it. I'd worked long and hard on my craft and, as deeply grateful as I was to have this acknowledgment, I knew I deserved it.

Aside from my chronic allergy issues, the post-nasal hacking that kept me awake for hours every night (resulting in the almost complete loss of my once-unique, rangy vocal-instrument), I was a very contended camper. Little did I know then that my greatest moment of fulfillment was yet to come.

Makin' Stuff Up

As I had never experienced the cocksure Keith rendering my song live in concert, I gathered up my wife, Stacey, and our (then-10-year-old) daughter, Glendyn, for the pleasant, three-hour-plus drive north across the width of the Bluegrass State. I was in such an accommodating state of mind, I actually found myself amused by the smoke-filled lobby of the Hyatt Regency as we checked in.

The pre-concert party crowd was lubricating itself liberally for the concert, due to start in an hour or two. Room service provided the only way Stace, Glenny and I could find a peaceful place to grab a family nosh. Since this "service" was not what one might define as "snappy," we were tardy for the opening set—much to the thinly disguised annoyance of my spouse.

As we made our entrance into the home of the storied Kentucky Wildcat college basketball dynasty, the boys from Rascal Flatts were already mesmerizing the audience with their beautiful, introspective, breakthrough ballad, *I'm Movin' On*.

Stacey tugged at my arm. "I *love* this song," she reminded me. It was clear that Stace wished she'd been present to experience Flatts' presentation from the get-go.

I chuckled smugly to myself, remembering how, that previous April, *My List* had not only held *I'm Movin' On* out of the top spot on the charts, but staved off Kenny Chesney's youthful rocker, *Young*, as well. No mean feat for a folk-country, mid-tempo, message-song.

We found our seats, about 20 rows back, on the center of the main floor. Ten minutes or so later, Flatts finished off their set to a respectful response from the hard-core TK crowd. Intermission was time for the meet and greet. Due to a mix-up, we only had two back-stage passes, so Stacey nobly held our seats, while Glenny and I found our way through several security check-points and commandeered our spot in a line that wound its way through the windowless, concrete corridors. There, my daughter and I waited to shake the superstar's oversized right paw and stand for a quick snapshot.

After being shuffled from one line to another several times, Glenny and I finally rounded the last corner. There was Toby, as always bigger than life, signing autographs, smiling, and posing with the most dedicated of his followers.

Now there's a hard workin' guy!, I was thinking. *He writes 90% of his songs, co-produces his own records, and then schmoozes hundreds of diehards every night—BEFORE he actually sets foot on stage to rock for two hours*. That's what it takes to be a pop icon in this modern world.

Makin' Stuff Up

"We're gonna make a boat load o' money together this year," Toby gloated, as he smiled broadly for the camera, his trunk-like arms hunkered over my shoulders to his right, and those of my youngest child on his left.

The main event was about to begin. I was gripping a large, plastic cup filled with flat, watery beer, and my belly was flip-flopping in anticipation. I looked down at Glenny. Her eyes were as wide as a lemur in a Madagascar jungle, as she soaked in the spectacle. Stace gripped my arm and grinned proudly at her man, the guy she'd stood steadfastly beside, through thick and thin, for 19 years. Then she guided my cup to her lips, and borrowed a tepid sip from my Bud Light.

The headline set began with a three-minute video starring a very confident bulldog strutting through the streets of town to be greeted by various colorful characters. The big finish had the canine making a pointed political statement, by urinating on a poster of the Dixie Chicks. The crowd ate it up. (My family-unit, however, was more than a little bit turned off by what seemed like a cheap shot at the trio, who'd recently been voted off country-music island in retaliation for one careless (but sincere) disparaging remark about our Commander in Chief.)

As the bulldog finished his business, lowered his hind leg and waddled off, the TK band kicked into their muscle-bound, up-tempo, opening number. The arena exploded. This first cooker was followed by another, then a third barn-burner, with no more than a split-second of air in between. As the lights flashed and popped, sweeping the walls, the rafters and through the crowd, each successive selection seemed to deliver more brute force than the one that preceded it. In a relentless bombardment lasting more than 15 minutes, Toby and his band brought the house to a veritable frenzy, with at least six consecutive, driving rockers.

Then, at the very moment when it seemed virtually impossible for the intensity be raised any higher, the entire atmosphere in the hall abruptly pacified, and the entire crowd breathed a deep, slow sigh of relief.

The lights stopped flashing and sweeping the room, mellowed, and took on a warm, golden glow. A finger-picking acoustic guitar played a familiar descending chord pattern, as an electric sitar offered the signature phrase of *My List*. Couples, who'd only just a moment before been dancing and pumping their fists in the air, embraced and began swaying gently to the musical vamp.

Makin' Stuff Up

Then, Toby's powerful baritone rang through the vast space, with the very words that had spilled almost effortlessly out of my mouth on a morning nearly three years before—a morning that had seemed nearly identical to so many others.

> *Under an old brass paperweight*
> *Is my list of things to do today*[xlvii]

I'd seen Springsteen, Tim McGraw, Mick Jagger and so many other stars at the top of their game, pointing their microphones out over sold-out houses, implying the unsaid instruction, "Take it!" Knowing every word by heart, those devoted legions invariably chimed in without abandon. Whether it was *Born to Run, Don't Take the Girl* or *Start Me Up*, the singers had as much enthusiastic, amateur, choral support as they could ever ask for.

Super Nashville song-scribe, Kent Blazy tells the story of being on tour in Ireland with a quartet of Garth Brooks hit-men. There, on foreign soil, he was picking his way into an understated, acoustic arrangement of *If Tomorrow Never Comes*—a song that had hit number one in the UK two separate times; first by Garth, then again by Ronan Keating. The audience immediately, spontaneously joined in and, by the first chorus, the songwriter couldn't even hear his vocal monitor—his back-up choir was *that* loud.

"Good thing, too," says Blazy, "'cause I was so emotional, I could hardly sing a note."

Hearing stories like that from my fellow creative souls, I'd feel an electric shiver going up my spine, imagining what an awesome emotional charge it must be to know that your work has touched so many lives. And sometimes I wondered if, in my lifetime, I would ever know that feeling myself.

Here I was now, standing between my proud, adoring wife and my starry-eyed daughter, in the middle of packed-to-the-rafters Rupp-frickin'-Arena. On the enormous platform-stage was a big-time superstar performing my song—the one he'd made into a major copyright.

The big, fat checks in the mailbox—they were great! I was truly honored by the Grammy Nomination, the BMI Awards and the Million-Play certificates, along with the plaques from the Country Music Association and NSAI. Without a doubt, though, the greatest reward in my entire songwriting career came while standing in a sea of swaying bodies, as over 17,000 people sang along with every single word of a little song I had brought into being.

≈   ≈   ≈

The following March, I was invited to play at Tin Pan South, NSAI's annual week honoring songwriters. Filling out my "writers-in-the-round" were three other journeymen tunesmiths, Jon Robbin, Casey Kelly and Alex Call—each a gifted writer in his own write, each having experienced at least one visit to the top of the charts.

The audience at the small coffee shop/venue comprised a mix of curiosity seekers and music die-hards, mostly songwriters, many with yet-to-be-realized aspirations of their own, who came out to appreciate the handiwork of four mature professionals. I recognized one fellow in the crowd who had two Number Ones to his credit but, for the most part, the faces were shiny and eager as they lapped up our glib repartee and admired the evening's exhibition of song-craft.

I played *Don't Mention Memphis*, the song Tim McGraw recorded in '95, and *Happy With The One I Got*, which was then due to be David Ball's next single. I figured I was probably the only Music Row song-scribe to have scored an Indigo Girls cut, so I broke out a sprightly version of *Wild Wild Party in the Loquat Tree*, replete with the requisite falsetto mouse-squeaks and growling bee-buzzes. Alex Call played his Huey Lewis hits, Robbin his Lorrie Morgan masterpiece, and Kelly regaled the crowd with long, cleverly constructed stories *and* his Tanya Tucker hit, *Soon*.

It's tradition to save your most recognizable selection for the last time around the circle.

"Break out the big stick, Rog," Max T. Barnes once said to songwriting legend Roger Cook, at Douglas Corner Tavern, as the final round was announced. (For Cook, who has a bushel-basket full of international smashes, the big stick is *I'd Like To Teach The World To Sing*.)

The four of us all had one heavy club left in our bag, the song most everyone in the crowd had paid U.S. currency to hear. For Robbin, it was *I Breathe In, I Breathe Out*, Chris Cagle's only chart-topper to date. Kelly has George Strait's classic, *The Cowboy Walks Away*, and Call nearly always closes with one of the great party songs of the last 35 years, Tommy Tutone's *876-5309*, which Alex always stretches out into a studied piece of performance art, with audience sing-alongs and plenty of snappy patter, guaranteed to get any house rockin'.

Until such time as I have another (even bigger) hit, I customarily save *My List* for my finale. I looked out over the wide-eyes and optimistic smiles glowing on the faces of the admiring crowd.

As I began picking that downward-moving chord pattern, I said, "This next song has been very good to me. I only hope that every one of you is blessed with the experience of writing a number-one song."

And that, dear reader, is exactly what I wish for you—that you fully develop your talent and apply your gifts with honesty and vigor. I hope that, one day, you'll find out what it feels like to be a hit songwriter. There is no more blessed life than to be a writer. To be a successful writer? That's a life experience beyond blessed. It's transcendent.

≈ ≈ ≈

My next truly meaningful personal appearance took place when I was invited to render a short set of tunes for my daughter's sixth-grade class at St. Bernard's Academy. The kids were attentive and receptive, not yet jaded enough to consider me, or my songs, totally uncool. I completed my brief program with the final cadence of *My List* and accepted the children's polite applause.

"I'm 53 years old," I told them, "and that was my first number-one song in the United States. What does that say to you?"

Curious as to what profundity this query might provoke from a room full of 10 and 11-year-olds, I acknowledged a lad, who eagerly waved his hand in the air as if he was about to spontaneously combust with the perfect answer. After being called upon, however, the young fellow's confidence seemed to wane somewhat, and his response came more in the form of a rhetorical pot shot, a stab in the dark:

"Never give up?"

I was impressed with this boy's ability to sum up so succinctly the most important reason why I had, after nearly 40 years of writing songs, finally co-composed and co-published a chart-topping song. His answer contained the wisdom of Winston Churchill wrapped in the innocence of a prepubescent child—one who stood, champing at the bit, wearing a pair of brand-new sneakers, ready to take his first strides down a yellow brick road leading to a magical future filled with unlimited potential. *I was that boy once*, I thought to myself.

"Yes, that's right." I said, with a chuckle to chase away the tears that wanted so much to be set free. "*Never* give up."

THE END

Makin' Stuff Up

INDEX

Makin' Stuff Up

Endnotes

---

[i] *My List*, by Tim James & Rand Bishop, © 2001,
Song Paddock Music, ASCAP/Weightless Cargo Music, BMI

[ii] *My List* again

[iii] *My List* again

[iv] *That's The Way I Like It* © 1975 (Harry Wayne Casey/Richard Finch)
EMI Longitude Music

[v] *The Song Remembers When* © 1993 (Hugh Prestwood) Hugh
Prestwood Music/Universal Music Careers

[vi] *She's A Woman*, © 1965 (John Lennon /Paul McCartney) Gil Music
Corp./ Sony/ATV Tunes LLC/Beatles

[vii] *A Little Help From My Friends* © 1967 (John Lennon/Paul
McCartney) Sony/ATV Tunes LLC/Beatles

[viii] *Save Me The Trouble* © 2007 (Jon Robbin/Rand Bishop)
Zone Ranger Music/Jon Robbin Songs, ASCAP/Zone On The Range
Music/Songs From The Finn Zone, BMI

[ix] *That's The Way I Like It* again

[x] *Get Down Tonight,* © 1975 (Harry Wayne Casey/Richard Finch) EMI
Longitude Music

[xi] *My List* again

[xii] *My List* again

[xiv] *We Gotta Get Outta This Place*, © 1965 (Barry Mann/Cynthia Well)
Screen Gems EMI Music Inc.

[xv] *You've Lost That Lovin' Feelin'*, © 1965 (Barry Mann/Cynthia Weil/Phil Spector) Screen Gems EMI Music Inc./ABKCO Music Inc./Mother Bertha Music Inc.

[xvi] *Just Once*, © 1981 (Barry Mann/Cynthia Weil) Mann and Weil Songs Inc/Sony/ATV Songs LLC

[xvii] *Johnny B. Goode*, © 1958 (Chuck Berry) Arc Music, Inc./Isalee Music Publishing Company

[xviii] *I Like it, I Love It* © 1995 (Mark Hall/Jeb Stuart Anderson/Steve Dukes) EMI Full Keel Music/MPCA Lehsem Music/Publishing Two's Music/Tier Three Music/State One Songs America

[xix] *Sympathy For the Devil* © 1968 (Mick Jagger/Keith Richards) ABKCO Music Inc.

[xx] *I Can't Make You Love Me*, © 1991 (Mike Reid/Allen Shamblin) Almo Music Corp./Rondor Music International Inc./Brio Blues Music/ICG Alliance/Universal Music/MGB Songs

[xxi] *Loves Me Like a Rock* © 1973 (Paul Simon) Paul Simon Music

[xxii] *Sounds of Silence* © 1966 (Paul Simon) Paul Simon Music

[xxiii] *Across the Universe* © 1969 (John Lennon/Paul McCartney) Sony/ATV Tunes LLC /Beatles

[xxiv] *Big Yellow Taxi* © 1970 (Joni Mitchell) Siquomb Music/Sony/ATV Tunes LLC

[xxv] *Raised on Robbery* © 1974 (Joni Mitchell) Crazy Crow Music/Sony/ATV Tunes LLC

[xxvi] *Don't You Worry*, © 1974 (Randy Bishop/Doug Pringle) Warner-Tamerlane Music, BMI

[xxvii] *This Is Not A Real Song*, © 2004 (Rand Bishop/Julie Zeitlin)

Zone On The Range/Songs From the Finn Zone, BMI/Ash Street Music

[xxviii] *Wouldn't It Be Nice* © 1966 (Brian Wilson/Mike Love/Tony Asher) Irving Music Inc.

[xxix] *I Want To Hold Your Hand* © 1963 (John Lennon/Paul McCartney) Sony/ATV Tunes LLC/Beatles/Songs of Universal Inc.

[xxx] *Yesterday* © 1965 (John Lennon/Paul McCartney) Sony/ATV Tunes LLC/Beatles

[xxxi] *She Blinded Me with Science* © 1982 (Jonathan Michael Kerr/Thomas Morgan Robertson) Bienstock Publishing Company/Lost Toy People, Inc.

[xxxii] *My List* again

[xxxiii] *My List* again

[xxxiv] *Lovin' Arms* © 1973 (Thomas Jans) Almo Music Corp./Rondor Music International Inc.

[xxxv] *Help* © 1965 (John Lennon/Paul McCartney) Sony/ATV Tunes LLC/Beatles

[xxxvi] *You're The Top* © 1934 (Cole Porter) Chappell & Co., Inc/Warner Chappell Music

[xxxvii] *De-Lovely* © 1936 (Cole Porter) Chappell & Co., Inc/Warner Chappell Music

[xxxviii] *Hound Dog* © 1952 (Jerry Lieber/Mike Stoller) Gladys Music Elvis Presley/Gladys Music Joachim Jean/Gladys Music Julian Aberbach/Cherry lane Music Publishing Company/Universal Music Corporation

[xxxix] *Blowin' In The Wind* © 1963 (Bob Dylan) Special Rider Music

[xl] *The Song Remembers When* © 1993 (Hugh Prestwood) Hugh Prestwood Music/Universal Music Careers

[xli] *I Saw Her Standing There* © 1963 (John Lennon /Paul McCartney) Gil Music Corp./ Sony/ATV Tunes LLC/Beatles

[xlii] *I'm Not In Love* © 1978 (Graham Gouldman/Eric Stewart) Man-Ken Music Ltd.

[xliii] *I'm Not In Love*, again

[xliv] *I'm Not In Love*, again

[xlv] *Common Ground*, © 1988 (Rhythm Corps) The Pasha Music Co./Beet Pollen Music

[xlvi] *Light Of the Sun*, © 1992 (Rand Bishop/Kate Cunningham/Charlie Pullman) Weightless Cargo Music/Uncle Chuckles Music

[xlvii] *My List* again